ABDUCTED

This book is for the countless number of families who are presently struggling to cope with similar experiences. Take heart in the hope that we will one day have an answer.

I also dedicate this book
to Jason,
for his immense strength and courage;
to Daniel,
for his understanding and his humour which lifts us all;
to Paul,
for his continuing love and support;
and to Tony Dodd,
who is always there – for all of us.

ABDUCTED

The True Tale of Alien Abduction in Rural England

Ann Andrews and Jean Ritchie

HEADLINE

First published in 1998
by HEADLINE BOOK PUBLISHING

10 9 8 7 6 5 4 3 2 1

British Library Cataloguing in Publication Data

Andrews, Ann
    Abducted: a remarkable story of alien abduction in rural
    England
    1. Alien abduction – Great Britain
    I. Title II. Ritchie, Jean, 1946–
    001.9′4′0941

ISBN 0 7472 2121 9 (hardback)
ISBN 0 7472 7516 5 (softback)

Typeset by Avon Dataset Ltd, Bidford-on-Avon, Warks

Printed and bound in Great Britain by
Clays Ltd, St Ives plc

HEADLINE BOOK PUBLISHING
A division of Hodder Headline PLC
338 Euston Road
London NW1 3BH

Contents

Acknowledgements

The authors would like to thank everyone who helped with the research and writing of this book, in particular Jason Andrews. The impetus to write the book came from his commitment to finding the truth of his own experiences, and his strong feeling that by speaking out about his abductions, he would help other people – particularly children and teenagers – who may be struggling to cope with similar phenomena.

Special thanks are also due to Tony Dodd, whose expertise in this field is unrivalled, and to Maria Ward, James Basil, and Sue and Billy Rutland, all of whom happily shared their experiences with the authors. Many thanks, too, to Paul, Daniel and Vi, who gave their time and support to the project.

CHAPTER 1

A BIRTHDAY PARTY

To look at, Jason is an attractive boy: average height and weight for a fourteen-year-old. His bright blue eyes, fringed with dark lashes, are set in a round, intelligent face. His dark brown hair is carefully cut into a neat style for school.

He does everything that fourteen-year-olds do: he's average at school, gets bad marks for forgetting to do homework. He's cheeky and smart-mouthed when he can get away with it, terrific on a computer, hangs out with his group of friends and thinks money grows on trees. A normal boy – except that those beautiful blue eyes hide a terrible secret.

July 2nd 1987 was a big day in the Andrews household. Jason, the younger of the two Andrews boys, was four years old that day, and his mother and father had organised his first proper birthday party.

By the end of the day, stuffed full of birthday cake and crisps, and over-excited by the balloons and presents and friends who had milled around the cottage for several hours, Jason collapsed into sleep on the sofa. His grandmother, Vi (short for Violet), draped her coat over him as the night air turned chilly.

His mother, Ann, was relieved that everything had gone well, and settled down for a quiet cup of coffee with her husband, Paul, and her mother.

Their desultory chat was interrupted by a loud banging at the door of their cottage in Slade Green, Kent. All three were puzzled: it was ten o'clock on a Friday evening, too late for casual callers. The noise was urgent, insistent: louder than the sound of a fist, more like a heavy boot being thrust against the door with tremendous force, so that the frame seemed to shake with each blow.

1

Paul jumped up and flung the heavy oak door wide.

There was no one there. The noise of banging ceased the moment Paul's hands reached the door. He strode outside and peered up and down the narrow lane that ended at their cottage. The heavy clouds of a brewing storm made it darker than normal for a July evening, but even in the gloom he could see the roadway was empty. There were lights on in the cottage next door to theirs, but the curtains were drawn and the doors shut.

As Paul stepped back into the living room there was a loud crack of thunder, louder than Ann had ever heard thunder before. It was followed by distant rumblings which rapidly built into swelling crescendos, as if each roll were breaking right over their cottage. The noise was so great that they could not talk, and for a moment the strange knocking at the door was pushed out of their minds.

The storm woke seven-year-old Daniel, their older son, who had been asleep in his bedroom. He appeared at the foot of the stairs, sleepily rubbing his eyes, and climbed on to his grandmother's lap. Jason slept on, curled up on the settee.

Suddenly there was a flash of lightning, so fierce in intensity that even Paul, a big, unflappable man, jumped. As if on cue, Jason sat bolt upright, sending his grandmother's coat sliding to the floor. Both the dogs whined and cowered together under the dining table. Jason was staring, eyes open but oblivious to the room and the people around him.

He opened his mouth and started to talk, pouring out an incredible stream of numbers, as if he'd hit the jackpot on some weird mental fruit machine. Fantastic numbers, huge numbers, strange algebraic configurations, mathematical terms like 'pi' and 'binary codes', all spewed out of the mouth of a four-year-old boy who normally struggled to count up to ten in his picture books.

The loud banging at the door began again. Then it seemed to come from the window, then all the windows and doors at the same time, and the whole cottage seemed to shake.

Paul grabbed the phone to dial 999. Nothing happened. He had the dialling tone, but the emergency digits were not registering. He tried again, and after a third attempt threw the phone down in temper.

He began to stride towards the door when, just as suddenly as he had started, Jason stopped talking. At exactly the same moment, the banging ceased.

Then Jason slid from the settee and, still in a trance, started to walk towards the door. Paul put his hands on his small son's shoulders, gently restraining him.

'Where are you going, boy?' he asked. 'It's pouring down outside – you'll get soaked.'

The child looked up at his father and replied in a strange, emotionless voice: 'They're waiting for me. I have to go.'

As he spoke the violent knocking began again. Vi was crying uncontrollably. Ann grabbed Daniel from her, and hugged him tightly, a talisman of normality.

Jason shrugged free from Paul's light hold and walked towards the door again. This time his father grasped him firmly. Jason struggled and Paul, in desperation, shook him violently, commanding him to 'Snap out of it.'

At first, Jason fought harder and the knocking grew louder and stronger, reverberating through the whole house. Then he blinked his eyes and Paul, sensing the turn in the tide, gently slapped him, talking to him all the time.

Gradually Jason woke up, and as he did so the knocking receded, dying out completely as he looked up at Paul and asked innocently if he could watch television.

Within minutes the two children in matching Batman pyjamas were in their favourite position, lying in front of the television set, as if nothing had happened. Vi, following instincts bred into her during the London blitz, coped with all eventualities by putting the kettle on.

The two dogs emerged from their hiding place and patrolled the room, enormous tails wagging, before settling next to the children.

Paul picked up the phone again, and this time was able to get through to the police. He told them about the knocking, and they promised to get a car round as soon as possible. Even as he tried to explain what had happened, he was overwhelmed by the impossibility of making sense of it.

When the police arrived minutes later, he went through the story of what happened, without mentioning Jason's part in it. The two policemen and Paul went outside with a flashlight to look for signs of damage to the door or disturbance in the garden.

'It's the oddest thing,' said the older of the two policemen, standing in the doorway in order not to walk mud on to the carpet. 'There are no signs of anybody being about – not one single footprint in the mud. With all this rain, you'd think there would be footprints.'

Fog closes in around my car so tightly that I can see no further than the headlights' beam. The vehicle jerks unhappily along the deeply frozen ruts of the farm track. It is the winter of 1996 when Kent, the garden of England, has been snowed in for weeks.

With relief I see the five-bar metal gate straight ahead of me, with the warning notice 'Beware, dogs loose'. This is it, the smallholding belonging to Paul and Ann Andrews.

A large man in a lumberjack shirt emerges from the fog and swings the gate back on its hinge for me to drive in. The yard is as pitted and uneven as the track approaching it. To the left, vision tapers into nothing, but to my right there is the low bulk of a building, and a hazy yellow light from a caravan doorway.

It is easy, in weather like this, to imagine anything possible beyond the abbreviated limits of sight, but the sound of Ann's voice, coming from the doorway and only slightly muffled by the fog, dispels the eeriness.

'Kettle's on. Come in and get warm.'

How hard it is, at this first meeting, to take in the enormity of their story. I knew they would be a perfectly normal family to whom abnormal things have happened, have been happening for years, and are still happening now. Yet at some subconscious level I expect the mark of Cain, the stigmata, something that outwardly betrays their difference from the rest of us.

There is nothing. As we chat about the weather, their dogs, my dogs, their children, my children, I could be with any of a number of friends. Ann and I share the common problems of mothering adolescent sons, and as we talk I constantly have to remind myself that, overlaid on all this normality, she copes with something far greater than the predictable frictions of life with teenagers: Ann is Jason's mother.

Jason. He is the real reason I am here. Much as I looked forward to meeting Ann and Paul, it is Jason who intrigues me most. What

4

do you expect from a boy whose childhood has been so dominated by events beyond the comprehension of the adult world, let alone his peers? How has he coped with the magnitude of his experiences, and the stress of keeping them secret from a disbelieving world?

He breezes into the caravan. I did not see him when I arrived: he was across the field, hidden in the fog, talking to his beloved ponies. He's a good-looking, fresh-faced boy wearing a fashionable puffa jacket and with a bright red Arsenal scarf round his neck. He's mad about football, mad about computers, mad about Michael Jackson's music. He doesn't like bands like Oasis, describing their songs as 'girls' music', but the Spice Girls are OK – more than OK, he tells me.

Like his parents, Jason is resolutely normal. He has Ann's sense of humour – they tease each other all the time. He does what he's told, but in his own time, like most kids of his age. He has taken the teenage masterclass in getting away with as much as you can without getting into trouble: told to turn his music down, he twitches the volume control and the sound shades down by no more than a decibel or two; told to take the dogs for a walk he does, but is back in front of the TV twenty minutes later.

On this first day, it is the very normality of all three of the main players in this extraordinary story that makes me want to find out more. The Andrews family are no weirdos. They aren't fantasists. There isn't one dominant member of the group who is pushing the others into going along with a deception.

These are three down-to-earth, sensible, unimaginative people. I keep coming back to the words 'ordinary' and 'normal'. Because that's what they are. Unexceptional. Special in the way that all people are individual and special to their own family group, but average and typical and run-of-the-mill to everyone else.

This doesn't diminish them. It makes their story so much stronger, so much more powerful. If it can happen to them, it can happen to anyone. Perhaps it happens to far more people than we know about. Because there is one way in which the Andrews family *are* exceptional: they are prepared to tell their story, to let it be examined and questioned and probed. They want the truth to be exposed. If there's a rational explanation to be had, they're up for it.

★ ★ ★

Strange and inexplicable events have surrounded Jason Andrews from the moment of his birth, July 2nd 1983, but it was not until twelve years later, in the autumn of 1995, that Paul and Ann were given any lead on what was happening. At first, it was an explanation they could not accept: it was so far-fetched, so incredible, so outside anything they had ever considered, that they both refused to believe it. However, the more they found out, both about Jason's experiences and those of others in similar situations, the more they realised that his problems exactly fitted this theory.

The revelation came to them one evening when they settled in the living room of their home in Borough Green, Kent, to watch television. It was one of those debate programmes where the audience, on raised tiers of seats, was stacked with people who had a contribution to make, tracked down by newly-graduate researchers and bribed with travel expenses and the lure of the TV camera. The presenter ran up and down the aisles, thrusting a microphone in front of the chosen few who would have their thirty seconds of fame.

There was a loose structure to the debate. First, hypnosis as entertainment: professional hypnotists argued with those who believed that stage hypnosis was demeaning and possibly damaging. There were members of the audience who had volunteered to be hypnotised in front of their mates, and found nothing but fun in the five minutes they had firmly believed they were Elvis Presley. There were others who disliked it, and days afterwards still felt the aftershock in their brainwaves.

Then there was the serious use of hypnotherapy, as a tool to help overcome addictions like smoking, overeating, drinking too much, or to help conquer real but unfounded fears, like the fear of flying or of spiders. Ann and Paul were watching the programme with interest. Ann knew someone who had stopped smoking with the help of a hypnotist, and it fascinated her. Daniel and Paul were both lounging on the sofa, looking at magazines and occasionally glancing up at the screen.

Finally, the ragged debate moved round to the use of hypnosis to recover hidden memories. A man in his forties explained how he had been driving his normal route home from work one evening, a journey of thirty-five minutes, but on this particular occasion it took three hours and twenty minutes. He had no explanation of what had happened in the extra two and three-quarter hours, but since the mysterious time loss he had suffered inexplicable mood swings, depression, and an irrational fear of the dark. In the end, he had visited a hypnotherapist to recover his memories of the lost time.

Without warning, at this point in the programme Jason leapt to his feet, picked up a small china dog which Ann's mother had given her as a present years ago, and hurled it at the TV screen. It missed the television and exploded on impact with the video recorder, shattering into a thousand fragments.

Paul jumped from his seat and angrily demanded to know what the boy was doing.

Jason turned to face his parents. Tears were coursing down his cheeks and his breath caught between sobs. 'That man on there is so stupid, so stupid. He should be glad he can't remember. He should leave it like that. Because I can remember. I remember everything. I'm scared. They won't leave me alone. Why can't they leave me alone?'

He fled the room, slamming the door behind him. The sound of his urgent sobbing could be heard from the kitchen.

The three in the room looked at each other in shocked silence. Daniel spoke first: 'Do you still not understand?' He spoke to his parents with barely disguised contempt for their obtuseness. 'This guy on the telly was abducted by aliens. Don't you both get it yet?'

They didn't get it. They looked at their older son in stunned silence. Daniel never got involved in the family rows about Jason's strange behaviour. At sixteen Daniel was semi-detached from the family: taking GCSEs, working out what he wanted to do when he left school, his social life revolving around his mates and his first serious girlfriend. He communicated with his parents in a series of grunts, made excuses not to attend family meals, raided the fridge at odd hours of the day and night: he was, in short, a typical teenage boy. The very fact of him sitting in the same room and watching the same TV programme as the rest of them was noteworthy.

Ann's mind was racing. The strange behaviour that the man on the television described was just like Jason's: he had talked about scars appearing and disappearing on his body, a sudden and terrible fear of the dark, a need to be with someone during the night, an unexplained fatigue even after long hours in bed, mood swings that were beyond his control, an overwhelming sense of panic.

Surely it was just coincidence? Surely the man's retrieved memories, of being abducted and taken to an alien spacecraft, were just wild imaginings? Ann had seen stories in newspapers about people who claimed to be in contact with aliens, but she scarcely bothered to read them. The world was full of nutcases, she thought. There were no more likely to be aliens than there were fairies at the bottom of the garden. As for Paul: if Paul couldn't touch it, it didn't exist.

As these thoughts skidded through her mind, she became aware of Daniel's voice again: 'Mum, remember me telling you about my soldier guy, who sat on my bed when I was little? You thought I imagined him? Do you remember how upset I was when he said he wouldn't be coming to see me for a while, because he'd realised I wasn't the one he should be working with?'

Ann vaguely remembered Daniel, as a toddler, snuffling his tear-stained face into her shoulder and telling her that the soldier 'friend' he had talked about so often had gone away for good. She'd humoured him, never for one moment believing that his invisible friend was anything more than the product of an overactive imagination. Lots of children, especially lonely ones without brothers and sisters, have imaginary playfriends – and Daniel had started 'seeing' his soldier before Jason was born.

'The one he wanted was Jason,' said Daniel. 'I know now that my soldier guy was real. I think I've always known he was real.'

Ann wanted to know why Daniel had not said any of this before. Paul, on the other hand, made clear that he regarded everything Daniel had just said as nonsense.

Daniel leaned back in the armchair and laughed without humour. 'See? That's why I've never said anything. Dad would have me hauled away and certified.'

His voice grew serious again.

'I'm sorry, Mum. I wanted to tell you, but I thought Jason's shrink would get it out of him. I get weird stuff happening too, you know. Last night I was woken up by a very bright light, and when I sat up I felt I had been hit by something, all over my body. Almost like something had entered into me. I felt a hot energy running through me, but I was paralysed. I was scared. Then the next second I was asleep, and I don't remember anything till this morning.

'My soldier guy told me Jason had an original soul, whatever that means. I know, because I can feel it, that they won't hurt him, but he needs help, Mum. He can't cope with it; it's really screwing him up. He's terrified.'

It was the longest speech Ann had ever heard Daniel make. She was having a hard time taking it in. Daniel was often flippant, with the same mocking sense of humour as his mother and his brother, but it was clear that right now he was in earnest.

Paul rose slowly from the settee, put his hand on Daniel's shoulder and took him to the kitchen, where Jason was still sobbing. Ann sat still for a moment, the drone of the television running counterpoint to her thoughts, and every so often throwing out that incredible, unbelievable, unacceptable word: 'aliens'.

When she finally walked through to the kitchen nobody acknowledged her as she pulled out a chair and joined them at the table. Jason's face was buried on his arms, but he was speaking clearly, gulping back his sobs: 'It's always the light that comes first. It wakes me up. Then I see the tall one rise at the foot of the bed. Suddenly, there's lots of little ones everywhere. They're fuzzy and indistinct, and they move very fast. I can't move or speak, but I'm awake and I can see and hear and feel. I want to scream and run, but the sound doesn't come and my body doesn't move. Sometimes I think I am screaming – I can hear myself screaming – but it never wakes you, you never come to help me. I hate them. I hate them. I hate you for not coming when I need you...'

Jason sat up and stared accusingly at his parents.

'Why do you let them take me? I have to go with them. They take me to an operating theatre, like at the hospital. It's all white and shiny. Sometimes it's a circular room with a metal floor. It's always cold. I want to go home, I hate it. They're there, the big one touches me but I don't feel it, like as if I've had an anaesthetic. I hate it, I hate it . . .'

Ann put her arms round him and told him it was time to go to bed.

'But you don't believe me, you never believe me, you just think I'm a stupid kid making it all up,' said Jason vehemently.

'I believe you,' she said. 'I'll help you sort it out.'

Did she believe him? She knew instinctively that he was telling the truth as he saw it, but it was all too much to take in. She felt there must be another explanation, one that didn't involve tall figures rising through the floor, but she knew that Jason was not pretending: the events were real enough to him.

When he asked if he could sleep in the same room as his parents, Paul readily agreed.

After they had settled their son on a mattress on the floor next to Ann's side of the bed, Paul and Ann discussed the events of the evening. Paul was even more reluctant than Ann to accept everything Jason had told them, but he, like her, could see that his son was in deadly earnest about it. He also accepted that it was their duty as parents to do what they could to help. The first step, he suggested, was that they should find out as much as they could about the subject of abduction. He volunteered to drive into Dartford the next day and trawl the book shops, looking for relevant reading matter.

It was the first step for them in a long and bewildering journey, a journey that would help them make sense of many of the things that had happened to Jason.

I joined them on that journey fifteen months later, in November 1996. Like both Paul and Ann, I had no previous knowledge of alien abduction, but like them I realised that something very significant was happening to Jason, something that needed investigation. The Andrews family asked me to help because they wanted an impartial person to look at the events surrounding their family, somebody whose perspective would not be affected by personal involvement.

They wanted, more than anything, Jason's story to be investigated, tested, probed. Even though, by this stage, Paul had reluctantly accepted that the alien theory was the only one that seemed to come close to encompassing all the mysterious things that had happened to them, he would dearly have loved a rational, scientific explanation, an interpretation of events that fits in with his resolutely Newtonian view of the universe. He is hard-headed, down-to-earth, not inclined to wild imaginings. Ann is more sensitive, more likely to believe that there is more to life than we can necessarily see, but even she, preoccupied with running a home, bringing up a family, helping Paul with the animals on the smallholding, has little time for fanciful stories.

By the time I met them, they had already travelled some way on their quest. They were inured by years of coping with Jason's strange behaviour and the catalogue of paranormal events that had occurred around him, and they had read and spoken to some of the experts in the field of alien abduction. I had a lot of catching up to do.

CHAPTER 2

THE HORSE WHISPERER

The story of Jason Andrews goes back before his birth, before the birth of his mother, perhaps before the birth of his grandfather, Stan, a Romany who married out of his family traditions by settling down with Jason's grandmother, Vi.

Jason's great-grandfather was a full-blooded Romany who married a Gaiety girl who also had Romany blood. For a time they lived in a wooden bow-topped horse-drawn caravan that they built themselves, boasting that the only parts of it they had had to buy were the wheels and the stove. It was a way of life Jason's great-grandfather knew well – he was fifteen before his family settled into a house, and it took him years to accept it. Despite giving up the travelling life when their children were born, Stan's parents socialised with other Romanies and encouraged their children to marry into the race. Stan, who served in the RAF during the war, upset his family by choosing Vi, a pretty sixteen-year-old he met when he joined the Crosse and Blackwell tinned food company as a chauffeur after his demob.

Vi remembers seeing him on the first day he worked there. He was dark, handsome and exciting. The young girl, only a year out of school, went home and told her mother that she had met 'a nice man but he's too old for me'. Stan was twenty-three, worldly wise, but just as smitten as Vi. He nicknamed her 'Min', and for the rest of their life together would only call her Vi if they were having one of their rare rows. Stan's parents were dead by the time they married, but the rest of his family made it clear they felt that Vi was too young for him, and not a Romany. A rift developed, and although the two sides of the family met at weddings and funerals, Stan was never close to his siblings from then on.

To compensate, he was welcomed into Vi's family, and moved with his new bride into a three-roomed flat in the Walworth Road area of London, within walking distance of Vi's mother's home. It was here that their oldest child, Ann, was born, on July 11th 1956. Within a year the family moved to a basement flat in Peckham, south-east London. Although there was only one bedroom, Vi and Stan put a screen of furniture across the middle, effectively making two rooms. Ann was soon joined by two brothers, David and Stephen. While they were all small, sharing half the bedroom was no problem. The flat had an outside toilet and the bath was a big tin one that was filled with water from the kettle – there was only cold water supplied to the large white kitchen sink.

Ann went to the local junior school, where she was happy and did well. The family were relatively poor, but so were all her friends and because her father was never out of work, she was better off than many. Her mother Vi was everything a child could want: encouraging, supportive, and dedicated to giving her children a good home.

Despite living in one of the most densely populated areas of London, Stan never lost his innate love of the countryside. In Ann's words: 'He found nature in the middle of London.'

From the moment she could toddle beside him, he took his little daughter to the local park every weekend, reciting for her the names of all the flowers and grasses that they saw there, and how they could be used, medicinally or to flavour cooking. Later on, her brothers would come on the expeditions with them, but would be more interested in chasing balls and riding bikes than learning about plants. It was with Ann that he shared the Romany lore, the traditions and fairytales that had been handed down to him by his father, and it was with Ann that he shared another gift.

When she was six she developed a passion for horses. Living where they did, horses were pictures in storybooks for most Peckham children, but Ann's great love of them was fired by a trip to the New Forest. She and her father wandered among a herd of wild ponies, patting them and talking to them, while other trippers watched from a respectful distance.

It did not strike Ann, the child, as unusual that her father had a rapport with the wild ponies: she knew, from their days in the park, that dogs and birds liked his company, and she took it for granted that horses would, too. Vi, however, watching from a safe distance, knew that her husband Stan had a gift. He was a horse whisperer, a skill passed down through Romany families. He could speak to horses in a language they understood, calm them, soothe them, persuade them to do his bidding.

Ann the adult can look back now and appreciate what her father gave up to support his wife and his three much-loved children. After Crosse and Blackwell he became a postman, working long hours and demanding shifts to keep a wage packet coming in, living in a built-up tenement area, while all the time he longed for the freedom of the countryside. For Ann the child, her father's sadness was only a shadow passing across his face at odd moments.

His daughter's fascination with the wild ponies prompted Stan to arrange riding lessons for her. Peckham was not well endowed with riding establishments, so every Saturday morning he and Ann would climb into the old Thames shooting brake and drive out to Dulwich, where she joined the daughters of the middle classes for riding lessons at Dulwich Riding Academy. Vi was not sure this was a suitable pastime for her daughter, but gave in easily. Sometimes David and Stephen would tag along, hoping to see their big sister fall off. Sometimes they were rewarded, but Stan would always pick Ann up, dust her down and insist that she got back on. He stressed to her that the fault was hers, not the horse's. 'Be more understanding, Annie, earn their respect and give them your respect,' he would say.

On one of these Saturday outings the whole stableyard was reduced to chaos when a big red horse began rearing, bucking and lashing out with his feet at the stablehands who struggled to control him while a vet waited to examine him and administer injections. Stan watched the panic and confusion for a few seconds, then told Ann to turn her horse around so that he would not also be panicked. He strolled confidently to the middle of the drama, taking the lead rope from the man at the horse's head, at the same time telling the other staff to stand back. The sweating horse immediately calmed down as Stan murmured to it, stroking the huge head as he did so. Within a few seconds he was leading the seventeen-hand hunter around the paddock as if it were an old and trusting carthorse. He signalled to the vet, who carried out the examination and treatment with no further trouble. As he handed the lead rope back, Stan told the stablehand that the horse would be calm for the rest of the day.

Ann finished her ride, justifiably proud of her father's starring role in the drama. As they headed back to the car, the vet called out to them to wait, rushing breathlessly up. He held out a hand to Stan, and Ann, although she was only nine, remembers with clarity the words he said: 'Correct me if I am wrong, but I believe I have just had the privilege of seeing a horse whisperer at work, have I not?' Stan smiled, accepted the outstretched hand, then ushered his daughter into the car while he talked for some time to the vet. Not understanding what a horse whisperer was, Ann nonetheless felt smug and proud.

From then on, Stan was a celebrity at the riding stables, and Ann basked in the reflected glory for a few weeks, and then began to feel jealous of her father's attention. Soon, owners were asking for him to visit their horses, and it was when she accompanied him on one of these trips that Ann was astounded to see her father climb, bareback, on to a large horse. She had never realised he could ride, although with the logic of hindsight she realises it was natural that he could. This particular horse had been classified as unridable, but Stan spent a few hours persuading it otherwise.

It was not until years later that Stan and Ann discussed his remarkable ability with animals, and he eventually agreed to pass on some of his lore to his daughter. His great regret was that neither of his sons was interested in horses, nor in learning the ways of the horse whisperer. Vi remembers him promising Ann, when she was very small, that one day she would have her own horse. Living in a basement flat in Peckham it seemed a wild dream, but it was one that would eventually come true.

Stan's gift with animals extended to dogs, and the family pet was always well trained, never needing a collar or lead to keep it in tow. In later years, before his death, Ann would take her own dogs to Stan for training.

For Ann, her childhood memories have almost all been happy ones. Her parents both laughed a lot, sharing a sense of humour, and although there was never a great deal of money to spare, the family believed in fun. There were twice-a-week bus trips to her grandmother's, and big family parties where cousins and aunts and uncles all spilled out of her 'nan's' living room. Ann's grandmother kept open house, never locking the door of her ground-floor flat in the Old Kent Road, the real heart of London. The kettle was always on, the sitting room always crammed with neighbours, relatives and friends, and Ann's grandfather sheltering behind his newspaper in the corner. She remembers him as a kind old man with twinkly eyes, a little bit henpecked by his jolly wife, but enjoying it.

However, amongst the melée of jumbled childhood memories, there is one terrifying one that has dogged Ann, surfacing at odd times throughout her life, and the significance of which she has only appreciated since understanding Jason's problems. Quite small, she remembers being unable to sleep, and going past the partition to the adjoining bedroom, where her mother was settled into the big double bed. Stan was working that night, so it was easy for Vi to snuggle her daughter into the bed next to her and lapse back into a deep sleep. Pat, the brown and black mongrel dog, was snoring gently at the foot of the bed.

Ann lay awake, with a strong feeling that there was someone else in the room. She hid her head under the covers, then slowly lowered the bedclothes and peered out. A cloaked figure appeared to rise through the floor at the bottom of the bed, smoothly gliding up to the height of a tall male. Ann feverishly tugged at her mother's arm, in a desperate bid to wake her, but Vi was in a deep trance-like sleep. Pat the dog was silent and still, as if he had been tranquillised.

The tall figure moved around the side of the bed until level with Ann. Her last memory is of the hood of the cloak being pushed back, and finding herself looking up into two large eyes. The face was not human, dominated as it was by these two huge, black, shiny eyes. The feeling of terror is still very real to Ann: she clutches the arm of her chair as she talks about it, thirty-five years on. She has no other memory from that night, but the next morning she clearly recollects her mother comforting her and saying that it was all a bad dream.

Poignantly, she can recall the feeling of profound frustration that her mother did not believe her that it was real, did not believe that she could distinguish between dream and reality. Remembering that feeling, tears come to her eyes as she guiltily recalls the many times she has used the same words of comfort to Jason. 'It's only a dream', 'You've had another nightmare', 'Don't worry, it will be all right in the morning'.

She never told her father about it. Her mother's reaction made her push the memory away, deep inside. It has surfaced unbidden at odd times ever since, but she has always ignored it. Perhaps, looking back, if she had told her father, he would have been more understanding. Perhaps he, too, knew what it was like to lie awake in the dark while those around slept an unnatural and deep sleep, knew what it was like to be host to unearthly and terrifying visitors.

Stan died in 1983, two months after Jason was born. All the questions Ann would now like to ask him must remain unanswered, but she instinctively feels that he, also, was abducted by aliens. Vi remembers him telling her there were things she would never understand, that he could not reveal to her: she always assumed they were Romany secrets. Now she, too, wonders.

When Ann was very small, before the birth of her brother Stephen when she was four, she spent hours talking to herself, playing with a 'friend' that her mother could not see. Vi put little store by it, knowing that lonely children often invent imaginary friends. (Family history repeated itself when Ann took the same line with a 'friend' that her first son, Daniel, talked to when he was alone in his bedroom.) Stan, though, was intrigued and troubled by Ann's unseen visitor, and tried to get his tiny daughter to describe her 'friend'. In retrospect, Ann wonders if he suspected that her 'friend' came not from her imagination, but from another part of the universe.

Many years later, after discovering the truth about Jason, more childhood memories began to surface for Ann. Unlike her son, she is a typical abductee – she has very few conscious memories of being taken. Had it not been that Jason was so clearly able to recall what happened to him, with such devastating effects on family life, Ann Andrews could well have lived the rest of her life never knowing that she has, from childhood, been a regular abductee. There would always have been mysteries in her life – unexplained marks on her body, strange and troubling thoughts, a feeling of something being buried just below the surface of her consciousness – but with a family to rear, a no-nonsense attitude and a husband who has no time for such things, she would probably never have solved these mysteries.

It was only when the puzzling events of her own life slotted in with Jason's that she began to look again at the circumstances of her father's life, and to see a pattern there which suggests he, too, was an abductee. It is not a case of lightning striking three times in the same place. Just as doctors and scientists are ascribing more and more of our health problems to the genetic makeup we inherit, so it is with abduction victims. While medically we hand down conditions ranging from minor ailments like short-sightedness and weak ankles through to propensities for life-threatening diseases like cancer and strokes, so abductees pass on a devastating legacy to the next generation.

Abduction runs in families.

When Ann was twelve her family were rehoused by the council, leaving the flat in Peckham, where all five of them shared one bedroom, for a brand-new ground floor maisonette in Slade Green. Ann had been in secondary school, Friern Road Comprehensive, for just one year, so the move was potentially disruptive, especially as she left a single-sex school for a mixed one, Slade Green Comprehensive. However, although she was sad to leave her schoolfriends behind, she is equable and outgoing, and soon had a whole new clutch of girlfriends.

The new home seemed palatial. It had three bedrooms and best of all, for Ann and her father, it was nearly in the country. Slade Green is outside the literal boundaries of London – off the *A to Z* by a couple of miles – but still part of the sprawling conurbation. Yet it is green, well planned, and within minutes' drive of the oast houses of the picturesque tourist county Kent.

Ann enjoyed school, worked hard and left with five O level GCEs. The school wanted her to stay on, do A levels, and apply for university, but Ann was keen to get out into the world, and took a clerical job with the Inland Revenue. She went to Erith College in the evenings, and passed A level Art and English. She changed jobs a couple of times, always following her father's stern advice never to leave one job until you have another, and eventually settled to work she enjoyed, in an estate agent's office. Ideally she would have loved to work with animals, but as an unqualified assistant at a kennels or a veterinary surgery she would have been poorly paid.

Just after her eighteenth birthday, Ann met Paul Andrews. He was seventeen at the time – the twenty-day difference in their ages has given fuel to plenty of jokes about older women and toyboys down the years they have been together. They met on a blind date arranged by Ann's cousin Fay, who was going out with a friend of Paul's. The relationship did not get off to a good start. Fay and her boyfriend had a blazing row and both stormed off, leaving Ann and Paul together. It was only at the end of the evening that Paul realised that Fay's boyfriend had his keys. Back at Ann's house he rang around trying to track down his mate, but eventually – and with great reluctance – Ann's mother and father agreed that he should sleep on their settee.

The next morning Ann said yes to another date, more as a means of making sure that Paul left quickly, without antagonising her mother further, than because she wanted to see him again. It was at this second meeting that they both realised there was more to it than a casual date: Paul even announced that one day he would marry Ann. She laughed, but they were soon seen as a couple by their friends.

Vi was not a great fan of Paul. She had dreams of her only daughter marrying well. Ann had dated a doctor, albeit very briefly, but enough to give her mother ammunition. 'My daughter could have married a doctor,' was a sentence Paul would hear more than once during his three-year courtship of Ann. To Vi, Paul seemed rough and ready, uneducated, without many prospects. Even worse, he drove around on a motorbike, and she had preconceived ideas about 'bikers'.

Paul lived with his mother, Shirley, in a council block in Kennington, not far from the areas of London where Ann's early years were spent. His father left the family home when Paul was a baby, too small for Paul to have any memories of him. His mother worked full time as a seamstress, so his grandmother played a large part in bringing him up. By the time he reached his teens he was more interested in motorbikes and mates than in spending his days in the classroom, and he left school without any qualifications. He'd never been in serious trouble with the police, but he'd had a couple of warnings about his bikes. When Ann met him he had just started work at a company specialising in the refining of gold, just off Oxford Street in the heart of the West End. Over the coming years he would rise from teaboy through an apprenticeship in the refining trade, to become assistant manager.

Three years to the day after their first meeting, Paul and Ann married. Surprisingly, the romantic anniversary was Paul's idea. Big, bluff and straightforward though he is, he is also the romantic one of the couple, bringing home bunches of roses for his wife for no particular reason. By the time they married, in 1977, Stan had grown very fond of Paul, and Vi accepted him. To this day, mother-in-law and son-in-law rub along in a slightly edgy way, sparring good naturedly with each other a lot of the time but prepared to find fault, too.

The wedding was traditional and white, with the bride arriving late because she was feeding the horses which pulled the open landau that Stan had insisted they would travel in to the church. When the ceremony was over Paul, in his new suit, dashed from the wedding photographer's line-up to talk to the horses.

The honeymoon was less of a success. When they arrived at the caravan site on the Isle of Sheppey they were surprised to discover Ann's grandparents, an aunt, an uncle and a pregnant cousin, Vicky, all booked into an adjoining chalet. Cramped for space, the others suggested that the cousin – whose childbirth was imminent – share with Paul and Ann. The newlyweds spent their first night as man and wife listening to Vicky's breathing, and trying to decide whether she was snoring or in labour. The following day they moved on to a boarding house in Hastings, but the two single beds refused to be pushed together, skidding apart on the shiny linoleum flooring and bringing the landlady to their door.

'At least we started life together laughing, even if we couldn't do anything else,' says Ann.

Their first home was a semi-detached cottage in Crayford, just a few miles from Ann's parents. They put down the deposit with a lucky windfall: they had been with Paul's mum to one of her regular bingo sessions, and Paul had won £400. With the £100 they had already saved, and a council mortgage, they were able to afford the

140-year-old cottage, and pay to have work done to install an upstairs bathroom. Furniture was donated by relatives, and they learned the hard way how to decorate. By the time Ann became pregnant two years after their marriage, they were well established.

Daniel was born on October 10th 1979. It was a normal labour, and he was a healthy seven-pounder. Ann was happy to give up work to look after him full time, and Paul was delighted with the addition to the family. Daniel was not the only new arrival: when she gave up work to be at home with her baby Ann bought a delightful Borzoi-Newfoundland-cross puppy whom they christened Heidi. The main reason was that the cottage had been broken into, and they wanted a pet who would double up as a guard dog. Ann also knew that Paul, who had had even more of a city childhood than she had, had always wanted a large dog. Heidi launched his lifelong passion: he is now a respected and well-known breeder of Pyrenean mountain dogs. There are trophies, rosettes and diplomas all over the family home, and never fewer than four or five dogs in residence.

A year after Daniel was born they moved to Strood, near Rochester, to a bigger house. However, they were further away from Ann's family, the area was more built up, and Paul had even further to commute into the centre of London every day. He was leaving at 5.30am, and not getting home until after 7pm, five days a week. He was young and fit and took it in his stride, but Ann felt very isolated, on her own all day with only Daniel for company. By the time she was pregnant with Jason, they knew they wanted to move closer to her mum and dad.

Paul was doing well at work, promotions and pay rises following on each other's heels. Despite the collapse of the housing market, they were prepared to sell the house at Strood for a loss and buy the home of their dreams, a cottage in Slade Green. It was here, two months after they moved in, that Ann went into labour with her second son, Jason Simon Andrews.

CHAPTER 3

THE SOLDIER MAN

Jason's first home was Sweetbriar Cottage, Moat Lane, Slade Green, a house and location as pretty as its name suggests. When Ann took me there thirteen years later her description had already prepared me, but I was still astonished to find this scrap of rural beauty tucked away in the sprawl of housing estates along the Thames estuary. We drove through streets of postwar development, crossing a railway line, and turning into what looked at first sight like nothing more than an entryway, but was a narrow lane. Within yards of leaving the last house behind we were, it seemed, miles from anywhere, the sides of the lane bounded by hedges and fields. The only sign of habitation now was the tall lights above a floodlit playing field which we could see across the fields to our left: Ann told me this, and the houses around it, had not been built when they lived here.

About half a mile on the lane peters out at an imposing collection of semi-derelict agricultural buildings. It must have been a large, prosperous farm once upon a time, but the encroachment of the houses has vastly reduced the amount of land, and the site is now used only for storage of builders' materials.

On the other side of the lane from the farm stands a row of cottages, originally built to house farmworkers. Behind the cottages the River Darent flows to meet the Thames, and has been diverted to form a moated island just beyond the cottages. The island once housed a convent, and the hunched ruins of the buildings can still be made out under a dense covering of ivy. Today it is a nature reserve. It was in the stagnant water of the moat that Paul Andrews once found a dead body, as he walked his dogs early in the morning. The police later told him that the man who drowned had recently been released from a psychiatric hospital, and had, many years earlier, lived in the Andrews's cottage. In his confused state, he had being trying to find his way home and had stumbled into the water.

Originally there were four cottages in the row, but the couple who sold Sweetbriar to Ann and Paul had bought two of them and were converting them into one. Halfway through the conversion their marriage broke down and they sold cheaply to the Andrews. For both Ann and Paul it was a dream home: close enough to the station for Paul to walk there, but surrounded on all sides by fields; near to Ann's parents, the shops, schools, yet idyllically countrified. Exactly, they thought, the right place to bring up children and their growing collection of dogs.

The downside was that they took on the cottage unfinished. There were no floorboards in the living room, there was no staircase – the only way to get to the bedrooms was up a ladder, and Ann did not venture up until after Jason was born. Builders were hastily employed to do the essential work needed to make the place habitable, and then Paul and Ann spent the rest of the time they lived there working on the cottage. They loved it, and wanted nothing more than to stay there for ever.

Soon after they arrived they acquired their second Pyrenean mountain dog, and began breeding, keeping two of the pups from the first litter. Paul was beginning to show them, learning all he needed to know from books, other breeders and the experts they met at shows. Dogs were, and still are, his hobby. Neither he nor Ann drink or smoke, so the cost of the dogs is his main indulgence. He would unwind from his long hours commuting into London by walking them along the river bank.

Jason was born at Queen Mary's Hospital, Sidcup. It seemed to be a copybook labour until it stalled, and Ann was put on a drip to keep her contractions going. At the same time a foetal monitor, to check on the unborn baby's heartbeat, was set up – and instantly the labour ward became a centre of high activity. The nursing staff were rushing around, calling for a doctor, panicking. Even through the pains of her labour Ann was aware that something was wrong. Paul, at her side, looked very worried, but did not tell her until afterwards that the foetal monitor was failing to pick up any heartbeat.

Ann was taken through to the delivery room with a doctor on

stand-by and an incubator prepared: the staff were expecting the baby to be born with serious problems, if not stillborn. They were all surprised and delighted when a healthy boy arrived. Throughout her pregnancy Ann had been told she was carrying a small baby, but Jason confounded all expectation by weighing in at 9lbs 10ozs, a large lusty baby with a mop of jet black hair, a strong cry, and a good appetite.

Ten days later Ann took him back to a transformed Sweetbriar Cottage. While she was in hospital Paul and the builders had put in a massive effort to get the structural work completed, and she came home to floorboards and a staircase, leading up to the three bedrooms she had never seen before. She felt happier than she had ever been: two lovely healthy children, a marriage that got stronger and stronger all the time, and her dream home.

There was one major cloud on the horizon. By the time Ann was pregnant with Jason she knew that her father was seriously ill with a heart condition. Stan was aware that he was dying: in the weeks before Jason was born he talked about it a lot to Vi, but he was determined to see the new baby. He was also determined to fulfil a promise he had made to a small daughter many years before.

'I can't go until that girl has a horse,' he told Vi. Within weeks of Ann and Paul moving to Sweetbriar Cottage, he lived up to his word, and presented Ann with an ugly nine-month-old colt.

'He'll come good as he grows,' he said. The horse was named Craven, and, true to Stan's prediction, he grew into a handsome creature who has won a shelf full of trophies and rosettes for his good looks as well as his jumping ability, and, despite developing diabetes, is still enjoying life to the full on the Andrews's farm.

Two weeks after giving the horse to Ann, and two months after Jason was born, Stan died. It was a terrible time for all his family, but Ann felt the loss acutely. He had passed on to her some of his knowledge of horses, but not all his secrets. He told her that he wanted the ancient art of horse whispering to survive, but tradition forbade him to share everything he knew with a female. All horses, and particularly Craven, trigger memories of her father for Ann. Her skill with them has never been tested as acutely as her father's was the day he tamed the rearing stallion, but she has an undoubted rapport with them. On the day we revisited Sweetbriar Cottage a chestnut brown pony galloped across one of the adjacent fields – the field where Craven once lived – to greet her, nuzzling up to her as though she were someone he knew well. Jason too, has a natural affinity with horses.

Vi remembers her husband holding the baby boy for hours at a time. He was not a 'new man' and in general believed babies were best left to women to cope with. It was the only time in all their married life that Vi had seen him cuddle a baby easily and naturally. She believes he knew that Jason was special, different, the heir to his skills with animals – but also to something else, something he did not even discuss with his wife.

Apart from the grief at her father's death, Ann's routine was very settled for the first few weeks of Jason's life. He was a contented baby, and although there was the usual tiring round of broken nights, constant feeds and nappy changes, time passed in a hazy blur. Daniel appeared to have taken to the new arrival very well. A little brother was amusing, but nowhere near as exciting as his new country home, with its large garden which was regularly invaded by the cows from the field at the back, to his great delight. He loved the puppies, and the freedom he had to toddle about in complete safety outside. These distractions meant he did not seem at all resentful that his mother was so wrapped up in the new arrival, and besides, Ann had read the babycare manuals and went out of her way to make sure Daniel did not feel excluded.

It was a month or two after Jason was born, after Ann moved him from a cradle next to her bed into a cot in his own bedroom, that the mysterious happenings began. She would put him down in his cot for a sleep in the afternoon and then find him later lying on the floor under the cot. When he cried in the night, she would find him at the wrong end of the cot, even though he was too small and immobile to have wriggled down there. Twice she found him underneath a chair near to the cot. On one terrifying occasion she could not find him at all when she first went into the nursery bedroom. She screamed in alarm as she saw the empty cot, the tiny duvet neatly folded back. The noise of her scream brought an answering wail from behind the door, where Jason was lying on the floor. Ann snatched him up and cuddled him, feeling a mixture of relief and fear.

26

Daniel, she supposed, was the culprit. She thought his apparent adjustment to a junior rival was masking a deep insecurity, and he was secretly moving his baby brother about when Ann's attention was elsewhere. Or perhaps, she reasoned, he simply wanted to play with Jason. Whatever the motivation, he was the only possible suspect, and she worked out that, standing on the chair, he was big enough to reach into the cot.

It didn't add up, though. There were times when she knew Daniel could not have done it: on one occasion he was at his grandmother's house, on another he was with Ann in the garden the whole time; And what about the times the baby was moved in the middle of the night?

She and Paul puzzled over it late into the night, desperately trying to find a rational explanation. Ann told her health visitor and her doctor. Vi, too, witnessed it, and was baffled and alarmed, but in the end, in the absence of any other possible explanation, Daniel was blamed. He was nearly four years old, and vocal enough to express his denials and his indignation. Ann did not press the point: she did not want to make him feel guilty. The doctor's advice was not to tell him off or make a fuss about what he was doing, but simply to keep an eye on him, and he would eventually be bored with his 'game'.

Life was crowded and busy, with builders still arriving intermittently to work on the house, two children to care for, dogs to be walked, meals to be cooked, washing to be done: in all the daily hurly burly Ann was able to shelve the worries about how and why her baby son was moved. Besides, it did not happen all the time, only now and again, and after about two months it stopped. Ann and Paul were relieved, assuming that the doctor was right and Daniel had passed through a difficult phase. It is only with hindsight that they appreciate the significance of what went on.

In the first couple of years of Jason's life, all Ann's concerns seemed to focus on Daniel. It was just after Jason's birth that Daniel began talking to himself in his bedroom, chuckling and laughing for no obvious reason. There was nothing odd about this: many children do it. There was nothing alarming, either, when he announced to Ann that he had a 'friend' who came to see him in his room. Lots of lonely children have imaginary friends. Although

Daniel now had a baby brother, with almost four years' difference in their ages it would be some time before Jason could be a playmate for him. Sweetbriar Cottage was isolated, apart from the two neighbouring cottages, so Daniel did not have a clutch of friends around to play with. Ann accepted it without worry when he told her about his friend, who disappeared whenever she entered the room.

She was surprised, though, about his description of his friend. She expected the visitor to be another small boy, or perhaps a teddy bear come to life, or a character from one of the books she read to Daniel at bedtime every day. Instead, Daniel said his friend was a 'soldier man', and he would become exasperated with Ann when she came into the room, accusing her of 'scaring him away'. He told her his visitor was called Junus, and when, one evening, he saw a sci-fi programme on television he called to her and pointed at the uniforms the 'space explorers' were wearing: all-in-one costumes with epaulettes.

'That's what Junus wears,' he said.

Both Paul and Ann gently probed about his 'friend' and Daniel told them that Junus was teaching him about the stars and the sky. Daniel answered questions about him in a very matter-of-fact way: when his parents asked how Junus got into the room they were told through the window. However, if they asked whether Junus went to school with him, or whether Daniel would like to invite him to tea, their small fair-haired son would give them a withering look and tell them not to be silly.

The visits would stop for a couple of weeks at a time. Daniel would tell them in advance. 'Junus can't come for a little while,' he said. Sometimes he would tell them that he was expecting a visit that night, and invariably they would hear him chattering away. If they sneaked up to the bedroom door, Daniel would be sitting up in bed talking, but would always, somehow, sense their presence and stop. He seemed unperturbed by the visits, and was growing into a happy, relaxed little boy who was fitting in well at infants' school. When Ann told the health visitor about Daniel's 'friend' she was reassured that it was not unusual, and if Daniel's choice of imaginary companion seemed odd, Ann reminded herself that she, as a child, had a vivid imagination, and Daniel must have inherited it.

Ann expected the 'friend' to disappear when Daniel started at school, and new, real friends filled his life, but in fact Junus visited Daniel for three years, until he was seven.

He only stopped coming when other, far more mysterious, things began to happen in the Andrews household, and particularly to Jason. The starting point was the fourth birthday party, when Jason began to babble complex configurations of numbers, and the cottage was rocked by violent knocking. After the police and Vi left, and Ann and Paul were alone together, she broached the subject, but Paul was already putting up defences, trying to make sense out of the puzzling sequence of events: the knocking was thunder, it was heavy rain, Jason was just having a nightmare. Ann did not pursue it. She could see from Paul's frown that he did not believe his own rationalisations, that he was deeply troubled by the events of the evening, but she also knew that he would not accept a supernatural explanation.

If he could not touch it, see it, examine it, Paul did not believe in it, and Ann understood that the unlikely explanations he was coming up with were his ways of coping with the night's weird events – and she certainly had no better explanation to offer.

After the day of the party, normality was never fully restored. Sweetbriar Cottage would be flooded with bright lights in the middle of the night – lights which 'switched off' as abruptly as they came on, and always before Ann had time to investigate. Electrical equipment developed a life of its own: the television or hi-fi would come on in the middle of the day or night, when the switch was off. The TV even came on after Ann unplugged it from the mains. The electrician who had rewired the cottage was called out several times, but could never find a fault. Clocks around the house would gain or lose time, all misbehaving simultaneously, as though the cottage were on a different time system from the rest of the country. This development worried Ann more than most of the others: she watched Daniel carefully, to make sure he wasn't playing tricks. But she was forced to rule this out when the clocks skipped hours while Daniel was safely in school.

Keys, cups, plates and books would be found under beds, inside wardrobes, in the wrong rooms. Toothbrushes would vanish from the bathroom and be found inside a kitchen cupboard, balancing on a tin of baked beans. A pair of dirty walking shoes turned up inside a bed. At first they teased each other about becoming forgetful ('Must take more water with the whisky!') but they began to wonder if they were going mad. Then they started checking and double checking each other. If Ann left the car keys on the kitchen table she would get Paul to witness her putting them there. Yet regularly, in the morning, they were moved.

Nothing ever vanished completely, everything always turned up somewhere. There were exasperating times, especially when the car keys were missing when Ann was in a hurry to take Daniel to school, but there were no serious losses, just inconvenience, and a creeping feeling of being in the middle of something very strange.

The children, too, were aware of it, and Ann deliberately turned it into a joke. She decided they were victims of a poltergeist, and nicknamed their supernatural intruder Charlie, making light of his annoying activities in front of Daniel and Jason. Poltergeist is a German word meaning 'noisy spirit', and although Charlie didn't make too much noise (there were occasional unexplained bangs and rattles) he was naughty and intrusive, as if he wanted to catch the family's attention: typical poltergeist behaviour.

Ann knew little about the supernatural, but she had heard of poltergeists. She knew that the cottage was more than a hundred years old, and she was happy to accept that spirits from the past had left their imprint on the place. Paul was sceptical, but he missed most of the paranormal activity because of the long hours he worked. After walking his dogs, he would sleep like a log, rarely even waking when Ann nudged him to see the strange blue-white light that flooded their bedroom periodically. Often, Ann would make a point of not telling Paul the catalogue of strange events. She knew it bothered him; that unlike her he would never accept the existence of ghosts and spirits. As long as 'Charlie' was harmless, Ann felt there was no need to worry Paul.

Vi was another matter. Visiting her daughter and grandsons during the day, she was present when lots of strange things happened, and seriously begged Ann to get the place exorcised.

Ann didn't discuss the problem with her immediate neighbours, an elderly couple who did not take kindly to the Andrews's dogs and children. The boys nicknamed the old lady 'Grotbags' because she would complain if they left their bikes near her cottage gate. However, the cottage at the far end of the row was lived in by another young couple, and they, too, experienced some mild supernatural activity: enough to make the wife's parents refuse to sleep in the cottage. When they visited they came in a small motorised home, and insisted on living in it. They never fully explained what it was about the cottage that worried them, but they told Ann there was 'an unnatural atmosphere' there.

The poltergeist activity was, to Ann, harmless fun, and because Jason had been fine since the dramatic events at his fourth birthday party, she gradually put her worries about that night out of her mind. Then five months after the party, something else happened.

Like many harassed and overworked mothers, Ann was grateful for the invention of the video. A supply of cartoon videos was a lifeline for both her and Paul, who worked such long hours during the week. From Monday to Friday, every waking hour for Ann was filled with the demands of the boys, the dogs, a horse, and a house that still required a lot of work.

At the weekends, Daniel could be relied upon to put cartoons on the video first thing in the morning. From 6am onwards Ann would hear the squawks of the animated characters on the screen downstairs, and she'd know that both her sons were happily occupied, giving her and Paul a precious lie-in.

What instinct was it that made her get up to check on them, that Saturday morning in November 1987, when Jason was four? She doesn't know. When she got downstairs she found Daniel, but no Jason. She called upstairs to Paul, who went to check on his younger son.

As Paul walked into Jason's room, picking his bare feet between the cars and planes and Lego that littered the floor, the little boy rushed at him, arms outstretched, tears pouring down his cheeks.

Paul carried Jason downstairs and settled him on the settee. Ben, the huge Pyrenean mountain dog who regarded himself as Jason's bodyguard, went through his usual morning ritual of licking his little charge all over. Jason normally giggled with delight, especially when Ben's coarse tongue tickled his nose, but this morning there was no response.

Paul gently reassured his small son that he had only had a bad dream, nothing more, but Jason refused to be comforted. Tears welled in his eyes again, and spilled down his face: 'They came again,' he said. 'They came again and I had to go with them. They came again. They came again.'

'Who?' Ann and Paul asked simultaneously.

'The little men with big eyes. They scare me and I don't want to go with them but they make me. Please make them go away, Daddy. Don't let the little one take me, don't let them hurt me.'

Ann and Paul soothed him, telling him again that it was a dream, and reminding him that Father Christmas would be coming in a few weeks' time.

Jason stopped grizzling and began to cheer up. Within minutes Jason was tearing around the house with Daniel in a frenzied game of cowboys and Indians. Paul put the incident out of his mind, but Ann dwelled on the words her little son had spoken. Who were the little men that he dreamed of so vividly?

Eventually, she convinced herself that it had been nothing more than a nightmare. All children have nightmares. Is there a parent in the land who hasn't had to comfort a disturbed and sobbing child after a fevered private screening of an X-rated horror dream?

It was in the early hours of the next morning when Ann, finally drifting to sleep, was dragged back into consciousness by another burst of bright light. Despite the closed curtains, the bedroom was suffused with light, which seemed to come from outside, squeezing through the gaps around the edges of the curtains. It was a clear, pale blue light.

She quickly roused Paul. She had seen lights like this before, on other nights, and tried in vain to wake her sleeping husband, but this time Paul surfaced from his deep sleep.

He jumped out of bed and went to the window, pulling back the curtains and gazing out. The lane and the farm buildings were brightly lit, much more brightly than in normal daylight. The pool of light seemed to stretch about fifty yards in every direction around them, tapering off into the blackness of the night. There was nothing moving out there, not even a cat.

'What the hell . . . ?' Paul said, struggling into his clothes. Suddenly there was a terrified scream from Jason's room. Ann sprang out of bed so fast that she and Paul collided at the door in

32

their scramble to get to their son, who was screaming full throttle, his little face red with the effort.

'They're back, they're back!' he shouted to his parents between hysterical screams.

Ann pulled him tight against her, making a soothing shushing sound as she stroked his head. The screams subsided to sobs. The intense light went off suddenly, as if someone had clicked a switch, and the three of them were plunged into darkness.

Paul refused to admit to a connection between Jason's screams and the light. It was another bad dream, no more. But he was uneasy, and after patrolling around the outside of the cottage with a torch agreed with Ann that Jason should spend the rest of the night with them. He carried in the mattress from Jason's room and laid it on the floor next to Ann's side of the bed.

The little boy was still sobbing as Ann tucked him up, and she lay awake, her arm dangling over the side of the bed, clutching his hot fingers. Slowly his sobs subsided into the level heavy breathing of sleep. Eventually, despite herself, she slept, too.

The following day was wet and windy, and the boys were confined indoors. The house resounded to the whoops and hollers of the cowboy patrol, and again Ann and Paul looked at their mischievous, normal little boy and began to wonder if they had imagined the night's happenings.

As bedtime approached, however, Jason became fractious and difficult. 'They only ever come at night,' he said. 'Can I sleep with you, Mummy?' Paul and Ann agreed. There would be many more nights to come when the only place Jason would sleep was his parents' room.

Years later, I ask Paul what he had expected to find when he went outside, looking for the source of the light, what the explanation could ever have been, and he has obviously never formulated any convincing theory.

Car headlights? But they lived at the end of a lane that led nowhere, and even headlights on full beam would not reach their first floor bedroom. A police helicopter beam? Possible, but there was no sound of helicopter rotor blades, no local paper story about joyriders or burglars escaping down this remote lane. A meteorite? Paul the sceptic would willingly believe that the sky was lit up by the ionised trail of a chunk of rock burning into the earth's atmosphere. But checks with the Meteorological Office and the Ministry of Defence have shown that there were no meteorites recorded over Britain that night.

Jason changed over the next few weeks. The happy outward-looking four-year-old, who liked rolling around on the floor with Ben the dog or Daniel his brother, who confidently explored the fields near the cottage with Ann, terrifying her with his daredevil antics, who chattered excitedly at the prospect of joining Daniel at school, who loved to cycle up and down the deserted lane: this Jason disappeared. In his place Ann had a fractious, difficult, clingy child, who would not even go to the toilet without her – and who sat outside the bathroom whenever she was inside.

Bedtimes became a nightly battle ground. Jason refused to sleep in his own room. The Andrews tried putting him in Daniel's room, and this seemed to comfort him a little, but he was only really settled when he slept on a mattress on the floor next to Ann's side of the big double bed in their bedroom. Even this was a compromise: he wanted to snuggle in between his parents, but his fidgeting meant Paul was not getting enough sleep before his early alarm call. If he did fall asleep in Daniel's room, Ann would be woken by him diving on top of her and flinging his arms around her neck in the middle of the night, sobbing about 'them' taking him again. She'd comfort him, telling him it was all a nasty dream.

If the family were out, visiting family or friends, after dark, Jason would panic. He soon fathomed how to undo his car seat, and he'd launch himself at Ann, clinging to her as she struggled to drive. She'd get angry, worried about the safety of all the car's occupants, but Jason would shriek, 'I want you, I want you.'

The poltergeist activity continued, and there was a new dimension. One wintry evening, as she went into the bedroom her sons were now sharing at the back of the cottage, Ann recoiled in shock: a large white shape was perched on the window ledge, and two huge eyes were staring at her, unblinking. After a few seconds, while her heart raced madly, Ann made sense of the white blur. It was a snowy owl. It was a spectacular sight, its pure white plumage against the pitch black night. Eight-year-old Daniel, playing on the floor with some toy cars, seemed to take its presence for granted. Jason was slightly more wary, holding tight to Ann's hand.

After a few minutes the bird looked at each of them for a few seconds, then turned and flew away. Ann watched from the window as it wheeled over the top of the cottage and was gone. However, over the next few months it returned many times, sometimes two or three times a week. Always, the visits lasted no longer than half an hour. Daniel loved it, and when he opened the window it twice flew into the room and perched on the back of a chair.

Ann was nervous of it. It was a large bird, with alert yellow eyes that followed her round the room. But she did not question its presence: in retrospect she knows she was naïve, but her city upbringing had not taught her about wild birds. The only time she had seen an owl at close quarters before was in a zoo, although she'd seen barn owls and tawny owls at night, swooping silently among the deserted farm buildings. She assumed that visits from owls, including snowy owls, were a normal part of country life, and explained its tameness by guessing that it had been hand-reared and then released into the wild, and so was not nervous of people. She had no idea that snowy owls are rare birds, Arctic creatures whose natural habitat is ice-floes and bleak ledges in a treeless frozen landscape. Even in a bad year, when the supply of lemmings runs low, snowy owls never venture further into Europe than the coasts of Iceland, Greenland, Norway and the Murmansk region of the old Soviet Union. It should never have survived among the lush, and relatively warm, habitat of Kent.

The owl came sporadically for six months, sometimes two or three nights in succession, sometimes not for a week or more. When it stopped appearing at the window Daniel was quite upset. Then one night it appeared again, a solitary visit in which it seemed to fix its eyes on Daniel for a long time. It flew off, and was never seen again, but after that night, Daniel accepted its disappearance. Ann got the distinct feeling it had come to say goodbye to him, to make its peace with him for not coming any more, but she banished such a fanciful thought.

Years later, I discovered that 'owls' frequently appear in 'screen memories' of aliens, when people see their alien visitors in a more normal, everyday guise. Children, in particular, often refer to aliens in terms they understand: birds, cats, or other animals. Owls are a common choice, probably because they have large eyes which dominate their heads in the way that the eyes of aliens do, and because of their ability to fly silently. Some researchers believe the aliens deliberately shroud their own identities by taking on other forms; others believe that the human mind takes refuge in matching a frightening entity with something familiar. Even so, there are usually clues that it would not be possible for the animal or bird to be in the situation that it is seen. The Andrews's owl, for instance, was not a common British owl, nor – by coming into the room – did it behave like a wild animal.

Paul never saw the owl, but Ann told him about it. He, too, accepted it as normal country life. Besides, he was preoccupied with his own problems, and he was finding the constant presence of Jason a strain. Bed was where he and Ann, like most married couples, took refuge from the stress of bringing up small children, but there was no escape for Paul. Wherever Ann was, there was Jason. He tried to be understanding, but he really felt his wife was being too indulgent and warned her that she was spoiling Jason, that she was turning him into a mummy's boy. He could see Jason was genuinely frightened of sleeping in his own room, or even with Daniel, but felt that constantly giving in to his fear was making it worse. Ann tried to insist that the little boy slept in his own bed, but night after night she found it impossible to resist Jason's desperate sobbing.

She knew that it was damaging her married life, but she thought that Jason simply needed time to grow out of the terrible nightmares she believed he was having. After all, she and Paul would have years to be together: Jason needed her now, perhaps only for a few more nights. Inevitably, the few nights dragged on and on, and several months went by with Jason falling asleep on the mattress, clinging to Ann's fingers which she dangled over the side of the bed. If she tried to withdraw them before he was deeply asleep he would whimper pitifully.

For Paul, life was going badly. He had always been happy to work and travel long hours, getting plenty of job satisfaction as he rose through the ranks of the small family-run company, and knowing that the money he was earning was providing his family with a good lifestyle. It is hard to reconcile his huge physical size with the delicate work he did, taking raw gold and silver and turning it into chains and rings, but he took a real pride in it. Ann's wedding ring was handmade for her by her husband. He was rewarded for his loyalty and hard work by a steady stream of promotions and salary increases. They lived well: Ann could fill her trolley in the supermarket without worrying; when the car needed replacing they could afford another one; the dogs and the children got the best of everything. It wasn't a lavish lifestyle, but they were comfortable.

However, there were changes at the company where Paul worked. He got on well with the elderly couple who owned it, but when the husband died and the wife retired, the business was handed over to the next generation. This included an American son-in-law with his own ideas about how the firm should be run, ideas that Paul disagreed with. Never being the sort of person to bottle up his feelings, he expressed his opinions forthrightly. Too forthrightly: one day he blew up when he was told to do something he thought was idiotic and counter-productive. He told the new boss exactly what he thought, and was summarily dismissed. Because he left on the spot, he received no compensation or wages in lieu of his notice. He had worked there fourteen years, and left with nothing.

Ann was astonished when he walked into Sweetbriar Cottage at 11 am that morning, only hours after he had left for work. She teased him that it was a good job her toyboy wasn't popping round that day, but she could instantly see from Paul's sombre expression that he wasn't in the mood for jokes. Her first thought was that he was ill, but he sat down and calmly told her what had happened. He was dreading her reaction, expecting her to say, 'What about the mortgage? What about the children? What are we going to live on?'

Ann's first emotion, however, was great relief. She had watched the pressure building up, seen how tense and tired Paul was when he got home, realised that it was taking him longer and longer to unwind. She was glad that something had finally happened, forcing him to take stock of his life. She knew that he was not a natural nine-to-fiver, that his only real happiness was when he was grooming his dogs or Craven the horse, or walking the dogs alongside the river.

So she was supportive and unworried, and found Paul's presence around the house all day a great bonus. The tensions that had built up between them over the months of disturbed nights, of Jason's 'nightmares' and clinginess, dissipated as this real crisis drew them together. It was Paul who was more concerned, especially when job application after job application came to nothing. His age, at thirty-two, was against him: the only people anybody seemed to want to employ were trainees. Unaccustomed to doing nothing, he needed to fill his hours: the dogs were walked more than they had ever been before, their coats were groomed even more assiduously than normal, Craven's welfare was fussed over endlessly.

He was even on hand to shoo the cows out of the back garden when they got through the fence, and it was while he was doing this that he started chatting to the farmer, an old man who was close to retiring. The land where the cows grazed had been sold to developers (although, to this day, nothing has been done with it). In his remaining few months of working life, the old farmer was happy to allow Paul to lend a hand, unpaid, with his livestock, and it was in doing this that Paul discovered his true vocation. The boy who had grown up in a block of council flats in inner London, with only a mouse in a cage as a pet, turned out to be a natural stockman, with a flair for handling cattle. Paul loved it. No amount of bad weather could deter him: Ann jokes that he has no blood, because in the deepest of frosts Paul will work in a T-shirt. He was used to very early starts, and hated lying in bed, so being up to help with the early milking was no problem.

He told Ann that for the first time in years he was enjoying what he was doing. In return for his free labour, the farmer taught him a great deal about animal husbandry, and Paul lapped it up, but there was one day a week that he did not relish, the day he had to sign on for his unemployment benefit. The family income had been drastically reduced. Ann went round the supermarket with a calculator, to make sure that she only spent what was in her purse. They cut up their credit cards, but were saddled with hundreds of pounds' worth of debt from them, money that they had spent in the days when Paul's salary rolled in every month.

Ann informed all their creditors, but none were very sympathetic. She surprised herself by being remarkably calm and philosophical.

'If we haven't got it, they can't have it,' she told Paul, as he worried about their mounting debt. She has inherited a great deal of her father's gipsy spirit, regarding life as an adventure with inevitable surprises around each corner. Paul, on the other hand, blamed himself for their predicament, because it was his temper that had cost him his job.

Then the crunch came: nine months after Paul became unemployed the building society informed them that their home was going to be repossessed. Despite some help from Housing Benefit, they were falling more and more behind with the mortgage. This was a devastating blow: they loved the cottage, and had worked so hard to restore it. Swallowing his pride, Paul pleaded with the building society officials, but the men in suits would not listen.

'Bloody penpushers – what do they know about people's lives?' he muttered as Ann ushered him out of the office before his temper exploded.

Ann contacted the local council, who offered them a flat in a tower block. She took one look at it and turned it down, worried that she would lose her sons to the teenage gangs who roamed the estate.

They put Sweetbriar Cottage on the market, but they had not found a buyer as the date for repossession approached. The two children were unconcerned. When asked if he would like to move Daniel said, 'Yes – can I take my bike?' Jason, at four-and-a-half, was too small to understand. As the prospect of being homeless loomed, they were saved when a family fell in love with, and bought, Sweetbriar Cottage. It was a bittersweet moment for Ann when they offered to buy it: she knew she and Paul needed to sell, but she also knew it was the end of her dream home.

Thanks to the boom in house prices in the late eighties, the Andrews paid off their mortgage, all their debts, and ended up with £30,000 to put in the bank. It seemed like a lot of money, but it was not enough to buy another home, and with Paul unemployed there was no chance of them getting another mortgage. So, although one problem had been solved, they still had nowhere to live.

It was then that Ann came up with a suggestion that Paul leapt at. As Paul was so happy working with the local farmer, why didn't they go into farming themselves? It would have to be in a small way: they did not have the money for rolling acres and large herds of cattle, but they had enough to buy themselves a smallholding. They could live on the land, in a mobile home, and Paul could have cows, hens, pigs, goats, geese, whatever he wanted. They would not only be buying themselves somewhere to live, Ann said, but they would be buying themselves a source of income, and, most importantly, a way of life that would suit them all. They would be able to take all the dogs, and Craven. Paul would never have to work nine till five again, and the boys would grow up in the fresh air, surrounded by animals.

Ann also felt that, with a life like this, Jason would get over his fear of sleeping on his own. Preoccupied as she was with the major family problems, she had never lost sight of Jason's fears and worries. A change of surroundings would, she hoped, make a big difference. Perhaps her mother had been right about Sweetbriar Cottage, perhaps it was haunted.

When they moved away, Jason's difficult 'phase' would, she was sure, be at an end.

CHAPTER 4

HAWKSNEST

Hawksnest Farm in summer is a beautiful spot, the fields, liberally sprinkled with buttercups and daisies, stretching down to dense woodland. The Andrews's horses, six of them, graze in the bottom field, while four picture-book-pretty cows, Charolais and Jerseys, with their dusty pale brown hides, large brown eyes and great fans of eyelashes, munch the grass nearer the farm buildings.

Prudence, a huge Vietnamese pot-bellied pig, roams the yard, often escaping into the lane, to the consternation of passing hikers, who have been known to ring the police reporting sightings of a wild boar. There is nothing very wild about Prudence: she's a gentle creature who enjoys having her back scratched. Less friendly are the geese who cackle and hiss at intruders, perfect guardians of the ten-acre site.

The buildings include a burned-out barn, which the Andrews are busy replacing with a new structure, and some stables and pens. There is, today, a very small caravan on the site: the huge mobile home where Paul, Ann, Daniel and Jason used to live is no longer there.

It is easy to see why Paul and Ann fell in love with the place. Less easy, perhaps, to see why it had to be this particular smallholding, when they visited farms all over Kent, Cornwall, Devon, Dorset and many other counties in their quest for a new home. They both admit they saw other places just as pretty, and some which were better equipped: there's no water supply or power supply to Hawksnest Farm. Yet right up to a few days before they were due to move out of Sweetbriar Cottage, they had not found anywhere that they instinctively felt was right for them – and then they looked over the huge five-bar gate on to Hawksnest Farm, about a mile from the tiny picturesque village of Crouch, near Borough Green, in Kent. Without even going on to the land, they knew they had found the home they were looking for. They both felt the certainty at the same moment, as though some outside force zapped them with it.

They paid cash, £25,000, to the amazement of the estate agent, and took possession of the empty land, tucked away down a rutted track which crosses another farmer's fields of crops. The farm is a wedge-shaped plot, with buildings, put up by the Andrews, running along one edge, a pond in front of them and fields tapering away to thick woods owned by an absentee Arab landowner, whose estate managers turn up a couple of times a year to supervise felling and woodland management. Through the woods, with a barbed wire fence for demarcation, the land becomes the property of the Ministry of Defence, and opens out into Mereworth Training Ground, which, according to the MoD, is used for Territorial Army training. There are bridle paths through the woods, used by riders and occasional mountain bikers, but away from the narrow paths the undergrowth is thick and impenetrable.

With their remaining money the Andrews bought a large mobile home and building materials for a large barn and stables. The mobile home, purchased second-hand from another farmer, measured forty-eight feet by twelve feet, and had two bedrooms, a lounge, a kitchen and a bathroom. It arrived on a low loader, but because the track to Hawksnest Farm is rough, Paul towed it on to the site with his Range Rover. Daniel and Jason were very excited: they loved their new home, but most of all they loved being in the middle of nowhere with nothing but fields around them. Electricity came from a generator, and water was ferried in a huge plastic tank from a garage in Borough Green. The owner agreed that Paul could fill up from his tap in the evenings, when there were not too many customers about. It takes over an hour to fill the tank, a job which Paul had to do about once a fortnight, but even these inconveniences were an adventure.

Apart from the dogs, who loved their new environment, Craven and his companion, a horse called Shannon, were the first animals to arrive at the farm, followed by a dozen goats. Paul tethered the goats along the boundary fence and they gradually ate their way inwards, bringing the overgrown fields under control. He was delighted with the taste of goat's milk, but Ann and the boys preferred the sort they bought from the supermarket. Money was tight, they were still living on benefits until the business was established, but they both felt wildly happy to have no mortgage, no debt, and to be working towards self-sufficiency.

Before they bought it, Hawksnest Farm had been home to a motorcycle scrambling track, but it had not been used for years, and when they moved in the blackberry bushes were twelve feet high. It was only after the goats had done their work that Ann could fully see the boundaries of the property.

Pigs, geese and chickens followed the goats. Ann's hens supplied fresh eggs for a local bakery as well as for the family, Paul sold organic pork to a butcher at Tonbridge, and they gradually edged their way into a profitable existence. What they lacked in material wealth they felt was more than compensated for by the outdoor life, and the feeling of being their own bosses. As she walked around the farm collecting eggs Ann often thought of her father, and how he would have loved the life she was leading.

It was a very happy time for all the family, especially because Jason was able to sleep undisturbed in the bunk beds he shared with Daniel. Ann found herself thinking less and less about his old problems, and when she did remember it was to think of it as a phase that had passed. Jason settled in at the local Borough Green infants' school. He seemed happy, although sometimes Ann wondered whether it was natural for him to be so self-contained: he would spend hours in the fields talking to the animals, who all accepted his company. There were times when Paul would call for Jason to help him handle the stock, because the boy had an ability to relax even the most nervous animal.

Riding seemed to come naturally to Jason. The Andrews acquired several horses, usually because they were not wanted by their owners. With ample grazing space Paul was always willing to take another one in, and even the most difficult ponies seemed to fall under Jason's spell. He rode them bareback around the farm with a comfortable grace that made Ann smile and think how proud her father would have been of the baby he held in his arms just before his death.

There was a strange incident involving Shannon (whose real name, Shenandoah, was too much of a mouthful for Jason), which puzzled the vet, as well as Paul and Ann. The horse was standing stock still when Paul crossed the field towards him one morning. Close up, Paul could see that a large square flap had been cut in the horse's shoulder. There was a small amount of blood around the wound, but very little. It had clearly been done with a knife – it was such a neat cut – and when the vet got there a couple of hours later he confirmed that it was a deliberate incision, and that several layers of tissue below the skin had been removed. It was obviously not the normal work of a vandal. Most oddly, Shannon stood still and showed no sign of pain while the vet inspected and then stitched the wound. It was as if the horse had already been anaesthetised.

Apart from the mystery of the wound, Paul was also amazed that anyone could have got into their field at night without rousing either the geese or the dogs. At the time, the family knew nothing of the strange spate of animal mutilations which appear to have some connection with alien activity, and Ann and Paul eventually accepted that Shannon's injuries must be the work of a malicious and cruel vandal. They were surprised how quickly Shannon healed, and grateful that the horse did not appear to suffer.

Apart from this mystery, there was one brief interlude of unhappiness, in the summer of 1989.

One morning in late July, just before the boys broke up for their summer holiday, Ann dropped them at school and then made a special trip to the local chemist. Later that morning she sat on the edge of the bed and gazed in despair at the pregnancy test kit. It had changed colour, confirming her worst fears. She was expecting a baby. She'd known, deep inside herself, for a few days, but she'd tried hard to convince herself she was imagining it. Now she could not pretend any more.

That evening, with the boys out of the way, she broke the news to Paul. He was delighted. He'd always wanted loads of children, and Ann knew he would love to have a daughter. She looked at him in disbelief. Had he forgotten how much work a baby meant, the nappy-changing, feeding, all the expense? She was thirty-three, and Paul was only days from his thirty-third birthday. Their youngest child, Jason, was seven – hadn't it occurred to Paul that this meant starting again? Ann hated to spoil his simple pleasure, but she could not join in his celebration. With Daniel and Jason old enough to be physically independent, she did not relish the prospect of going back to having a tiny, totally dependent child. She'd long ago given away all the baby equipment: cots, pushchairs, clothes. She was looking forward to the family getting back on its feet, getting the farm running, and although she loved living in the mobile home, she was not sure she wanted to be confined to it with a tiny baby. Besides, they had just established their cattle programme, and Paul was up to his ears looking after the cows. A baby would mean she would not be able to help Paul as much. She was worried, too: she'd been in her twenties when she had the other two, and she knew the risks of pregnancy were greater over the age of thirty. Jason's had been a difficult birth, and he was a special child who needed so much extra time and help.

She said very little to Paul about her fears, wanting to give herself time to think it through. She knew that, without his enthusiasm, she would probably have sought an abortion, but did she have the right to deny him another baby? Paul could see she was upset, but he found it hard to subdue his happiness. He put his arm around her and told her that she was probably just low because she wasn't feeling too good – she'd felt queasy for the first few months during both her other pregnancies.

They agreed to talk it through again, the next day, but neither changed their position, and for a couple of weeks there was an uncomfortable silence between them. Then Ann made a decision: despite really not wanting another child, she would go through with it for Paul's sake. She did not want him to feel, for the rest of his life, that she had deprived him of a bigger family.

When she told him, he was delighted. They agreed not to tell the boys. A pregnancy is a long time for young children to wait for something as exciting as a new brother or sister, and besides, Ann had an uneasy feeling. There was something about this pregnancy that was not like the previous two.

It was only two weeks later, on a Wednesday night in August, that Ann felt very tired, and went to bed early. She did not think anything of it: the outdoor life of the farm meant they were all tired at night, and the early weeks of any pregnancy are exhausting. In bed, she found it hard to sleep. When she finally did, she had disturbing dreams.

The next morning Paul shook Ann awake. There was panic in his voice, and when she opened her eyes he muttered, 'Thank God.' Ann felt tired, weak, but Paul's strong arms helped her into a sitting position. He gestured at the bedclothes. A dark red stain had seeped through the duvet, and when Paul flung it back Ann could see that her nightdress and the sheet were soaked in blood. She felt no pain, and apart from being tired, did not feel ill, but Paul insisted she stay in bed. He phoned the doctor, who arrived fifteen minutes later and told them that Ann had miscarried.

Paul felt guilty about his attitude over the past few weeks, and apologised to Ann. In the few seconds before he roused her, he had had real fears for her, and he realised that her health was more important to him than his idealised fancy for another child. Ann forgave him instantly. While Paul fussed around her, changing the bedding and getting her into a clean nightie, they discussed what had happened in the night, both of them puzzled that Ann had slept so soundly through it. She did not tell Paul, but she had uneasy stirrings of memories, as if she had been dreaming something important, but just could not bring it to the front of her mind.

Paul was so attentive over the next few days that at times Ann felt suffocated. She needed time to think about her loss, to gauge her own feelings. There were days when she accepted it, and she had an eerie feeling of hearing a voice inside her head telling her it was 'all for the best'. Whenever she considered the reality of having another baby she knew this was true, but there were other days when, despite her rational feelings, she felt weepy and grieved for the child she had lost.

Life at the farm was so busy that she soon forgot about her pregnancy – or, at least, buried it somewhere beyond her conscious thoughts. Paul was doing well, and they were turning over enough money for him to fulfil his greatest ambition: they had bought some cattle. Paul had spent weeks working on the barn and outhouses, making them into suitable stalls, and when these were ready he bought his first four calves, which he raised successfully and sold for the top price at market. He was very proud, and Ann knew that he was finally completely happy: cows, of all animals, are Paul's first love, and he had learned enough about rearing them before they moved to Hawksnest to be confident in handling them.

Armed with a glowing market report on his first four cows, Paul went to see the bank manager, who was happy to lend him £20,000 to build a proper cattle barn and increase his stock to twenty cows. With the barn complete, he bought five or six cows at a time, always isolating them to prevent them bringing any infection on to the property. He took no short cuts, as each animal cost between £200 and £300 and represented a big investment for a small business. Injections were given, feed buckets were doused in disinfectant, each calf was inspected a couple of times a day. Paul was once again working from very early in the morning until late in the evening, but this time it was from choice, not because he faced a long commute into London. He rose easily and naturally at 5.30am, never needing an alarm clock, and at times Ann had to remind him to leave his beloved animals at bedtime.

Within days of the first batch of cows arriving Hawksnest Farm received an unexpected visitor, a council official who wanted to know how long the family had been living there. Ann was surprised by the question: they were paying their rates, sending their children to the local school, they knew all their neighbours – their presence was no secret. However, the man from the council explained to them that they had not been given permission to live on the land.

This surprised Ann even more, and she turned to her filing system to get hold of the deeds, to prove that they owned the land. The council official shook his head: the ownership of the land was not the issue. The family were living on land that had not previously been inhabited and, he said, they needed council permission to do that.

Both Ann and Paul looked at him in silence. They had naïvely assumed that if they owned the land, they could do what they wanted on it. It had never occurred to either of them that they had to ask permission before moving a mobile home on to the site. There are lots of similar smallholdings in this area of Kent, with owners living in caravans and mobile homes, and the Andrews assumed that they could do the same.

The man from the council was pleasant and sympathetic, telling them to get an application in as soon as possible. Without committing himself, he gave them to understand that it would be surprising if they were not allowed to live there. Ann filled in the forms the same day, confident that it was a formality, a piece of paperwork which she had missed, but which would now be sorted out. For once, Ann's instincts let her down: this was a problem that would not go away so easily.

The reply from the council said that to live on the land, the Andrews would have to prove that their smallholding was financially viable. Ann believed she had instant, easy proof: she had applied for Family Credit, a benefit paid to families on low incomes, only to be turned down because the smallholding was too profitable for her to qualify. She was sure that with this, plus the figures Paul had worked out for the bank manager, who had been happy enough to base his loan on them, the council would be satisfied.

While she was waiting for their reply, disaster struck.

The morning of Wednesday, September 13th 1989 is one that Ann will never forget. She had ferried the boys to school, fed and exercised the dogs, and was just beginning her regular round-up of the eggs, which the free range hens hid all over the smallholding. As she crossed the yard with the basket in her hand Paul came running towards her.

'One of the calves has died!' he shouted, dashing past her into the mobile home to ring the vet. Ann had a dreadful feeling of foreboding, a fear that clutched at her insides and was out of proportion to the death of one calf. They'd known there were risks, and they'd budgeted for the odd failure, but this felt like something worse. For the first time since moving to the farm, she felt fear.

As they waited for the vet, Paul shared Ann's worries: he had seen plenty of sick calves before; he had even been there when calves had died. But he had checked this calf the night before, and it was showing no signs of going down with anything. The death was so sudden that he could not explain it: he could only imagine that it had eaten something poisonous, and if that was the case, it was vital to find out what it was.

The vet, who arrived from a local practice in Borough Green, was also puzzled by the sudden death of the seemingly healthy calf, and arranged for the carcass to be taken to the Ministry of

Agriculture Veterinary Investigation Centre at Wye, near Ashford, Kent. She said she would call again the next day, but Ann explained they would not be there in the middle of the day, as Ann's grandmother was ill in hospital and they were going to visit her. Within an hour or two the vet rang them from her office, to say that she had checked with colleagues and that they should not go to the hospital, in case they were carrying the infection that had killed the calf. Again, Ann felt a powerful surge of fear: she wondered if the vet was hiding something.

When the report on the death came back it showed that the calf died from salmonella, a strain known as *Salmonella Typhimurium 204c*. By the time the report arrived other calves were showing signs of being ill, and over the next two weeks, all but two of the twenty-six cattle were wiped out.

For a month, it seemed as though the curse had been lifted and the remaining livestock were safe. But then it struck again: within eight days, at the beginning of November, all seven sheep on the farm also died. The following day, both the remaining calves died. Each time there was no sign of illness, no warning of what was to come.

Paul was devastated, and initially blamed himself, thinking that perhaps someone with more experience would have been able to avoid the disaster. The vet, herself at a loss to understand it, called in an investigating officer from the Ministry of Agriculture, who came after the deaths of the first nine calves, and a detailed study was carried out on the farm and the farming methods Paul was using. Apart from making a few minor recommendations to improve the cattle accommodation, the report gave Hawksnest Farm a clean bill of health, and Paul's farming standards came up to scratch.

However, a piece of paper exonerating him meant nothing to Paul, as the devastation continued. Alarmed by the scale of the outbreak, he was told at first to dispose of the bodies by incinerating them, and then he received a call from a man who introduced himself as a Ministry official, who instructed him to keep the carcasses. He was not told why, but assumed it was part of an investigation into the cause of the deaths.

The growing pile of bodies was a constant reminder to Paul of the farm's failure.

Ann's grief at the loss of their livelihood was made much worse by the death of her grandmother, who she had not been allowed to visit. She had always been very close to her mother's mother, and in her last few hours her grandmother had kissed one of Ann's cousins and called her by Ann's name. The pain of the loss was aggravated by guilt at not being there for the old lady.

In front of Ann, Paul tried to keep his spirits up. It was a struggle to always sound optimistic, but he knew how much he owed to his wife: not many women would leave a comfortable cottage for life in a mobile home without a word of reproach. He knew it was a long time since Ann had bought a new dress, splashed out on a lipstick, treated herself to something new for the home. All the money they made went on vet's bills, buying animals, getting the food and clothes two growing boys needed.

Now it had all come to nothing. Alone on the land, Paul came close to despair. This was his dream, and he'd worked hard day and night to get it up and running. Now the pasture where the cows had grazed was empty. The sheep had gone, too. The pigs survived and, looking back, Paul can see it was the pigs that pulled him through. They, and the poultry, were all he had left to make a living for his family. Without them there would have been no reason to carry on. Animals don't ask questions, want to see bank statements, demand early repayments; they want food and shelter and attention, and Paul could provide these.

As he worked he kept his eyes averted from the corner of the field, where the carcasses of his dead calves were waiting for collection. All his calves: a big enough herd to make a living, yet small enough for him to know every one individually. He'd only had them a few weeks, and he was professional enough to know that they would have been driven away to slaughter one day. But to die this way: it wasn't right.

Paul knew it wasn't his fault. but he worried at the problem. How had salmonella got into his herd, after he had so carefully isolated each batch of new cows? The Ministry report gave no clue as to where the strain of salmonella might have come from, and he was at a loss to explain it. Why had it run rampant? The odd death from salmonella happens, but to lose a whole herd just did not add up.

An ADAS official, talking about the outbreak to me years

later, said this was the most puzzling part of it.

'Salmonella gets on to farms – it's easy to buy an infected calf without knowing it. It is possible for a calf or two to die, although most respond to antibiotic treatment. But it is very rare for it to run right through a herd like that, and for them all to die.'

Paul the pragmatist wanted answers: if it could happen once it could happen again, and he needed to know how to prevent it.

He was feeding the big sow on a cold afternoon as the winter light was failing when a dark Transit van pulled into the rutted yard. The mid-November weather was chilly but there had been no rain for a few days, and the ground was compacted. Paul strode towards the unmarked van, puzzled. Hawksnest Farm was so far off the beaten track that they did not get passing visitors, and Paul knew his few regular callers.

The Transit door slid back on the driver's side, and to Paul's astonishment a tall, thin man dressed from head to toe in a pristine white coverall suit, complete with hood, jumped down.

'We're from the Ministry,' he told Paul, as five more 'spacemen' in white suits emerged from the back of the van. They began to inspect the barns and outbuildings, moving together as a group, not speaking to one another.

'What are you looking for?' Paul asked, bemused and hopeful. Perhaps now he would get the answers he wanted: these men certainly looked like business. The men ignored him. When he tried to follow them they turned him back with outstretched arms.

Only one of them spoke: the thin man with pale grey eyes who had first alighted from the van. He asked Paul to get the records of all the movements of the cattle which had died. Paul made his way to the mobile home, where Ann was peeling vegetables for the evening meal. She hadn't heard the van arrive, but when Paul told her she followed him outside, taking the carefully filled-in lists of animal purchases and movements. It was Ann who did the paperwork for the farm, and she was meticulous. She did not have to search through files for these documents: she and Paul had been worrying away for days at the salmonella mystery, and she'd been checking through the details of where each calf was bought and how it had been transported to the smallholding.

The thin man was speaking into a walkie-talkie. They did not

51

hear what he said, but when they appeared he snapped it shut and held out his hand for the sheaf of papers. He thanked Ann and said that they would be checking out the movement details.

As he spoke a large lorry lumbered up to the gate of the yard. The white-suited men began loading the dead carcasses, each individually wrapped in plastic sheeting, into the back of the lorry, then the doors were locked. Immediately the men in white suits clambered back into the Transit, and the two vehicles nudged their way, bumper to bumper, out of the yard and along the dirt track towards the road. Paul watched until the tiny convoy disappeared.

'Who were they?' asked Ann.

'They said they were from the Ministry,' said Paul. As he spoke it dawned on him that the silent men had not told him which ministry. 'It must be the Ministry of Agriculture,' he said more to himself than to Ann.

For a few minutes the couple did not speak, both unable to articulate the strange unease they felt. The spell was broken by Daniel and Jason scrambling over the gate as they returned from school. They'd been dropped at the bottom of the dirt track and had walked up, but they had not seen the van.

'That's weird,' Paul said. 'It's all weird.'

Shaking his head, he walked back to the pigs. Ann went back to the kitchen, trying to hide her worry from the boys.

The cattle dealers at Sevenoaks Market who sold Paul the calves were very concerned when they heard what had happened. Paul warned them that the men from 'the Ministry' would be getting in touch to check on the cattle movements, and they all made sure they found the relevant paperwork. Months later one of them asked Paul if he'd heard any more from the 'officials' who took the carcasses away and Paul was surprised to find that none of the dealers had been approached. He himself heard nothing more. Five years later, when he was dealing with ADAS, at that time a government body responsible for advising farmers, he asked about the mysterious men in white suits from 'the Ministry' – only to be told that the Ministry of Agriculture did not have a flying task force of vans and men, and that the normal procedure after a salmonella outbreak is to burn the carcasses on the farm, to prevent any risk of contamination when they are moved.

However, although they heard no more at the time about their cows, the Andrews did hear more from other sources. First was the council who, on discovering that they no longer had cattle or sheep, ruled that the smallholding was definitely not viable and that they could not live on it.

This bad news was compounded by the action taken by the bank. After the death of the cattle they increased the rate of interest on the loan, and demanded that it be paid off as rapidly as possible, tripling the repayments from £100 a month to £300. Even without the cows, his chief source of income, he could have handled £100 repayments from the profits from the pigs and poultry, but £300 was too much.

Worse, the family once again faced the prospect of being homeless. It was as if all their hard work and careful planning had come to nothing, and Ann felt she was back at square one, as desolate as she had been when they faced eviction from the cottage. They'd watched their savings disappear, but, hardest of all to bear, their dream was in ruins.

As they hung on for a couple of months, fighting the council's decision that they had to leave the land, life was bleak. The only income was Child Benefit of £15 a week, plus whatever they could make from the eggs. The pigs were not ready to be sold, and they and the horses and dogs had to be fed.

Paul solved this problem: he found a local bakery which was happy to let him take away all the stale stock. The cakes went to the pigs, the meat pies went to the dogs and the bread went to the horses and poultry. With money so tight, insurances were allowed to lapse, and in the bleak winter weather a large tree fell across the mobile home, crushing one end of it. The family were reduced to a kitchen, bathroom and living room, where all four of them had to sleep.

In February 1990 they accepted defeat and allowed the council to rehouse them, in a three-bedroomed ex-council house now owned by a housing association, on a neat well-maintained council estate in Borough Green, just ten minutes' drive away from Hawksnest Farm. The council gave in to Paul's stipulation that he would not move without the dogs, and all three Pyrenean mountain dogs they had at the time moved with them.

The speed with which they were rehoused – and on their own terms – amazes them, especially as they know of families who have been on the waiting list for years before being offered a council home. There were pointed questions from neighbours who had friends and relatives desperate to be housed. Ann regards it as particularly ironic: when they faced eviction from Sweetbriar Cottage they would have loved to have been offered a decent council house, but were told they could only have a two-bedroom flat in a tower block (albeit by a different local authority). Yet when they didn't want public housing they were forced to take it, and in the event were given a good house on a large corner plot, with room to build a shed for the dogs and for Paul to park his cars.

She and Paul are also baffled by the council's attitude to their mobile home. When they were living in it, they were told it was environmentally detrimental; but when they moved out, they deliberately did not get rid of it, and nobody from the council insisted that they should. It stood for five years on the farm, until Paul eventually broke it up, and in that time there was no complaint about the 'detriment to the environment'. Yet when, in 1996, they bought a small caravan to use as a feed store and somewhere to sit for a cup of tea when they were at the smallholding, an official from the council turned up the same day to make sure they had no plans to live in it.

It seemed to both Paul and Ann that there was a strange determination to keep them from living at Hawksnest Farm, and an astonishing intelligence network that meant the council was somehow informed within hours of the small caravan being delivered.

For the boys, living in a house was a novelty – especially for Jason, who was too young to remember much before the mobile home, and was fascinated by light switches that gave instant light, without putting the generator on first. He was also excited to have his own room, which made Ann smile when she remembered how hard it had been to get him to sleep on his own just a couple of years earlier.

Paul immediately looked for work, taking any job that allowed him time to spend at the farm. At first he worked nights as a cleaner,

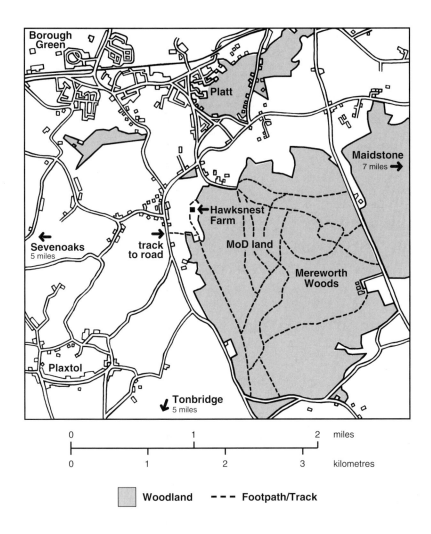

Map showing the site of Hawksnest Farm.
Behind are the dense woods leading to the MoD land beyond.
The half-mile track to Hawksnest leads from Long Mill Lane through
isolated fields. The Andrews family now live in Borough Green.

A happy Paul and Ann on their wedding day in 1977. They had no idea of the problems ahead of them.

Tony Dodd – the internationally acclaimed expert on UFOs and aliens, and the man who never let Ann and Jason down.

The Horse Whisperer. Ann's father Stan, as she remembers him from her childhood, when his uncanny ability to tame wild horses meant he was in demand with owners and riding instructors.

Ann's parents, Stan and Vi, photographed the year before Stan's death, which came just weeks after he held his precious newborn grandson, Jason. Ann believes he knew that Jason was special.

Jason at 18 months, with his five-year-old brother Daniel. This was at the time that Daniel was being visited by his mysterious 'soldier man'.

Jason, photographed on the day of his fourth birthday party, when a strange sequence of events shocked the Andrews family.

and then found himself a job as a self-employed taxi driver, an ideal arrangement which enables him to work evenings and nights, leaving the daylight hours free for the smallholding. To pay off a substantial chunk of the money they owed to the bank, Paul and Ann sold one and a half acres of the farm to a motorbike club, which holds a rally there for three days in August. The rest of the year this land is used by the Andrews to graze their animals, so they have effectively lost very little.

The temptation to sell the whole farm has been strong, but after spending time with Paul and Ann, I know how hard they would find it. For both of them, Hawksnest Farm is where real life starts. They may be more comfortable in their rented house than they were in a mobile home, but they would both move back on to the farm tomorrow if they were given the chance. So would Daniel and Jason: Jason, in particular, misses the everyday contact with the animals, even though he spends most of his free time there.

Ever since the day they were rehoused, Paul and Ann have fought hard to be allowed to live on their own property. They have today, after many battles with officialdom, resigned themselves to not being allowed to move back there. However, they have had an even tougher battle on their hands, for the right to build the smallholding back up into a profitable cattle unit. Every attempt they have made has been inexplicably thwarted. Someone, somewhere, is determined that they will never live on their own land again, or run it as a well set up unit for cows.

They wonder if it has anything to do with the other inexplicable things that have happened there – things that Ann has chronicled in her diary for the past few years; things that Jason himself attempted to explain to me, things that they brought with them when they moved to Hawksnest Farm. The Andrews cannot figure out why – unless of course, the farm was in some mysterious way especially selected as a magnet for this remarkable family.

CHAPTER 5

THE WATCHERS IN THE WOOD

The first time I visited Hawksnest Farm in good weather, Ann and Paul walked me round the boundaries, greeting the horses and shooing away the nosey pot-bellied pig, Prudence. At the edge of the farm the trees are thick and slightly menacing, even in bright sunshine. The undergrowth is a dense tangle of brambles, and you would need a machete and a great deal of determination to carve a way through it. There are footpaths and bridleways through Hurst Woods, but none that border or come close to the Andrews's land. On another occasion I walked the nearest pathway, and again the web of briar and bramble crowding on to it was so thick that it would be impossible to stray away from the trodden path.

Yet, as we walked around the perimeter of the farm on that warm afternoon in the spring of 1997, we, all three of us, stopped in amazement as we clearly heard the ring of a mobile phone from the woods alongside us. It could not have been more than a hundred yards away, and it was silenced after two rings. We heard no sound of voices. After a second or two Paul could not resist shouting out, 'It's for Yoo-hoo.' There was no reply, and the only rustling in the undergrowth was the normal mix of sounds, probably caused by the wind and small animals and birds.

It was the strangest of feelings. Perhaps, in that impenetrable vegetation, someone was lurking, observing us. It shocked me, and it shook Paul and Ann – but not for long. They looked at each other, shrugged their shoulders, and Ann laughed.

'Sooner him than me, spending an afternoon in there,' she said.

I was astonished that she and Paul accepted the mysterious presence so calmly, but they had already told me that, on several occasions, they had seen figures on the boundary of their land, and heard strange noises from the woods. For me, though it was a deeply unsettling first-hand encounter with the bizarre happenings at Hawksnest Farm. Although I had never doubted Ann, Paul or Jason, it was this moment that brought the full horror of their situation home to me. This was only one small incident, relatively trivial to them. But from then on, I would never feel at ease at the farm however serene the weather and idyllic the landscape. For me, there would always be an awareness that we were being watched, from deep within the wood. For the first time, I could appreciate the strain that pervades the Andrews's life at all times.

Ann laughed about the phone ring that told us there was someone there: but the more I know of the Andrews, the more I am aware that they use humour as a defence, a mask to hide behind instead of giving in to fear.

The first occasion when they realised they were under observation was September 12th 1995, a Tuesday. The boys were at school, and Ann and Paul drove up to the farm together, along the access lane through the field belonging to their farmer neighbour. The crop was high, waiting to be harvested, and Paul was commenting to Ann how the pouring rain was damaging it. As he spoke he noticed to his left two figures standing in the middle of the wheat. At first it was hard to make them out, but as the car passed to within fifty yards of them he and Ann could clearly see they were two men, tall (at least six feet) with dark overcoats and dark hats. Their clothes were not the rough gear of farm workers – and besides, Paul knows the farmer and all his workers well. Paul and Ann drove into the farm, parked, and went about their daily round of feeding and checking on the animals, but every few minutes Paul, feeling very uneasy, observed the men, who were still there, strangely immobile and silent, not speaking to each other. After about thirty minutes in which the strangers did not move, but kept their faces towards the farm as though watching everything Paul and Ann were doing, Paul decided to challenge them. He walked towards them, but as he did so they turned slowly and vanished into The Spinney, a dense patch of woodland. Although they seemed to walk ponderously and slowly, they moved away faster than Paul could follow them. Paul walked to the edge of the wood but could see no sign of them, nor could he understand why, with the path so close, they had chosen to go into this thick tangle of brambles. It was a wild, wet, windy day , and he had no inclination to follow them further, but he was puzzled. Ann felt deeply uneasy, and she was aware that the horses were restless, the way they are before a storm breaks.

The following Saturday the watchful strangers were there again, and this time it was Jason who spotted them first. At weekends he always goes with his parents to the farm. As he saw the two strange figures standing in the middle of the crop he turned to his father and commented that they'd better move or the farmer would have plenty to say to them about flattening the wheat. This time, Paul wasted no time in approaching them. He stopped the car on the farm track, as close to them as possible, jumped out and made his way towards them as quickly as he could. For a few seconds the men stood stock still, looking straight at him. Then, without communicating to each other, they turned simultaneously and walked into The Spinney.

Watching their retreating backs, Ann felt a shiver of cold fear run down her spine. But to Jason she put on a brave face, telling him that Paul was chasing the men because he suspected they were vandals. Jason turned towards her and held her gaze for a moment, and Ann knew that he was not fooled.

It was the summer of 1996 before the next mysterious intruder was spotted. It was on August 26th, an important day in the saga of strange happenings at Hawksnest Farm, as we will see, and Ann is not sure whether, in view of what happened that morning, she isn't reading too much into this sighting, because the man she and Paul spotted was dressed conventionally for the situation: he was wearing a tracksuit and trainers, which is the standard gear of the few walkers who pass by the farm. However, he was standing against the boundary of the farm, with his back to thick woodland, through which he must have forced his way. Only a hundred yards away is the bridle path, which would be a much more likely location to spot a rambler, and from where he would have had an equally good view of the farm, if he was just a nosey passer-by. He – or she, because from the farm buildings Ann could not be sure that it wasn't a woman – vanished back into the thick undergrowth. Looking at the spot the same time of year, when the brambles and briars are at their maximum summer growth, it is impossible to see how anything apart from the smallest rabbit could comfortably disappear into this vegetation.

It was in February 1997, a couple of months before I heard the phone ringing in the woods, that Ann and Paul first heard the same sound. Again, after two rings, the phone was silenced. On that occasion, from the other side of the plot, Paul and Ann were unable to be sure that there was no reply to the ringing: they heard nothing, but were so far away that a whispered conversation would have been lost among the sounds of the winds in the trees. They were together, just climbing out of the car, when they heard it. After the second ring Ann turned to Paul, but before she could say anything he simply nodded and said, 'Yep, you're not going mad, there's someone out there with a phone.'

They puzzled over the possible explanations, as they walked towards the small caravan they use for storing feed and giving shelter on cold days. When they went into the caravan they instantly realised someone had been in there, although there was no sign of a break-in. Paperwork had been moved around: it was not strewn everywhere but was piled neatly in a way that Ann was unfamiliar with. She knew it was not how she had left it. The cupboards, too, where she keeps cups and plates, had been rearranged. Nothing was taken and everything had been put back tidily – too tidily. The mugs that she and Paul use for coffee every day were at the back, behind some cups and saucers which are rarely used. There was a strong, lingering smell of aftershave, not one of Paul's.

'Tidy vandals – that's unusual,' Paul said, before striding across to the edge of the woods where they had heard the phone. Ann, feeling uncomfortable in the caravan, went outside to watch him. When he came back across the field he was shaking his head.

'God knows how anyone can get through those brambles,' he said.

Later that day, Ann made enquiries to find out if there was any forestry work being carried out in the woods: there was not.

Twice more in the next few weeks the phone was heard ringing in the woods, and on one occasion Paul, who was near the boundary fence at the time, crashed into the undergrowth to try to find the source of the sound. The ringing stopped, deadly silence ensued, and he had to claw his way back to the farm through bushes which snagged his clothes and scratched his hands and arms.

At the end of March, Paul and Ann spent a full day at the farm, working on the fences. They left just before dusk, as it became too dark to carry on. They were twenty or thirty yards up the dirt track in the car when Ann remembered that she had left a letter that she needed in the caravan. It was routine: she wanted the telephone number from the letter-heading to order some animal feed. Paul made a joke about her memory, turned the car engine off, and the pair of them walked back. As they turned the corner of the track just before reaching the gate, they almost collided with a man who was startled to see them. He was an incongruous sight: he was wearing a white shirt, a tie, green corduroy trousers, immaculately clean green Wellington boots and, oddest of all, a camelhair coat and brown leather driving gloves. Even the wealthy country dwellers in the area, who dress in uniform Barbours, jeans and dirty boots, would have found his outfit strange, and in the thickening twilight meeting anyone on the path, so far from the road on a damp and cold March evening, was eerie. Unlike most of the walkers who pass the farm and give a friendly greeting, the man did not speak, but hurried along the lane away from Paul and Ann, looking over his shoulder several times to see if they were still watching him.

It was a couple of days before I heard the strange sound of a mobile phone in the woods, on May 8th, that Ann had a terrifying experience at the farm.

Paul was in the field looking at Craven, because they were worried he was unwell. Suddenly he realised that all the horses were staring at a corner of the farm, where some equipment is stored. Ann was in the caravan, so didn't see anything at this stage, but Paul told her afterwards that he looked across, following the gaze of the horses, and thought he saw something, a shape that could have been a human figure, behind the equipment. He could not make it out properly, and before he had time to go across to it Craven moved away, and Paul got on with attending to him. When he looked again, the shape had vanished, and Paul decided reluctantly that it must have been a trick of the light.

About twenty minutes later Ann was walking across the field to get a bale of straw for Craven's bed, when she saw, out of the corner of her eye, a 'head' peep out from behind one of the large trees, and then disappear again. She watched the spot closely and the head – she was sure this time that it was a head – reappeared, and then ducked back. It was only four feet off the ground, but the head, which was white and with such indistinct features that Ann could not make them out from twenty yards away, was bigger than a human head. For a few seconds Ann was rooted to the spot, but when she was sure there really was something there, she called anxiously to Paul, who was working a few yards away. She hastily explained what had happened, and while she watched the tree Paul, with a garden fork in his hand, went towards it. As he got nearer a figure fled from behind the tree and crashed noisily into the undergrowth, where the vegetation could be heard rustling for a few minutes.

The figure was full grown, human size, but seemed to dart with a fluid, unnatural movement. Paul, aware of vandals and opportunist thieves who raid smallholdings like his, later rationalised that it could have been a teenager looking for something to steal or wreck. But the intruder must have come on to the land while they were there, and as they were both working in the open air they were easy to see – vandals and thieves would be more cautious. And, again, the route of escape was through thick brambles. It did not make sense. Ann was shaking when they talked it through, over coffee, in the caravan. She knows that what she saw was not human.

'The face was so pale, almost luminous. Even though it was too far away from me to make out features, the head seemed hairless and too big for a human head. The movement was really odd, a gliding motion that was smooth even though it tacked across the field, changing direction once or twice. It was as if it was hovering just inches above the ground. There was no sense of it jogging up and down like a human would if they were moving so quickly, and it moved easily through the brambles and the tangled undergrowth.'

Apart from the distinctive ring of a mobile phone, other noises have been heard from the overgrown woods. One warm July Monday in 1997 both Paul and Ann heard a sneeze. They thought it came from the woods, but Ann looked up and down the bridle path by the gate in case they were mistaken about the source of the sound. Ann and Paul were working together, strengthening a fence, and when they returned to their labours they clearly heard two more sneezes, definitely from the bushes near to where they were working. Paul shouted 'Bless you,' but there was no response from the watcher in the wood.

This, however, all came much later: let us carry on with their story in logical order. Settling into their new life, away from the farm, preoccupied all the Andrews family for some time. The boys did not have to change schools, and in some ways life was easier for them: they could get to and from school without having to be taken by car and they had other children of the same ages around them on the estate to play with in the afternoons and weekends. For Ann it was easier, too – they were close to shops, they had more room, there was electricity at the flick of a switch – but for both her and Paul there was a great feeling of sadness, which was soon overtaken by a determination to get the family back on to the farm one day.

With all the financial worries, Paul working all the hours he could to meet the demands of the bank, and Ann having to take on a lot of the responsibility for the animals still on the farm, it was a stressful and busy time.

Then, within a few weeks of moving away from the farm, they suffered another blow to their morale and their finances. To supplement the money he earned at night, Paul was buying second-hand cars, working on them, and selling them at a profit. He stored them at the farm, in the barn buildings which were empty since the death of the cows. Towards the end of May, Ann went with him to buy a second-hand bumper, the final piece he needed to complete a Ford Sierra he had been working on, and for which he already had a buyer lined up.

As they arrived back at the house, they saw a policeman on the doorstep. Ann went into such a panic that at first it was a great relief to her to hear that he was there because the barn had burned down – at least nothing had happened to either of the boys. Then the news sank in. The barn, containing the farm van, the farm pickup truck, the Ford Sierra and another car which Paul had been about to start work on, had all been destroyed. The fire brigade officer who saw them later told them it was clearly arson: the barn had been broken into, and a piece of burning cloth had been stuffed into the petrol tank of the Sierra. With no insurance cover, the family were once again badly hit. Predictably, nobody was arrested for the offence: it could, possibly, have been the work of opportunistic vandals, but to Paul and Ann it seemed to be yet another part of the orchestrated campaign to keep them from the farm.

It wasn't many months before Ann noticed that Jason was again having very disturbed nights. She would wake him for school in the mornings and he would look as tired as he had the evening before, struggling to surface from his sleep. Sometimes, to her astonishment, he would climb out of bed dirty, with muddy streaks down his legs and arms, yet she knew he had bathed before going to bed. When she told Paul he, as usual, would look for a rational explanation: 'Oh, I daresay he skipped the bath – just ran the water to fool you. Or he jumped in and out so quick that he didn't have time to get clean. He's a boy, after all – remember how Daniel used to avoid water like it was the plague when he was smaller,' he'd say, but Ann would know this wasn't true. She'd supervised bathtime, she knew Jason had, however reluctantly, been soaped all over and emerged clean.

Sometimes, too, Jason's pyjamas were streaked with mud, and his feet and hands were covered in scratches. Again, Paul would look for an explanation, suggesting that perhaps one of the dogs had got into the bedroom with Jason, and scratched him in play. Knowing this wasn't possible, Ann would nonetheless agree – Paul had enough to worry about without Jason's problems.

It was Ann who woke when Jason cried in the night, Ann who took him into her bed to cuddle and soothe. Paul was working nights, so it was easier for Ann to let Jason slide in next to her than make up a bed for him on the floor, as she had done so many times before. He would come to her crying, terrified and at the same time angry with his mother for not being able to help him. Looking back, Ann realises with guilt that she did exactly what her mother Vi had done with her so many years before: she took him in her arms, comforted him, and assured him over and over again that the terrible things that had happened to him were nothing more than a bad dream, and that everything would fade back to normal in the morning.

Jason, older now and more articulate, would argue with her, insisting that it wasn't a dream, but Ann would brush it off gently, telling him that all children had nightmares. Eventually he would drift off to sleep.

There were physical problems, too. He complained frequently of stomach pains, and Ann took him to their GP several times when he was eight and nine years old. Each time, nothing was found. In September 1992, a couple of months after his tenth birthday, the GP arranged for him to be admitted to Maidstone Hospital for tests. He was there for three days, but no reason for his stomach ache was diagnosed.

Ben, the big old dog who had been with the family throughout Jason's life, died when Jason was eleven. Bought for Paul to breed from, he had been more of a family pet than a stud dog: more than any of the dogs, Ben lived at the heart of the family. Jason learnt to walk by pulling himself up against Ben, clinging to the long thick coat and staggering unsteadily along, while the dog plodded very slowly and gently across the room. It was Ben who had appointed himself Jason's guardian, sleeping on the landing outside his bedroom door while the other dogs were kept downstairs. It was Ben's neck that Jason clung around in the depths of his misery, when the adult world dismissed his night-time problems as dreams and nightmares. Ben and Jason had an instinctive understanding, and his death hit Jason hard.

Ann had tried to prepare him for it. Knowing that the old dog must be very near the end, she encouraged Jason to take an interest in the other dogs, letting him choose one to have as his own, but nothing could compensate for the inevitable loss of Ben. So when, soon afterwards, Ann was summoned to Jason's new school – he had transferred to Wrotham School, a secondary school, at the age of eleven – to talk to his teacher about his behaviour, she felt she understood the root cause of it. Jason was being disruptive, throwing tantrums, bursting into tears for no apparent reason, flying into tempers and lapsing into silent, sulky depressions. The staff were finding him hard to handle, and were genuinely concerned about him.

Ann and Paul were concerned too. Their easygoing son was metamorphosing into a surly, uncommunicative, badly behaved problem child, and they were not being spared his mood swings at home. After telling the teacher how she felt the death of his longtime companion Ben was at the bottom of it, Ann tackled Jason, explaining to him that, however upset he was, it was unfair to take his pain out on others.

Jason looked at her and, with a slight sneer in his voice, said: 'You just don't understand, and you don't want to understand.'

Ann assured him she did want to understand, but she and Paul found it increasingly hard to accept his outbursts of anger, followed by real desolation in the middle of which nobody, not even Ann, could reach him. Perhaps it would have been easier had it been Daniel, who was by now an adolescent, but Daniel had never had mood swings like Jason's, even in the midst of his teenage angst.

Ann went backwards and forwards to the school, as she and Jason's teacher both tried to make sense out of his behaviour. For weeks at a time there would be an improvement. Then the disturbed nights would start again, and with them the letters from school complaining about erratic outbursts. Some mornings, sensing that Jason was once again very tired, Ann would keep him at home, rather than risk his frayed temper landing him in trouble again. She talked to their doctor about the problem, and was told it was probably just a difficult pre-teen spell, and to be patient.

His physical problems continued, too. In November 1994, Jason woke Ann in the night, complaining of severe stomach pains. He was hot and feverish, so Ann gave him junior Dispirin and sat with him in his room. He tossed fitfully and could not sleep, his temperature was not coming down and he was obviously in pain, so she called to Paul to ring the local surgery. A doctor arrived and after a brief examination decided to send Jason to hospital with suspected appendicitis. Paul drove them, to save time waiting for an ambulance, and when they arrived the staff were ready with a trolley to whisk Jason in as an emergency.

At Maidstone Hospital the staff were reassuring and attentive. After a much more thorough examination Ann and Paul were told that it was not appendicitis, but that the doctors did not know what was causing the pain and fever. Jason was admitted to a ward, so that further tests could be carried out. His parents were relieved that he did not face an operation but at the same time were worried about the outcome. After three days in hospital Jason felt better, and nothing had shown up on any of the tests, so he was allowed home. On the final day Ann was asked a puzzling question. Why, one of the doctors wanted to know, did Jason have a six-inch-long scar along the right-hand side of his body? Ann had never seen the scar before, and had no idea what had caused it.

A week later, Jason was again suddenly struck down with acute stomach pains, and again his temperature shot up. He was readmitted to hospital. There was no sign of the scar on his right side, but there were several red fresh-looking scars on his stomach. He had no idea what had caused them, and nor had Ann. The hospital staff were puzzled, but sent him home after three days because the pain had subsided. For three months he was better, but the pains returned violently in March 1995, and another stay in Maidstone Hospital yet again revealed nothing. Each time, apart from the pain, he was feverish and had swollen glands in his neck.

Jason's strange moods and angry outbursts continued. Some of the time Ann shielded Paul from the extent of the problem, making light of it in order not to worry him, but there was no way Paul could avoid knowing about it – Jason's fiery outbursts weren't restricted to when his father was not at home. Most of the time Paul was gentle and forbearing with his son, and was as baffled as Ann about what was happening. Alone together, the worried parents would talk it through, and reassure each other that Jason had simply hit adolescence early, that time would sort it all out, and that one day they would look back on this unhappy spell and laugh about it.

The school authorities, however, were in no mood to laugh about it, and in the summer term of 1995, before his twelfth birthday, Ann and Paul were summoned again. This time, they were told, Jason's temper tantrum had upset so many other pupils, disrupted a whole morning's work, and had involved him being verbally abusive to more than one member of staff, and the school would put up with it no longer. Jason, they told his parents, would not be allowed back to Wrotham School after the summer holidays – he would, in fact, be suspended – unless the Andrews family agreed that he should be referred to the school psychiatric service.

Ann was momentarily shocked, but then was overcome by a feeling of relief. She had a touching belief in doctors and scientists, and she felt that at last something serious was being done about Jason's problems. It was obvious that her son was deeply troubled, but now he was going to get the help he needed. Paul was not so happy about it – he was suspicious of anything that smacked of weakness, and he found it hard to cope with normal physical illnesses. He resented any suggestion that his son was 'not all there', as he put it, and it took all Ann's powers of persuasion to help him see that this could be something beneficial for Jason. Besides, as she pointed out, they really did not have an option: if they did not go along with the referral to the psychiatrist, the school would not accept Jason back for the autumn term. If he were found a place in another school it would be much less convenient, as he would have to travel by public transport, and he would be separated from Daniel. It would be even more unsettling for him, and hardly like to help.

The appointment for the first session with the psychiatrist arrived. It was to be a family session, with Paul and Ann also expected to attend. They were all nervous: there was a feeling of the family being on trial. Ann felt defensive, as though all her skills as a mother were being questioned; Paul felt defiant, still seeing no reason for the intervention of a psychiatrist; and Jason – well, he, like Ann, was nervous, but he was also hoping that something was going to be done to help him. He, too, thought that treating his 'bad dreams', which he knew were not dreams, would be possible. That there would be a pill or a medicine he could swallow, just like there would be if he had a physical illness.

The meeting went well, Ann thought. The psychiatrist was good at her job, and soon had the reticent Jason chatting away about every aspect of his life. Another appointment was made, and then three or four followed after that. With Paul and Ann, there were questions about the family environment, about relationships within the family, about how they felt towards each other, about Daniel and how well he was getting on. Then there would be long sessions with Jason, while Paul and Ann waited outside. When they questioned her about how well it was all going, the psychiatrist said she thought Jason was holding something back: that he talked openly about all areas of his life, but she had a feeling there was something that he wasn't yet ready to tell her.

There were some things which he did tell her, about which his mother Ann had no knowledge at the time. Although he had never been told about the miscarriage Ann had suffered when he was seven, Jason talked to the psychiatrist about 'the baby that never was'. He also spoke of 'seeing his mother's coffin' and was so worried about Ann's health that, at the suggestion of the psychiatrist, her GP called her in for a thorough medical to reassure him. Five days after the dream in which he 'saw' her coffin, a very close friend of Ann's died: she believes it was this funeral that he had a premonition about.

There did, at first, seem to be an improvement in Jason, after he started his sessions with the psychiatrist, but Ann knew from experience that, whatever it was that upset her son so much, it came in cycles. She was hopeful that the psychiatrist was helping, but realistic enough to know it could simply be a quiet time for Jason.

She was right. After the first few appointments Jason again began to have disturbed nights, to wake up tired and miserable, to struggle to find the energy to cope with a normal day – and to have temper outbursts. He wanted to sleep either in his parents' room or with Daniel, and he was always jumpy and nervous at bedtime. Ann checked on him every night before she and Paul went to bed, and despite the difficulties in getting him to go to bed he was always sound asleep. Then something weird began to happen: in the mornings, Jason would be found deeply asleep somewhere else in the house. Sometimes he was on the floor at the foot of his own bed, just as she had found him on the floor when he was a baby. Sometimes he was in the living room. Once he was stretched out on a hard kitchen worktop, asleep.

Paul put it down to sleepwalking, and refused to be as worried as Ann was, but even he became very alarmed when, early one morning, he got up to go to the bathroom and, on impulse, poked his head around the door to Jason's bedroom. The bed was empty. He checked Daniel's room, but his older son was sleeping there alone. It was only after checking every room downstairs that Paul woke Ann. Heart racing, she quickly and quietly double-checked everywhere, looking underneath beds, pulling the sofa away from the wall, even opening kitchen cupboards where there would be no chance of a large twelve-year-old being concealed.

Desperate, she told Paul to get in the car and drive around the housing estate, believing that if Jason were sleepwalking he could not be far away. She picked up the phone to dial the police, and then remembered that they had not checked the sheds in the back garden, where Paul kept supplies of dog food. Calling Paul back – he had reached the car but not started the engine – she rushed outside, unlocking the back door as she went. The shed was also locked, and there was no sign that it had been recently opened. Despite this, Ann started to strain at the heavy bolts, and then Paul took over from her, jerking them back. The door opened with a rush and as the light poured in, Ann could make out a huddled shape in the corner, on the concrete floor. It was Jason, sound asleep. He didn't waken even when Paul picked him up and carried him back inside.

Paul and Ann puzzled over it: it would have been impossible to close the bolts from inside. Paul had fitted the bolts because he occasionally used the shed to isolate one of the dogs that was ill, or about to give birth, so he had made it secure from outside. If Jason had been sleepwalking he would have needed all his strength to open the bolts, but even if he had, there was no possible explanation for how he had closed them again. The wooden shed was strong, there were no windows and no other way into it.

Again, after discussing it for a few minutes, Paul shrugged and put it out of his mind, but Ann could not: she was desperately worried that one morning they would not be able to find Jason at all.

The appointments with the psychiatrist continued. When Ann asked her for guidance in how to deal with Jason at home, she advised them to treat him with patience and tolerance, but when Jason arrived home from school one day with yet another letter complaining about his behaviour, and threatening him once again with suspension, Paul – this huge, gentle man – reached the end of his tether.

He'd gone along with Ann and the psychiatrist for months, tackling the problem her way, with patience and tolerance. Now he'd reached the point where he could no longer play this game: he was angry, and he felt it was time to show Jason that his behaviour was unacceptable. How could he be patient and tolerant with a boy who had been sent home from school, yet again, with a letter summoning his parents to see the head teacher? How could he be patient and tolerant in the face of being told that Jason's sullen cheek would no longer be tolerated by the staff, that his temper outbursts were upsetting the other children, that he refused to concentrate on his work?

Paul knew about trouble – he hadn't been a model schoolboy himself – but he also knew that, as a parent, he wanted his sons to have chances he never had, and that meant chances that school could give them. Daniel was doing well, thriving at school, making the most of his skills – and still having a good time with his mates. Jason wasn't. Ann was visibly worried, and this added to the pressure on Paul. He felt his wife had suffered enough, losing two homes and with the future of the farm in doubt. Why should she have this extra load of worry?

Patience and tolerance had been tried, and now, Paul's instincts told him, it was time for another tactic. He didn't think it through rationally: when Jason walked in from school at 3.30pm with the letter he could control his temper no longer. He blew up.

Ann, out in the garden, heard the raised voices and hurried inside. Paul was brandishing the letter an inch away from Jason's face. The boy was flushed but defiant, shouting back at his father, and Ann's interruption went unheeded.

Just at that moment Daniel appeared at the top of the stairs and screamed down, 'Mum, my goldfish. My beautiful fantails. They're gone.'

The violent shouting ceased and everyone turned towards him. Cochise, one of the huge Pyrenean mountain dogs, trotted down the stairs, tail wagging. As he came near to Ann and Paul they saw the large loose jowl on the side of his face begin to quiver, as if being tickled from the inside. Then it started to vibrate quite violently.

Paul, always the best at handling the dogs, gently prised the huge jaws open and four golden fantails plopped into his hand, still very much alive. He ran upstairs with them and tipped them back into the tank, which Daniel moved to the top of his chest of drawers, too high even for a dog of Cochise's huge size.

It was a brief comic interlude, but it defused Paul's anger. When he came downstairs again, he spoke to Jason in a different tone, pleading with his son to tell him what was wrong.

'It's the dreams, Dad. I'm getting the dreams, like I did when I was little.'

This time, Paul had an answer. If it were dreams that were bothering Jason, he must be encouraged to share them with the psychiatrist. Perhaps this was what he was holding back, and if he could just tell her about it, she would be able to sort everything out.

They were late for the next appointment – one of the dogs had decided to go walkabout and Paul had struggled to catch it – but when they entered her office, it must have been obvious that both Paul and Ann were bursting to tell her something. They quickly explained what Jason had told them: he was having dreams which seemed to disturb him profoundly, and he had promised he would share them.

Left alone with the psychiatrist, Jason talked at length for the first time about what was happening to him in the night.

Jason's first memories of abduction go back to the very early years of his life, when he was still sleeping in a cot. Like all early childhood memories, they are patchy: like snapshots, rather than a continuous film of his life.

'The first memory I have is just the hands,' he says, telling me the same things that he shared with the psychiatrist. 'I was crying for some reason – I've no idea why – and I can clearly see some long fingers reaching down into the cot and picking me up. They were very different from Mum's hands, the hands that usually picked me up if I was crying. These fingers were much longer – at least twice as long as Mum's – and they were thin with large joints at the knuckles. They were dark in colour: not black or brown, not even grey. I've never seen a colour like it, like a dark dolphin colour. I don't know what happened after they picked me up.

'The next memory I have is when I was a bit older, able to walk. Again, I remember the hands lifting me. I was old enough to know about fairies and elves and demons – Mum read stories to me every night – and I thought I was being taken by elves.

'Another time I saw what I thought was a soldier on the landing. The house where we lived was near an old ruin, which when I was little I believed was an old castle, and I thought that this little person – he was only about two feet six inches tall, the same size as me – was the ghost of a soldier who had died there. All I can remember is seeing him. I don't know what happened next.'

Jason has other, confused, memories of those early years, when the family lived at Sweetbriar Cottage. Almost all of his memories include the hands reaching out for him. He remembers seeing 'small people' in his room, and he remembers the terror he felt when they appeared, but each memory stops at the moment they made contact with him: he does not know what events followed.

As he gets older, the memories naturally become clearer and more cohesive. When the family moved to live on the farm, he shared bunk beds with Daniel, sleeping on the lower one.

'I can remember being terrified one night, I don't know why, but I ran through to Mum shouting, "They're coming to get me." By then I knew what happened – I knew I was being taken away – and I never wanted to go. I couldn't remember where I went or what they did to me, but I know I hated it, and all Mum would say was that it was a dream, and she'd cuddle and comfort me. It made me so mad that she wouldn't believe me that it wasn't a dream. I kept trying to think of ways of making her believe me, then I realised it was no good.

'I can remember the horrible feeling I had when I knew they – Mum, Dad, everybody – would never believe me. I felt so lonely and miserable.'

On one occasion, Jason remembers running through to his parents' room in terror. The fear was always the same: something huge that he was unable to articulate, a compelling feeling of helplessness, and a dreadful frustration when his worries were dismissed as nightmares. However, on this occasion he also felt a sharp pain in the left side of his body, and when Ann pulled his pyjama top up she saw a red weal running from chest height to his hip.

'I was pleased there was something there, even though it hurt, because I thought Mum would take it seriously. She was very worried, but she eventually got me back to sleep, and in the morning the mark had completely gone. She said it must just have been where I was lying on my side, but I knew it wasn't, and I felt angry again.'

Marks on Jason's body have appeared throughout his life – and disappeared just as quickly. The usual pattern is for five red dots to appear, four in a square with one in the middle, on his shoulder or behind his knee. They last for a couple of hours at the most: on several occasions Ann has made appointments with the local GP, only to cancel them later when all signs of the marks have disappeared. Over the years she contained her worry by persuading herself that Jason had the sort of flesh which was easily marked, perhaps by folds in his bedding as he lay on it, and just as easily cleared up. Paul did not take the marks too seriously, mainly because they had usually vanished when he looked for them.

By the time the family moved to the estate in Borough Green, Jason's memories were becoming even clearer. He was no longer sharing a room with Daniel.

'There is a pattern to the bad nights, the nights when things happen to me. I settle down to sleep, in a low bed. (I've now got a high, cabin bed, but for the first few years I had a low one.) I've got a very good alarm clock, a state-of-the-art digital one, and it always stops at 3am. That's the time it happens. I lie in bed, awake although I don't know what wakes me, and the dogs are always growling. Then, suddenly, they shut up – all of them, which is very unusual for our dogs.

'I always try to go back to sleep, in the hope that nothing will happen, but then I see something at the end of the bed, almost out of the corner of my eye. It rises up through the floor. It's the big one. There's only ever one big one. It's about five feet four inches tall, just a bit shorter than me. The head is large, with big black eyes on a slant which go round the side of the head, and a very small nose and mouth. It's thin, and it has the long dark fingers that I remember from my baby days. That's all I notice, really, the fingers. Even more than the face.

'It's not always the same one, although I don't really know how I know that, because they look the same. Once, one had a strange zig-zag shape to the top of his head, as if a lump had been chopped out. I nicknamed it Zig-Zag. It never came again.

'Then, when I've seen the big one rising up, I'm aware of the little ones. I never see where they come from, they're just there. They are similar to the big one, grey in colour, but smaller, and they scuttle around, busy, busy, busy. They never stay still. There are usually about half a dozen of them. Sometimes they bring some other creatures with them: I call them koalas because they are small and furry like little bears. They don't seem to have a distinct shape, they're fuzzy at the edges, and they don't seem to do much – as if they are pets for the others.

'My Mum used to have a collection of teddy bears, with a couple of koala bears among them, and I can remember even when I was tiny I wouldn't touch the koalas, because they reminded me of these creatures.

'I see the creatures in my bedroom, and I see the big one stretching out its long fingers, just like it did when I was little. Then I never remember what happens immediately next. Sometimes I don't have any more memories at all of that night – except that when I wake up in the morning I am very tired, and the alarm clock is two hours slow.

'But sometimes I wake up somewhere else, somewhere cold. I can't move my body at all, only my eyes, and I can't speak. I'm lying on something smooth and cold. It feels like marble, but I don't think it is. It doesn't have corners, everything is rounded and smooth. The room is dark but there is a light, but I can't see where it is coming from.

'Sometimes all I remember is being there, but other times they are with me – I can remember seeing a big one holding something about eight inches long, like a metal ruler. Sometimes I can see the big one touching me, but I can never feel anything, as if my body is paralysed. I'm always terrified.'

Jason remembers vividly one of the nights when Ann found him, the next morning, with scratches on his arms and legs, grass stains and mud on his pyjamas, and very dirty feet. Although this memory has more of the qualities of a 'normal' dream, Jason knows that it was real.

'It started the same way, with the creatures coming into my room. Then there is a blank, and I don't remember what happened next, but I found myself up at the farm, about three miles away from our house. I've no idea how I got there, but I knew that I was being chased. I didn't see what was chasing me, except that it was big and brown and somehow I knew it was an animal. I ran for a hole in the hedge, which I knew was there, and dived through it just as the creature caught up with me. It stretched out a claw towards me and scratched me, but I was through the hedge before it could catch hold of me.

'I can remember the horrible feeling of not being able to run any faster, and knowing that it was gaining ground on me, but I could also feel something else, as though the aliens were with me, experiencing what I was feeling. I felt, for the first time, that they were protecting me, looking after me. When I woke up I was at home, and I have no memory of how I got back there. Mum saw all the dirty marks on the sheet the next day and asked me if I had been out in the night to see the dogs. She was quite cross, but then she saw the scratches on me, some of them quite deep, so she put antiseptic cream on them. She kept asking me what happened, but there was nothing I could tell her, because she wouldn't believe me. I had a strong feeling that they – the aliens – had saved me.

'I used to lose my temper and scream at Mum, "You must believe me." I think she and Dad just thought I was very badly behaved. Sometimes they would try to be understanding and sometimes they would get cross, particularly when I was in trouble at school, but while they wouldn't believe me, I couldn't help it.

'At school I used to get frightened. I hated sitting by the window, because I was sure "they" could see me there and come and get me. Once, when there was a lot of lightning, I locked myself in a cupboard. I'm not frightened of thunder and lightning, but the lightning reminds me of beams of light I sometimes see when I am with "them", and I really thought they were coming for me again.

'I got into so much trouble at school because I was tired, and when I'm tired I get grumpy. Also, I didn't see any point in being nice to anybody. Nobody believed me; they treated me like I was some kind of idiot who couldn't tell the difference between dreams and things that really happen. So I hated them all.'

It was his bad behaviour at school which led him to the office of the psychiatrist, where he poured out his tale. She was interested, and probed for more detail. She appeared to be very open-minded – she did not dismiss what Jason was saying out-of-hand. He felt encouraged: at last he had somebody to talk to.

Within days of opening up to her, another amazing breakthrough happened for Jason. He watched the hypnosis television programme with his mother and father, and suddenly they, too, seemed to be taking him seriously. His mysterious movements in the night, his terror of the dark, the inexplicable scars on his body which appeared and disappeared so rapidly, the clocks in the house all losing time simultaneously: it all, at last, added up. They weren't saying they believed everything he told them about abduction, but for the first time in his life, they weren't fobbing him off with the words 'dream' and 'nightmare'.

Ann and Paul were on the threshold of accepting that something very odd indeed was happening to their son.

CHAPTER 6

HELP AT LAST

The day following the television programme, the one which finally gave a name, 'abduction', to Jason's experiences, was a Friday. Ann kept Jason home from school: she could see that he was tired out by the emotional evening they had all spent, and she did not want to make things more difficult for him by a fraught day at school. He was pale and listless, and had to be coaxed to go up to the farm to help Ann collect the eggs.

Paul, in the meantime, had been shopping for books. He arrived home that afternoon with four, of varying degrees of usefulness. The whole family, Daniel included, spent a couple of hours browsing through them. For Ann, the very existence of the books brought an overwhelming feeling of relief, the relief of finding their problem was shared, not just by the man on the television programme, but by many hundreds of other perfectly normal, sane people. Paul, still sceptical, was prepared to concede that others were obviously having very similar experiences to Jason. He still balked at the word 'alien', hoping that there would be a simpler, more rational explanation, but he could see that this was the closest they had ever been to solving Jason's problems, and they owed it to their son to carry on finding out about the subject.

In the appendix of one of the books was a short list of useful phone numbers. Paul and Ann decided that they would ring the number given for Quest, an international UFO investigation organisation based in Britain. It was Ann who dialled the number – Paul could not bring himself to do it, afraid of appearing 'round the bend'. Ann, too, felt ridiculous as she explained to the well-spoken gentleman on the other end of the line that she thought her twelve-year-old son was being abducted by aliens. She was expecting a derisory laugh, or perhaps a kind but insistent suggestion that she should see a psychiatrist. Instead, the man she was speaking to was calm and understanding. He did not ridicule her, or humour her: astonishingly, he reacted as though everything she was saying was perfectly familiar.

He gave Ann another number to dial, and once again she found herself speaking to a reassuring and sympathetic man, who told her he would put one of his investigators in touch with her. He asked for her number, and for a moment Ann panicked. She refused to give it and put the phone down, overcome by a sudden sense of the bizarreness of the situation. Here she was, making arrangements with UFO experts as normally as if she was speaking to the council about fixing the drains. She suddenly felt embarrassed and ridiculous. Worse, perhaps they thought she was mad and only wanted her number so that they could send the men in white coats round to take her away.

It was Paul who talked her into ringing back.

'What have we got to lose?' he asked. 'If someone rings and you think they're making fun of us, just tell them it was a mistake and that the boys made the original call, as a joke. If the worst comes to the worst, we can change our number – but if we don't try it, we'll never know. Besides, I like the idea of an investigator – it sounds like our best chance of getting to the bottom of this.'

When she did ring back, the man perfectly understood her fears. This time she left her number, and that's how, later that evening, Ann answered the phone to Tony Dodd, the person who, perhaps more than any other, has helped the Andrews family cope.

Tony Dodd is Director of Investigations for Quest International, an organisation which produces a magazine, called simply *UFO*, and organises conferences and seminars on the subject. Quest came into being when Graham Birdsall, who set it up, found himself wondering who to turn to about his own abduction experiences. He soon found that there was a need for an information forum for others in the same boat as himself: intelligent, rational people who had found themselves drawn into something beyond the frontiers of normal life.

Tony Dodd became involved in the subject in 1978, when he

was a serving police sergeant. He spent twenty-five years in the police, leaving with an exemplary service record, and has the cynical, hardbitten attitude common among officers who spend their working life dealing with the problems of humanity. He is not, in other words, a fanciful, sensitive person prone to imagining things. He is hard-headed, down-to-earth, practical. The combination of being a police officer and being a Yorkshireman leaves little room for self-indulgent fancy. Meeting Tony Dodd and hearing his story, presented phlegmatically and without any evangelical zeal, is enough to make even the most hardened non-believer question their incredulity. Tony Dodd does not care whether you believe him: he knows what happened to him, and knows what has happened to thousands of others. He has dedicated his life to researching the subject, and he is now acknowledged as one of the world's greatest authorities on UFOs and abduction.

It all started with an astonishing incident as he was on night patrol across the Yorkshire moors, with another police officer sitting in the car with him and, by coincidence, another police car with one officer in it approaching from the opposite direction. It was 2.30am, and as they rounded a bend in the road both Tony and his colleague saw, one hundred feet away from them, a large bright object about one hundred feet in diameter. No sound came from it – in fact the whole area was eerily silent, as the engine in Tony's car died away. A glow of light surrounded the object, which was moving slowly, at no more than 10–15mph, away from the road. The policemen watched it until all they could see was a ball of light.

Tony Dodd had been in the RAF for three years before joining the police, so he was very familiar with the shape and dimensions of aircraft in current use. He knew this was not a plane. It clung to the contours of the hills as it moved, yet it was further above the ground than was possible for a hovercraft.

As soon as they overcame the shock of seeing it, Tony and his colleague tried to make contact with police headquarters on their car radio. The only noise they could get from the set was a loud buzz of static – and yet Tony regularly used the radio on this stretch of road with no problems. As soon as the craft had reached the distance, the radio crackled back into normal reception, and Tony registered the strange sighting. He then contacted the local airports to see if anything had been recorded on their radar, but drew a blank. He was not surprised, because the UFO had been below the radar range all the time he and his colleague watched it.

Later, he discovered that the policeman driving towards them had also witnessed it, and his account tallied very closely with theirs. Baffled but intrigued, Tony was determined to get to the bottom of it – expecting, as Paul Andrews would years later, a rational explanation. Gradually, his search for this explanation has taken over his life, and after retiring from the police in 1988 he now works full time on UFO research. He is in charge of all Quest investigations in Britain and has lectured across the world, including twice in America.

At first his interest was in, quite literally, UFOs – unidentified flying objects. There can be no doubt that UFOs exist: even the most hardened sceptics admit that there are lights and objects seen in the skies that cannot be identified. The sceptics may not accept that these are alien in origin, but they acknowledge that no plausible explanation can be given for some of them, although many can be explained, in terms of aircraft, weather, reflected lights, etc. This core of unidentified objects – including the one he had seen himself – started Tony Dodd off on his life's work, and has brought him now to a set of beliefs which go far beyond the earth being bugged by alien craft.

Tony now feels that his initial experience of the UFO – followed by several more sightings on the moors in the subsequent few years – was a deliberate introduction engineered by the aliens. He himself, he believes, has been regularly abducted for many years. Unlike Jason, his memories lay dormant until triggered by the UFO activity around him, but now he is aware of waking up, his limbs paralysed, with a bright light suffusing the bedroom. He remembers no more the next morning, but gradually memories come to him in flashbacks. His contact with the aliens, he believes, has a definite purpose: he has been chosen to pass on messages promoting world peace and greater understanding of the cosmos. The messages 'appear' in his brain, and are so unlike any of his own, familiar, down-to-earth thought patterns that he feels sure they are planted there by benevolent aliens. Many abductees (including, later, as we will see, Jason Andrews) have similar 'messages' delivered to them.

Tony does not believe all aliens are benevolent, nor does he think the earth is simply being buzzed by one particular race of space beings, but by several. He subscribes to the view that world governments are involved in cover-ups, that they know far more about alien activity than they admit to the populace at large.

Whatever his own beliefs, Tony Dodd approaches his investigations with rigour, never assuming that there will be anything more than a rational explanation. He lives in the picturesque small North Yorkshire town of Grassington, a centre of Dales walking country, and an unspoiled haven for tourists looking for a traditional market town. Driving there is an uplifting experience from the moment that the M62 and the industrial areas of Bradford are left behind.

In the scrupulously organised sanctuary of Tony's office, an answering machine beeps continually, recording messages of strange sightings across the country. Each one will be investigated and the caller will be replied to.

The majority – an estimated seventy-five per cent – will have a perfectly logical explanation. Most of the rest will not be detailed enough for any conclusion to be drawn. Others, although he will not be able to prove it, strike Tony as natural phenomena. That leaves a small core of cases, perhaps only a couple in every hundred, which intrigue him, and which contain enough possible evidence for an investigation to be carried out.

The call from Ann Andrews fell into this category. He questioned her, gently and sympathetically, but with a policeman's thoroughness, about what made her suspect her son was being abducted. Her answers rang true. He describes his first reaction to talking to her:

'I am very suspicious of people who state that they, or someone in their family, are being abducted. Ann didn't state it: she put it forward as a possibility, because of Jason's reaction to the TV programme. Most of all, she wanted help, and she was very willing to consider any other possible explanation. I got a strong feeling, as I usually do in genuine cases, that she sincerely wished it would all go away. She would like it not to be happening to her son: there was no way that she was enjoying it, seeking publicity, or had anything to gain from it.

'She sounded, to be honest, distraught. She was at the end of her tether with worry about her son, and her only concern was to get to the bottom of what was upsetting him. From the moment he told them he was being abducted she and Paul tried to understand, but when they rang me they were bewildered. The most important thing I could do at that first contact was reassure her that they weren't all going mad, that it was possible that Jason was being abducted, and that there were lots of other people having similar experiences.'

Ann's memory of this long, first phone conversation with Tony is that he asked her a great many questions, many of them seemingly irrelevant. Tony admits that many were asked simply to put Ann at her ease, but among them he included several key questions.

'There are certain things which abductees are aware of, trigger points, which are rarely present if people are fantasising an abduction scenario. I don't want to reveal what they are, because they are of enormous help to me in deciding whether or not I am dealing with a genuine case. What I do is to ask a series of questions around the subject, to see if these key points come up, but I make sure it is they, not me, who introduce these points: in other words, I am very careful not to feed them their answers. That's why I ask so many questions, often nothing to do with the experience under discussion.'

Although he is keeping some of these key points up his sleeve, Tony will list some of the more obvious ones that come up time and time again in abduction cases:

1. Noises in the ears.
2. Nose bleeds.
3. Increased psychic abilities – being able to predict events before they occur.
4. Strange, unexplained marks appearing on the body overnight, and usually disappearing quickly.
5. Waking to find odd things have happened in the night: e.g., finding night clothes removed, or inside out; waking in the wrong bed or wrong room. In one case Tony dealt with, the abductee woke wearing a completely different set of clothing, not belonging to them. Another, a middle-aged woman, on several occasions woke in the garden with no clothes on, and with the doors to the house locked.
6. Fear of the dark.

7. Strange lights appearing around the home, and other paranormal activity, usually electrical.
8. Animals behaving strangely, for instance, dogs barking at unseen objects.

In his experience, the person at the focus of the alien activity sleeps restlessly, and often wakes up in a sweat, with damp pillows. Those around them (often, in the case of a married abductee, actually sharing the same bed) go into a deep trancelike sleep and cannot be woken by the abductee.

Although Tony Dodd is a committed believer in alien activity and in abduction, he is at pains to dismiss any cases which he suspects are deliberate hoaxes or fantasies. He wants to convince the world, including the scientists, of the constant traffic between alien civilisations and our own, and does not think this cause will be well served by encouraging the making-up, or elaborating, of stories of possible abductions. He wants, in other words, the best quality evidence he can muster, and he is visibly annoyed when he talks about 'abductees' whose stories have been successfully challenged.

'It sets us all back, if one person admits to lying, or is discovered to be a fraud,' he says. 'We have enough genuine cases without needing people jumping on the bandwagon for their own, suspect, reasons.'

That is why he carries out such a thorough interrogation, and then sends investigators to look more closely at the cases which he believes stand up to scrutiny. Jason's case was especially important to him, because of Jason's age.

'If children are making up stories it is usually very easy to trip them up – they are not sophisticated deceivers. Nor are they likely to have read lots of books and newspaper reports about the subject, so their memories are unpolluted. Sometimes adults quite innocently mix things they have read with their own memories, and it becomes hard to distinguish the real facts. I rarely have that problem with children.'

Another of the unusual aspects of Jason's case which makes it important is his conscious memory of a lot of what happens to him. In Tony's own personal experience – and that of hundreds of other abductees – memories only surface sporadically and if triggered by some other event, usually appearing in a series of vivid flashbacks. Often, the full memories are only released under hypnosis – the subject of the television programme that finally offered Ann and Paul a key to Jason's problems.

The controversy surrounding the use of hypnotherapy will be dealt with more fully in the next chapter, and is fascinating as part of an overall study of abduction cases, but it does not affect Jason, who has not been hypnotised and who will not be, not if Tony Dodd and his parents have any say in it.

Tony Dodd's refusal to recommend hypnotherapy for Jason is partly to keep the case clear of any accusation of input by the hypnotic therapist – although Tony on the whole cares more about helping the abduction victims than answering the critics – but is much more a response to Jason's age. Tony and the organisation he represents, Quest, regard it as wholly unethical to suggest hypnosis for anyone under the age of eighteen, and would hesitate to recommend it even for someone under twenty-one.

Ann and Paul agree: they see no point in Jason recovering any more memories, as he finds it hard enough to cope with those he has, and Ann herself, who fits into the much more classic model of an abductee, with memories triggered very slowly and not until she reached adulthood, sees no value in it for herself. If hers and Jason's testimony are to be of any use to others in the same situation, she believes, there should be no suggestion that their memories have in any way been corrupted. She, too, feels that her memories (of which we shall hear more) are as much as she can cope with, and are surfacing unprompted without help of hypnotherapy. There are gaps in her memory – and Jason's – but she sees no possible advantage in filling them.

Her motivation is different from that of Tony Dodd. Although, like him, she would dearly love an explanation of the whole alien abduction phenomenon, and she is now fascinated by the subject, her main concern is not to satisfy the scientific demand for proof but that her teenage son should be able to sleep easily in his bed at night. If she cannot stop him being abducted, she wants to be able to help him come to terms with what is happening to him, and create a framework in which he can live in harmony with it.

The most dispiriting and depressing moment that I had while

researching this book was when I asked Jason what the future held for him. He shrugged his shoulders and said that he did not see it ever getting any better, nor did he see himself ever learning to accept it. Chillingly, he told me how he had seriously contemplated suicide, even going as far as to take a rope into the woods in an attempt to hang himself. He talked about it laconically, with apparent indifference, describing it as though it happened to a third party. Then, suddenly, the reserve broke, and tears came to his eyes as he shouted angrily at 'them', the uninvited strangers who have robbed him of so much of his youth. It was a very sad moment, the sort of moment that a great many of the UFO sceptics and debunkers choose to ignore. They demand proof, and use the lack of it to dismiss the whole subject as bizarre and cranky, but for Jason, and many thousands of people across the world like him, the quest for proof is an irrelevance. What matters is the quest for a way of life.

'I wish I could promise Jason that it will stop one day,' says Tony Dodd, 'but it is unlikely. Having been selected for multiple abductions, I feel the aliens will follow him for many years to come, probably all his life. But he will come to terms with it. He'll find a way of coping.

'I think he may, eventually, prove to be a very important abductee. Some of the experiences he has had [which will be explored later in this book] make me think he is being groomed as a "teacher", a human who is entrusted by the aliens with messages for the whole of mankind.'

In learning to live with it, Jason and his family have already taken the first, huge step. The day Ann rang for help was the day they all faced up to speaking to outsiders about Jason's experiences. By coming out into the open with it, they began, from that day on, to learn to cope.

There are, the experts believe, many thousands of others who have similar experiences to Jason's who are struggling on in silence, terrified of being thought unstable, mad, or of being laughed at. Coping with abductions entirely alone makes them miserable and in some instances they question their own sanity. In America there are cases of abduction that have been identified when a victim has sought the help of mental health professionals, only to be found to be sane and normal. This reassurance that they are not psychiatrically ill has encouraged them to admit to their abduction experiences, even if consciously they have only a few clouded memories.

In the USA it is quite possible to get help. There are psychiatrists, psychologists, scientists and many other professional people who accept abduction, and who can provide strategies for coping with it. One of the best of these strategies – as it is for so many other problems – is group therapy, where the victim meets others who have had similar experiences. Sharing memories with others who empathise is often the greatest help that can be had.

Such groups do not exist in Britain, but Tony Dodd provided the next best thing for Ann and Jason. He has always been there for them, returning Ann's phone calls as soon as he is able, and offering explanations and help whenever he can. He pulled no punches with Jason, admitting from the beginning that there was no 'cure', no magic potion which would make the abductions stop, but by being frank and open with Jason about his own experiences, he has helped the boy come to terms with what is happening. Over the phone he described his own abduction to Jason, and admitted he was scared.

'Don't be embarrassed, Jason,' he said. 'We are all scared, not just you. I travel the world, but I'm too afraid to sleep alone in the dark. I have to have a light switched on all the time. I'm too afraid to enter a darkened room on my own. They still come for me, and although I now know that they mean me no harm – and have accepted it – it still scares the hell out of me. It's easy to be calm and rational in the cold light of day, but when night comes, so does the fear.

'Having seen their crafts and the awesome power they possess, I know that we can never stop them. How the hell do you fight something which can not only paralyse you, but can levitate you and float you out of the house through solid walls? All we can do is try to understand why.'

It was a speech which brought a great deal of comfort to Jason. If a grown man could admit he was scared of the night visitors, he had nothing to be ashamed of, he could accept his own fear as natural.

As well as offering this sort of counselling, Tony Dodd also performed another great service for the Andrews family: indirectly, he was responsible for putting them in touch with other abductees, including one teenager who has been able to help Jason a great deal. It may not have been within a formal support group, but it was the same, very effective therapy: sharing the problem with another person who has experienced it.

Recognising that Jason was being abducted was a huge step for Ann and Paul, and one that set them on the right track to being able to help their difficult and disturbed son. It was also the point at which the paranormal activity surrounding the whole family escalated and the following few months were a very difficult time for all of them.

However, before we go any further with their individual story, perhaps this is the right moment to set it into a general context of what is known about alien abduction and UFOs. The next chapter provides a summary of the masses of serious research which has now been done on the subject.

CHAPTER 7

WHAT'S IT ALL ABOUT?

I came to the subject of alien abduction a complete beginner. Like Ann and Paul before me, I had preconceived ideas and prejudices that made me turn the page quickly whenever I came across a newspaper or magazine interview with an abductee. I dismissed such people, quite unfairly, as self-publicists or cranks. Films and TV programmes about the subject were interesting, but largely, I believed, fictional.

I was, and am, prepared to accept that there are more things in heaven and earth than are dreamt of in our philosophies. At both the smallest and largest extremes of human knowledge there are essential puzzles, which make it impossible to rule anything out. The unpredictable, ungovernable realm of quantum physics, which has brought an almost spiritual, mystical dimension to the work of hard-headed scientists (all that stuff about the observer in the system affecting the outcome), coupled with a sense of the magnitude of space, and the haphazard chances that led to the development of life on this particular planet, means that, yes, anything is possible. But the leap from the grand theory to the hard facts of spacecraft parking off earth and aliens travelling down to take back selected individuals for their own purposes? That all seemed too fantastic, too farfetched – until I met Jason and Ann, and started to research the other, many, well-documented cases of alien abduction.

It was the sheer plausibility of Ann and her family that first convinced me. I quickly realised that she was not lying, exaggerating, or being manipulated. Paul's resistance to the idea of abduction added even more conviction, and so did Jason's own telling of his story. He was not boastful, nor did he seem in any other way to be given to fantasies. As a family they are believable, and puzzled to

91

find themselves at the centre of something they did not seek nor enjoy. I was soon to discover that they are not unique: there are now hundreds of abductees who have come forward across the world, and the vast majority are as honest and straightforward as the Andrews family. That's not to say there have never been hoaxes, but, interestingly, there have been fewer than might perhaps be expected around such a controversial subject.

Although some of the abductees have immersed themselves completely in the world of UFO research, many others have only reluctantly recognised what is happening to them, and are uncontaminated witnesses – in other words, their testimony is their own, not the result of watching too many *X-Files* programmes and sci-fi films, or reading books and magazines covering other abductee stories.

The more I read about the subject, the more it became clear that the common threads running through the abduction reports were there long before the Hollywood producers moved in on the subject. We may think of UFOs as a modern phenomenon, but they have been around for centuries, probably from the beginning of life on earth. There are legends from every known civilisation of strange sights in the sky, and there are some uncanny parallels between modern stories of abduction and folklore stories – from all cultures – of being taken by 'fairy' folk. All the classic abduction symptoms are echoed in the old tales. French author Jacques Vallee, a scientist and mathematician, was one of the first to explore the close links between the old tales and the modern UFO-linked events, and since he pioneered the way there have been many fascinating collections of research from all over the world, all echoing a common theme: missing time, visits to strange worlds, small creatures with inexplicable powers.

There are also legends from many different ancient civilisations which talk of god-like creatures with very advanced technology coming from the skies to teach man. The ancient Egyptians believed the whole structure of this planet was created by sky gods who raised the land above the water, and laid down laws and wisdom which they handed to the Pharaohs. In Japan there are statues more than three thousand years old of figures very like the aliens described today. The Babylonians and Sumerians believed there was another planet in our solar system, orbiting so far away that it is rarely within range for viewing, from which visitors came to earth to shape our development. The Bible, in Genesis, makes reference to the Nephilim, believed to be a race of super-heroes born of human mothers by fathers who were not of this earth.

There are Incan, Aztec and Mayan legends, all about godlike creatures coming from the skies. In India there are stories of man being descended from gods who arrived in fiery chariots in the skies, and Vedic writings about gods from other planets. An ancient Tibetan book tells of superior beings from other planets who visit earth to monitor our progress. Native American Indians believe earth has been visited by beings from another star system since time began.

And so on. The common theme running through all these stories is uncanny, especially as they date from an era when the dissemination of news was so different from today. One modern criticism of abduction stories is that they spawn each other – that a TV or newspaper story brings more people forward to tell the same, or a very similar, tale – but you cannot level this criticism at ancient writings dating from long before modern communications existed. Each of these documents grew up independently of the others: there can have been no cross fertilisation (at least, not unless it came from these 'gods' or 'aliens').

Modern stories of strange sightings and encounters have mushroomed in the past hundred years, and particularly in the last fifty. This may mean that we are living in the middle of an epidemic, and that the growing number of abduction cases means that we are on the verge of some apocalyptic intervention by the aliens. More simply, it may mean that it is becoming easier to talk about strange experiences that, as Tony Dodd says, in previous years would have resulted in questions being asked about the sanity of the abductee. The latter half of the nineteenth century and most of the twentieth has been an age of science and rational explanation: anything that could not be explained was dismissed.

Increasingly, these values are being questioned, and scientists are much more open-minded. There is now a growing number of distinguished academics who are prepared to treat the subject of UFOs and abduction seriously – although, it is important to note, there is still a much bigger body of sceptical opinion among the scientific community. However, there are more and more brave souls who are prepared to risk ridicule by their peers, just as there have in history been those prepared to stand up and be counted for the earth being round, the evolution of the species, the sun as the centre of the solar system.

Early UFO sightings, from the latter end of the nineteenth century, are difficult to evaluate. There seem to be some which looked like airships, and, although airships were unknown for several more years, it is always possible that prototypes were being tested (just as, in recent years, the Stealth and Aurora jets have given rise to a great many so-called UFO sightings). Yet just because reports are old and cannot be verified does not make them invalid, and among all the early reports are many that coincide with modern experiences: bright balls of light which seemed to attract witnesses towards them; flying objects of incredible speed with the ability to hover and change direction instantly; horses and other animals being spooked by the strange aerial objects; sightings of small (less that four feet high) inhabitants of these craft.

However, it is in the last fifty years that the UFO phenomenon has been closely monitored and documented, with specialist groups springing up all over the world to study it, and with governments becoming involved in investigating (and covering up) the extent of the contact between other life forms and this planet. The stories that came out of the Second World War, when both Allied and German planes found themselves being pursued by strange lights which appeared to be under intelligent control, sparked the first official interest in the subject. Pilots from both sides believed that they were dealing with a new super-weapon developed by the other side: when they discovered that the enemy was similarly deluded, it aroused scientific curiosity. In fact, over the years, a vast number of reliable sightings – at least 3,000 – of unexplained lights and objects in the skies have been made by experienced pilots and navigators, trained observers who are accustomed to the bizarre patterns of the weather, and who risk their professional standing by coming forward to report what they have seen.

The first modern reference to a 'flying saucer' came in 1947, from an American pilot who was describing a formation of crescent-shaped objects which he encountered in the Cascade mountain range in Washington State. They were travelling very fast, much faster than any contemporary aircraft, and the pilot, Kenneth Arnold, assumed they were some new top-secret military aircraft under development. When he reported what he had seen, coining the neat phrase 'flying saucer', it caught the imagination of the American news media and was soon being used all over the world.

Within weeks one of the biggest UFO mysteries ever broke in the newspapers. It was the story of a UFO crash at Roswell, New Mexico, from which debris and bodies of aliens – possibly dead, possibly some of them still living – were allegedly recovered. To this day, controversy about it rages, and a lot of it is centred on the role of the American government in ordering a cover-up: the official line is that the only thing that hit the ground was a weather balloon. There is neither time nor space here to go into the details of Roswell (there are plenty of books and films dealing with the subject), but it is impossible to escape the conclusion that something a lot more interesting than a weather balloon was involved, something that the US military and government officials have been determined to conceal.

From Roswell onwards there is extensive and undeniable evidence of cover-ups, not just by the American government but by other governments worldwide. It is the USA, though, which has been at the forefront of official investigation into UFOs, and therefore also in leading the way in failing to be open and honest with the public about sightings and contacts. Interestingly, the best evidence of alien activity obtained here in Britain involved an American Air Force base, and the main witnesses were American Air Force personnel. The Bentwaters case, which is also known as the Rendlesham Forest case, happened in 1980 close to the Bentwaters base, near Ipswich. It lasted for two days, with strange lights being seen in the forest, a small triangular-shaped craft being observed on the ground, and another, much larger, circular craft hovering. Again, a great deal has been written about the case, especially because the reports included such high-quality witnesses as the deputy base commander, a Lieutenant Colonel in the USAF, and again, the case was subject to a massive cover-up. Since the 1950s a great deal of credible evidence has been assembled on cover-ups, and official investigations which are hushed-up.

A large number of abductees and witnesses report sightings of what has now become a UFO cliché: the 'men in black'. There can be no doubt that there are sinister visitors who turn up after UFO activity: strange men, dressed uncomfortably, sometimes making contact with the witness and sometimes just observing them. The Andrews have seen them, so have many other abductees. They seem to be most evident when there has been a report of visible UFO activity. One possible explanation is that they are from national or international bodies monitoring the contact between aliens and earth (and many UFO experts now believe that all the major world governments are working in league against what may turn out to be a far greater threat to the earth than natural disasters or even world wars). Another explanation is that these strange men are actually aliens, adopting the uncomfortable and ill-fitting guise of human clothes to allow them to observe the aftermath of their own activity.

There have been earlier reports of abduction, but the one which first hit the headlines, and encouraged others to come forward with their stories, was the case of Barney and Betty Hill, an American couple who were returning from a short holiday in Canada in the autumn of 1961. They were close to their home in New Hampshire when they saw an unusual bright light. They followed it in their car, and then stopped and Barney climbed out and walked towards it. Using binoculars he could see small figures looking out of what appeared to be windows in the crescent-shaped craft. As it began to descend towards the earth, Barney Hill went back to his car and drove off.

When the couple arrived home they found the journey had taken two and a half hours longer than it should have done. They both felt strange: Betty insisted on bathing immediately, and bundled up the clothes she had been wearing as if they were contaminated. They reported what had happened to the nearest US Air Force base thirty-six hours after the incident. It was only years later that it was revealed that the base had registered an 'unknown' on its radar at exactly the same time that the Hills were having their encounter.

Both Barney and Betty experienced a whole range of physical and psychological side effects, including nightmares, high blood pressure, exhaustion and, for Barney, a strange ring of wart-like growths in his groin area. They were eventually put in touch with a respected psychiatrist and neurologist who carried out six months of hypnosis sessions with them, and under hypnosis it was revealed that they had both been taken on board the alien spacecraft and various medical tests had been carried out on them both, including a needle being inserted into Betty's stomach, which she believed was 'a pregnancy test'.

The Hills's story was not made public for some time: they did not seek publicity, they wanted help. Eventually, when their account surfaced in the media, it provoked a great deal of controversy, but after it there followed a mass of other abduction reports, some following the same outline as the Hills's case and others with different elements but some common factors. It is clear that nobody doubted their sincerity, even the most sceptical of commentators. Everyone who met them was convinced that they were respectable, sensible people who had nothing to gain (they paid out of their own pockets for their hypnosis sessions).

Since the Hills's case, in the early 1960s, there have been many others where hypnotherapy has been used as a tool to unlock memories which some believe have been deliberately 'masked' by the aliens, but even at this stage in the research, experts were urging caution about the use of hypnosis.

Its use in abduction cases (in fact, in all cases) is controversial. Some investigators believe it is the only way to release true memories of what happened, others that under hypnosis people can fantasise. There have been some tragic examples of 'false memory syndrome' among young women who have accused members of their family – usually their fathers – of sexually abusing them when they were young, memories which have apparently been blotted out by the trauma and only released under hypnotic therapy. Families have been divided, parents have been publicly shamed, and then the whole 'memory' has been discovered to be false.

Sceptics argue that abductees can equally conjure up fantasies while under hypnosis. An experiment in 1977, in California, used regression hypnosis on a selected number of abductees, and also on a group of people whose knowledge of UFOs and abduction was no more than might have been gleaned from everyday sources like newspapers and television. They were not abductees, nor were they people with an interest in UFOlogy. They were asked, under hypnosis, to imagine an alien abduction. About half of them came up with stories similar to those of the genuine abductees, a conclusion which inevitably cast doubt on the use of hypnotherapy (to the sceptics it cast doubt on the veracity of the 'real' abduction stories, too).

The experiment was fundamentally flawed. It would have been difficult in California in 1977, a time when there had been a lot of publicity about a few striking abduction stories, to find a cross-section of people who had no idea of the basic components of an abduction. In fact, the 'made-up' abduction stories were not classic abduction scenarios, they simply contained some similar points which were stressed, and the other differing details were ignored. The experiment also took no regard of certain very important differences between the two groups: the placebo group, those who were not genuine abductees, were all aware that they were imagining the experience. When they came out of the hypnosis they had no sense of having unlocked deep-seated memories. It was no more real to them than becoming Elvis Presley for two minutes is real to the volunteers who go up on stage with professional hypnotists, and find themselves singing 'Blue Suede Shoes' while strumming an air guitar. It was a game, they treated it as a game, and it had no lasting effect on them.

The abductees, on the other hand, were all overwhelmed by the reality of what they had found in their memories. They were deeply traumatised by their experiences, and the emotional upheaval was ongoing and long-lasting (for most abductees, it appears to be a permanent condition of life).

So, hypnosis has its advocates and its critics. It is probable that the solution is a compromise, just as it has proved to be in forensic work. Hypnosis can be used to help release information, but cannot be the only evidence. American police forces, when hypnotic regression was first used on witnesses, went overboard, and were putting people into the witness box whose only contribution to evidence in the case had been obtained under hypnosis. It was soon proved that it was possible to lie under hypnosis, to present imaginary scenarios, just as the volunteers did in the abduction experiment, and the whole system was discredited.

However, in Britain and many states of the US, hypnosis was quietly being used as an aid in the collection of other evidence. For example, when a young newspaper delivery girl was viciously attacked and left for dead in the Greater Manchester police area, detectives soon worked out that her father, walking to the newspaper shop because she was late in coming home, must have passed the attacker's car leaving the scene of the crime. Several cars had gone by and the father could not recall them clearly. Under hypnosis he was able to retrace his journey and describe to the police each car. They tracked them all down, and with the help of other evidence (bloodstained clothing, etc) they found the attacker. He was convicted: and the use of hypnosis was not an issue at the trial because it had been used only as a tool, not as evidence in itself.

Another celebrated case involved the murder of a young boy in the West Midlands, again while he was out delivering newspapers in the early hours of the morning. Detectives established that the killer was likely to be the same man who had carried out twenty-nine other attacks on boys in the area and had tried to approach two other newspaper boys in the weeks leading up to the murder. The boys gave descriptions of the man and his car – but, under hypnosis, one of them was able to give such particular details about the car that the police came up with a reasonably short list of similar, customised, vehicles. The driver, a paedophile with previous convictions, was found and admitted his guilt. Again, the hypnosis was a tool, not an end in itself.

So it should be in alien abduction cases. If it can help trigger memories that release other, conscious, memories, then it is valuable – but those memories may well surface anyway, as they have for Jason and, to a lesser extent, Ann Andrews.

Throughout the sixties and seventies more and more abduction cases were being reported throughout the Western world (they are doubtless still being subsumed into the local folklore in under-developed countries). Most reported cases were American, but this probably reflects a willingness to accept and discuss (and publicise) the cases rather than an actual difference in the numbers of abductions occurring.

The popular idea of abduction is that it is a one-off experience, something that happens suddenly, without warning, and usually in a public place at night-time – for example, while driving along a dark road. There are, indeed, hundreds of such stories in the abduction literature. However, Tony Dodd is far from being alone in believing that most abductees are, like Jason, abducted regularly over a period of many years, and one of the first researchers to realise and highlight this was Budd Hopkins, an American artist who has pioneered a great deal of serious work with abductees.

He first became involved in 1975, when the subject was still comparatively new. He, with his wife and a friend, had spotted a UFO years before, in 1964, and had remained puzzled and interested in the subject. When, in the summer of 1975, there was a spate of sightings of UFOs near his summer home in Cape Cod, he began investigating. By chance, and certainly without specifically seeking an abduction case, he found himself looking into a UFO landing which had been witnessed by several people, one of whom had a 'missing' chunk of time. This man refused to try hypnotherapy when Budd suggested it, but by finding out more about the possibilities of it, and talking publicly about it, Budd unwittingly became one of America's best-known UFO names. Because he was one of the few experts available to the media, his name was often the first to be known to American abductees in need of support, and wanting to tell their stories to someone who would believe and help them. Consequently Hopkins was contacted by many victims, and has written books about some of the more important American cases.

He discovered, while working with a psychiatrist who used hypnosis, that many abductees had not just one but a whole series of abductions locked in their memories, usually starting when they were children. There were other common factors, one of the most striking being the appearance (and disappearance) of scars on their bodies, with no known cause.

Budd Hopkins is very important to the whole history of abduction research because, while the subject of UFOs in general was attracting serious scientific study by the 1980s, aliens themselves were still regarded as beyond the pale. Yet, as nuclear physicist Stanton Friedman pointed out, the UFOs themselves are fascinating because of their technology, but if they are a means of transport then their pilots have got to be of far greater interest. 'Never mind the saucers, what about the occupants?' he said.

Nick Pope, a British researcher who came to the subject while working for the Ministry of Defence, carrying out investigations into UFO sightings, puts it more graphically: 'If the Queen called at your house, you probably would not be interested in the car in which she arrived.'

It took Hopkins, and his methodical approach to the subject, to bring credibility to abduction research. Perhaps his single most important convert to date is Professor John Mack who, like so many other academics, was drawn reluctantly into the abduction field, aware of the risk to his considerable professional reputation by becoming involved in something so generally disregarded.

John Mack is Professor of Psychiatry at Harvard Medical School, and among the many books he has written is a Pulitzer prize-winning biography of T.E. Lawrence. He enjoys enormous peer respect, and gambled it all by championing the cause of the abductees. When he published his seminal work, *Abduction: Human Encounters with Aliens*, in 1990 he was hugely criticised, and the Harvard Medical School held a formal inquiry into his work. His job, despite over forty years of experience in the clinical practice of psychiatry, was on the line. In the end, although the inquiry criticised some of the methods he used, he was vindicated, and kept his post.

It is unlikely he would have faced the same problems if the subject of his book had been less controversial. Professor Mack could understand the view of his fellow academics: when he was originally invited to meet Budd Hopkins he declined, because he felt the whole subject sounded just too weird. His instant reaction was that Budd Hopkins must be 'crazy', but he could hardly reject him for that – the work of a psychiatrist must embrace helping the crazy – and he eventually met the New York artist who was doing so much to help the victims of abduction.

After the initial meeting Professor Mack was convinced there was something that required investigating, and he was fairly confident at this early stage that he would find a specific psychological cause for people to 'imagine' they had been abducted. Budd Hopkins welcomed the input of such a distinguished professional and was happy to put abductees in touch with the professor, who subsequently examined more than a hundred of them in depth, both under hypnosis and in lengthy interviews.

The abductees Mack studied come from all walks of life, with differing levels of education and skills, and with different attitudes, spiritual beliefs, and ambitions. Their ages, gender and family circumstances throw up no common patterns. Although, now, there are books and magazines which cover the subject, many of these victims came forward before abduction was widely discussed and there are common themes in their experiences. Perhaps the most striking is that they have usually been involved in a continuing series of abductions.

Professor Mack's chief interest was to discover whether this wide cross section of people were suffering from a recognisable mental illness. He and others have carried out many tests, and come to the conclusion that, apart from the stress and trauma caused by the actual abduction experience, these are perfectly normal, sane people with no psychiatric problems. From his initial standpoint of deep scepticism, he now believes that the abductees are telling the truth.

He lists five 'basic dimensions' which need to be part of any explanation of what happens to abductees, whether it is the alien abduction explanation or another, more prosaic, one. To satisfy him, any theory would have to include:

1. Why there is such a high level of consistency between the accounts of abductions as well as the reliability of most abductees.
2. The absence of detectable psychiatric or psychological illness among abductees.
3. The physical manifestations, including cuts, bruises, lesions, scars.
4. The connection between the abductions and UFO activity, often reported by independent witnesses.
5. Abduction reports from young children, whose memories cannot have been contaminated by reading or seeing television programmes about the phenomenon.

This five-point list runs very much in line with Tony Dodd's own thoughts about why alien abduction cannot easily be dismissed. The fact that here in Britain, as well as in many other countries across the world, the experience of abduction is so similar to the American experience means that it is unlikely to be a self-generating response to publicity. The increased scepticism of the British, the language and culture barrier with so many other countries, and the lack of publicity (until recent years) mean that cases were coming forward spontaneously, and producing common threads.

'I have now investigated a lot of abduction cases,' he says, 'and I get the same or very similar scenario running through each one. They can't all be part of some huge conspiracy, and many of them have never read about or heard about other abduction cases.

'Under hypnosis, why do they all have the same delusion if it is not genuine? They have marks on their bodies, they find themselves surrounded by other paranormal activity, mostly electrical. Jason is not the only child I have dealt with: I have heard abduction stories from much younger children, too young to say the word, even if they had a clue what it meant. They can't be making it up.'

One difference between British abductees and Americans is the gender profile: in the USA half of all victims are male, but in Britain approximately eighty per cent of those who come forward reporting an abduction experience are women. Tony believes this is because the British male is particularly concerned not to 'make a fool of himself', attracting derision from his mates. American males are more upfront, more inclined to discuss their feelings and emotions, less buttoned-up. It is a difference in reporting, not in actual abduction patterns.

Professor Mack and Budd Hopkins are just two of scores of American professionals who now work with, and believe, abductees. There is a chain of support groups, where abduction victims can meet one another and share their problems. When Professor Mack set up his first support group it was in order to get victims talking to each other without the interference of outsiders who could, however unintentionally, be guilty of implanting ideas and thoughts. However, the support groups have done far more than offer the researchers access to 'uncontaminated' reports. They have, like all such groups covering other problems, brought a great deal of comfort and relief to the abductees, many of whom have been ridiculed and disbelieved. Some have even found themselves (as Jason has) in the hands of psychiatrists and psychologists, trying to pin labels on their 'condition'. Others have kept their experiences strictly to themselves, for fear of the reaction of others. The support groups have allowed them to talk, in an uncritical atmosphere, about their memories and fears.

Such organisations do not exist in Britain, but increasingly serious UFO researchers are putting abductees in touch with one another, with much the same results: there is an instant feeling of relief at being able to share experiences with someone else who has 'been there, done that'. Many abductees are very lonely: sometimes even their partners remain sceptical and hard to convince, and those friends and relatives who are sympathetic can have no real appreciation of what it is like to be abducted. Jason Andrews understands only too well the value of having someone to talk to: his life improved dramatically after a colleague of Tony Dodd put him in touch with another abductee, who in turn referred him to another.

There has not been scope in this chapter to do more than skim the surface of abduction research: this is a very brief summary of the masses of work now available on the subject. I spent a great deal of time reading, talking to experts, and attending conferences in the weeks and months after first meeting Ann and Jason and, had I harboured any doubts about their story, the sheer volume and meticulous detail of the material would have been enough to convince me.

There is a groundswell of belief in UFOs and aliens: a reputable survey in America in 1996 showed that forty-eight per cent of the population believe in UFOs, and almost one in three people believe that contact has taken place between aliens and humans. A much less scientific study in Britain came up with a higher figure: seventy-three per cent believe extraterrestrials have visited this planet.

More significantly, the number of scientists, doctors, mental health professionals, pilots and other aviation workers who now admit that they believe in (and have evidence of) alien life approaching earth is growing all the time. Most politicians have yet to show the courage of their convictions and speak out about it, although there are several in America who are prepared to stand up and be counted, and there is a UFO research group within the Houses of Parliament in Britain.

It can only be a matter of time before the alien 'problem', which governments undoubtedly discuss behind closed doors, appears on the public agenda, which is why it is important that stories like that of Jason Andrews are made available. The Andrews family do not talk in terms of high-flown ideals, but they do see an important, altruistic purpose to making Jason's story known. They hope that, on a small scale, it will help other abductees. I believe, on a much larger scale, it will help push forward understanding and acceptance of the abduction phenomenon.

CHAPTER 8

THE FINGER LADY

The relief of being able to talk openly made a big difference to Jason: for a few weeks after the first contact with Tony Dodd he slept better at night, and school was going quite well. He had a couple more appointments with the psychiatrist, but in the end, after eight months, she said she felt she had not been able to help him.

After being sympathetic and receptive the day he unburdened himself about his night-time visitors – and, remember, that was before he had seen the television programme or even heard the words 'alien abduction' – she was more sceptical at later appointments. She told him that his experiences were dreams, which Jason had heard many times before.

Then, at last, the programme gave him the key, an explanation, and he refused to be fobbed off, as he had been for years, with 'dreams' and 'nightmares'. He told her about it, and about Tony Dodd. Ann even arranged for her to ring Tony, so that he could pass on some basic background information about the whole subject, but, even after two hours on the phone, she maintained to Tony that she believed Jason was dreaming, and said that she felt she could do little more for him as her insistence obviously antagonised him.

Ann believes that the psychiatrist, like so many other professionals who come across the subject of alien abduction, was initially interested and open-minded, but may have realised after talking to colleagues that it was a controversial and generally derided area. She found herself unable to accept the abduction and fell back on the insistence that Jason's night-time experiences were simply dreams.

They had even shown her one of the mysterious scars which

appeared on Jason's body after an abduction, and she was unable to explain it: she wrote to the Andrews's GP describing it as a perfect two-inch triangular patch. On that visit she described Jason as pale and scared.

Like all the other phenomena that surround Jason, the marks on his body come in runs, several occurring within a short space of time, then a gap of weeks or even months before the next one shows up. For example, Ann's diary for September 1995 includes the following notes:

20th. Jason complained of a pain in his side this morning. Lifted shirt to show me a red triangular-shaped mark, very angry-looking, on his rib cage. I wanted to phone the doctor, but Jason said leave it. By the time he came home from school, there was no sign of it. [This was the scar that Jason showed the psychiatrist.]

23rd. Jason limping slightly. Showed me a mark at the top of his leg – as if the flesh had been scooped out. But there was no cut or broken skin, although the whole area was red. Later, at the farm, I tried to show the mark to Paul but it had vanished.

1st October. Jason has the dice mark on his left knee.

The dice mark was the square of dots, with one in the middle, that Ann often saw on Jason's body, usually behind the knee – although on this occasion it was on the front of his knee. Each dot was about quarter of an inch in diameter, and perfectly round.

An earlier set of marks, in June of that year, was seen by the Andrews's GP, who described it in a letter to the psychiatrist: 'Jason has shown me marks on his left side, stating that this is where the "creatures" cut into him. I do not know what to make of them. I haven't seen anything like this before.'

Jason became very annoyed with the psychiatrist when he realised that she was not giving him the help he had hoped for, and he clammed up again, refusing to talk to her about the abductions. The psychiatrist was clear that Jason is not mentally ill: she wrote to his GP in November 1995 stating that in her opinion, Jason was not psychotic. This unambiguous endorsement of his sanity echoed what the psychiatrist had already told Ann, that Jason was not hallucinating. She prescribed an anti-depressant for him, to help him sleep.

His behaviour at school now became a problem again, and he was once again threatened with suspension. It was mutually agreed in January 1996, by the psychiatrist, Paul and Ann, that the sessions were going nowhere. The psychiatrist wanted to refer Jason to somebody else for treatment, but admitted that she had no idea to whom she should send him, and by this time, as we will see later, he was getting a great deal of support from another abductee, Maria Ward, who was counselling him.

Both Jason and his parents believed that continuing to see the psychiatrist was fruitless: she was always going to contend it was all in Jason's mind. He would emerge from his talks with her in tears, insisting to his parents that he wasn't making it up. As they now had, for the first time, an understanding of what was happening, they felt these sessions were counter-productive. If Jason was to learn to live with his abductions, he first had to accept them.

Tony Dodd says, ruefully, that Jason's dealing with the psychiatrist taught him a necessary tactic: to keep quiet.

'Adults do it, because they know if they talk openly about what happens to them they'll be regarded as loopy. Twenty or thirty years ago, people were sent to psychiatric institutions for less: luckily, we are living in a more enlightened world, but there is still not a general acceptance of the subject. So most older people don't invite ridicule: they only discuss UFOs and abductions with those they know understand. Jason has, sadly, learned the lesson that there are still an awful lot of people who don't or won't treat the subject seriously.'

The psychiatrist's reluctance to accept the abduction explanation hardly mattered to Ann and Paul: they were so relieved to have found out what was happening to their son, and to have discovered that he was not unique, nor would he come to any harm.

'The most important thing that Tony told me,' says Ann, 'is that among the many hundreds of reports of abductions across the world, there are none of people failing to return, or of them being permanently physically harmed. It made Jason's night-time disappearances so much easier to accept. It may sound strange to other parents, but there have even been nights when Paul and I have been able to sleep, knowing that Jason was not there, but also knowing he would be back by the morning.'

However, the psychiatrist's apparent rejection of his explanation upset and angered Jason. He was building up confidence, thanks to Tony Dodd and the other abductees he was speaking to, and he did not understand how some members of the adult world could accept his experiences, while others were still treating him like a little boy frightened of his own nightmares: 'It's all very well for the doctor to insist on a rational explanation for everything,' he told his dad, 'but she can't tell me what the rational explanation is! That's all very well for her, but I've got to live with it.'

He always referred to the psychiatrist as 'the finger lady', as every time she spoke of the aliens she would hold up two fingers on each hand, bowing them a couple of times in what Jason felt was a condescending manner, to indicate that the word 'aliens' should be in quotation marks, and thereby not taken as necessarily correct. She did it in a flippant way, as if by even talking about it she was playing Jason's game. (From January 1996 until the summer of 1997, Jason was not provided with any psychiatric help, much to his relief, but in August 1997 he was again assigned a psychiatrist, a different one, and has attended meetings which he does not feel are helping him at all. The new psychiatrist described Jason in a letter to his GP as a most interesting case, and said that she was 'trying to help him cope with his experience of alien abduction'. Ann is happy for Jason to see anyone who is trying to help him, but she believes he gets the best support from those who know about, and believe in, the abduction phenomenon.)

His behaviour at school deteriorated, with sudden explosions of anger, door-slamming, cheek to teachers, and once again he was briefly suspended. This time Ann was less worried: she hesitated to tell the staff at the school what the real problem was, but at least she herself understood her wayward son. She talked seriously to him about the need to contain his anger. Tony Dodd, counselling him, asked why he erupted so much at school and Jason's reply surprised him for its maturity: 'They talk down to me, as if I'm an idiot. Yet I know more than they do about so many things. I've been shown so much...'

It confirmed what Tony already suspected. The aliens who were 'borrowing' Jason in the night were grooming him for a reason of their own. He was being shown things and taught things which, so far, he had not revealed to anyone. It was possible that they were buried deep in his memory and not easily retrieved, but Tony stuck to his guns about not using hypnosis. Jason, he was sure, would be allowed to remember when the right time came.

For a few weeks after their first contact with Tony, the only problem disturbing the Andrews household was Jason's behaviour – but not for long. It was a smell that heralded the restart of paranormal activity.

A sweet sickly odour pervaded the whole house. It was something like the smell of burnt sugar, but much stronger, and very unpleasant. It made them all feel sick. Even the dogs spent as much time as they could out in the garden. Ann bought every room deodoriser on the market, but only managed to mask it temporarily. They'd had the smell before, but never this bad and never in the house.

They'd noticed it at the farm, in a corner of the field, near the woods, soon after they had spotted the strange watchers in the neighbouring field. Paul had first smelled it, and called Jason and Ann across to confirm it: later that night all three suffered stomach cramps, and diarrhoea. Then the sickly, sweet smell had taken over Ann's car, so strongly that for a whole day none of them could bear to use it. At the same time, the car battery mysteriously went flat.

In the house the smell was much more difficult to cope with. It seemed to permeate everywhere. The weather was not warm enough for them all to spend their time in the garden, or to have the windows and doors permanently open. It was so bad that Ann's mother Vi refused to visit them. In the end, in desperation, the family sat with their heavy coats on and the windows open. The dogs had never had so many volunteers to take them for walks, as everyone tried to get away from the nauseating odour. Carpets were lifted, cupboards cleared out; Ann searched everywhere for something that could be causing the smell, but found nothing.

Then, suddenly, the smell was gone completely. Relief was short-lived, as it was succeeded by a spate of paranormal activity.

Light bulbs exploded, electrical equipment switched on and off, the hi-fi played bursts of loud music, even when not plugged in. Ann began buying large packs of light bulbs, as all the bulbs in the house would blow at the same time. Council workmen checked the wiring but could find nothing wrong. Objects were being moved, sometimes even to different rooms.

At times all the dogs would start to growl, hackles up, as if there were an intruder, but Paul could find no sign of anyone near the house. One evening in September 1995 there was a power surge, and all the dogs dashed into the living room, as if spooked by something. The four cockatiels that Ann keeps in a cage in the hall began to squawk in terror, flapping their wings and scattering feathers everywhere.

Jason became tired, bad-tempered and frightened. The night-time visits, he told his parents, had started again. It was the same routine: at 3am by the digital alarm clock he kept by his bed, he'd wake and hear the dogs growling, and then, suddenly, they'd go completely quiet.

Then he'd see one of the aliens, one of the grey ones, rising silently at the foot of his bed: a smooth action, as if it was coming up through the floorboards, the large head with the big black eyes, slanting round the side of the smooth head, appearing first. After the 'big one' he became aware of many smaller ones, busying around, and then sometimes the 'koala bears', fuzzy and furry.

He never remembered the journey, but he would find himself again on the smooth cold slab with rounded edges, unable to move anything except his eyes. There was never more than one of the larger aliens there at a time, and it was obvious that this one controlled the little ones. On several occasions the senior one seemed to be holding an implement, about eight inches long. Then Jason would lose consciousness, and would awake at home, though not necessarily back in bed. The alarm clock would be working, but two hours behind the right time. All the other clocks upstairs would either have stopped or be two hours slow, yet the ones downstairs would still register the right time.

The barking dogs woke the neighbours, but they never woke Ann, Paul or Daniel – yet on normal nights, Paul would stir and stumble downstairs if one of his precious dogs so much as whined. One of the neighbours was so impressed by the instant silencing of the dogs that he asked Paul for the trick of shutting them up so effectively.

The solution seemed simple to Paul. He would stay awake all

night, keeping vigil by Jason's bed. He managed it, only dozing off for brief moments a couple of times, but on these occasions nothing happened. Jason slept soundly. By this time Jason was able to predict when he was going to be abducted. He gets a 'funny tingly feeling' in his head, and 'just knows' when his abductors are coming, and on those nights Paul made an extra special effort to stay awake, arming himself with a flask of strong coffee and a good book. Used to working long hours – at weekends he rarely finishes driving his taxi until dawn – Paul is more able than most to keep his eyes open all night (Ann tried but fell asleep every time), but on the nights when Jason predicted an abduction, Paul invariably fell into a deep dreamless sleep, remembering nothing when he woke. Like the dogs, it was as if he had been zapped by some powerful external force that rendered him unconscious. On one occasion Jason, awakened by the strange light which usually precedes an abduction, shook his father violently but failed to wake him.

As the activity increased again, so did Jason's misery. Ann could not persuade him to change his clothes – he told her he did not deserve clean clothes. His self-esteem went right down, and again Ann became deeply worried. She kept him home from school, unsure whether this was wise but not wanting to risk him being suspended again if his mood led to bad behaviour. On one occasion, she was so worried about the risk of him committing suicide, that she put him on the phone to Tony Dodd. Tony's bluff, down-to-earth approach, coupled with his understanding of the problem, always seemed to work wonders for Jason.

The bizarre electrical activity increased. One day, as she passed along the landing, Ann heard a noise from Jason's room. Gingerly pushing open the door she found a power car, a toy that he prized, zooming up and down the carpet, its lights flashing. Somehow, uncannily, it managed to swerve away from the skirting boards, as if someone was controlling the steering. Ann watched in amazement for a few seconds, then she bent to switch it off, but before she could touch it, it suddenly stopped.

One evening, when Ann and the boys were watching television together, they all simultaneously fell asleep, although it was early and none of them was aware of being particularly tired. When they woke, the television was picking up a French channel: they could hear the sound but there was only the shadow of a picture. Daniel was the first to notice that one of the dogs, Milly, was missing. She'd been stretched out next to him on the settee before they all went to sleep. The other three dogs seemed upset and nervous.

The only possible explanation Ann could come up with was that Milly was outside, and that they must all have been mistaken when they thought she was on the settee. The dogs are of similar size and colouring, and at a glance it is easy for anyone not familiar with them to mistake one for another, but Daniel was adamant, and affronted that his mother would even suggest he did not know which one was which. Nonetheless, Ann went outside with a torch, calling Milly, without success. She was about to ring Paul, feeling slightly apprehensive because she knows how much he dotes on the dogs, but as she walked back into the house she glanced into the living room, and there was Milly sprawled on the settee, asleep. Both Daniel and Jason swore that she could not have got back in without them seeing her, yet there was no other explanation. Milly was very deeply asleep, and did not stir for the rest of the evening or the night. The following morning she was dopey, as if she had been drugged.

On the night of Tuesday 3rd October there was a violent thunderstorm over Kent. The boys were in bed, and Ann and Paul were preparing to go upstairs when a huge clap of thunder broke across the rooftops. The dogs growled and shifted uneasily: they do not like thunder. Paul was soothing them and Ann was unplugging the television when Jason appeared at the foot of the stairs. He walked into the living room, sat on the sofa, but with his back ramrod straight, as if he was sitting on a hard-backed chair. Ann spoke to him but he did not reply. He did not look at her, but stared straight ahead. Then he started to mumble, and the words became stronger and clearer as the storm overhead grew louder and wilder. Jason was again spouting numbers, huge sequences of figures, in a terrifying reprise of the incident on the day of his fourth birthday party. Paul came back from seeing to the dogs and he, too, tried to speak to Jason, but he just continued, in an emotionless delivery, to spew out numbers. He mentioned mathematical concepts way ahead of his years: fractals, theorems, algebraic formulae. He talked in massive numbers, mentioning billions and millions, and at one point announcing that he was working to six decimal places, but he did not sound as though he was making calculations: it was more as if he was reading these incredible numbers off a screen in his head.

Shocked, but less upset than they were eight years before, Paul and Ann looked at each other, neither sure what to do. Paul went out of the room to find a tape-recorder, and Ann sat herself next to Jason, not touching him because there was a remoteness about his voice and posture that made her uncomfortable. Before Paul could return, the thunder rolled away and all that could be heard was the odd, distant grumble. As it faded, so did Jason's voice, until in the end he was mumbling softly to himself, although still sitting bolt upright and staring straight ahead. Then he went quiet, his body slumped, and he leaned back against the settee, rubbing his eyes as though he was just waking up.

'It's OK, Jason, you're downstairs, and the storm's gone now,' said Ann, putting her arm round him. Jason gazed around the room, then at his mother.

'I wasn't frightened of the storm,' he said, hastily, with a twelve-year-old's bravado. Ann realised that he had no idea what had happened, no memory of spewing out numbers in such a bizarre fashion.

''Course you weren't frightened,' she said. 'You came down to comfort the dogs, then you dropped off to sleep.'

''Night, Mum. 'Night Dad,' he said, and went off upstairs.

Before Ann could say anything Paul shrugged his massive shoulders. 'We could tire our brains out trying to make sense of it – or we could go to bed and get some sleep. I'm voting for bed,' he said. Ann, resignedly, nodded in agreement.

Jason's depression deepened over the next few days, and at Tony Dodd's suggestion Ann decided to take him on holiday for a week. It would mean a week away from school, but he was missing such a lot of teaching anyway that it would hardly matter. If it gave him respite from the abductions, which seemed to be happening with even greater frequency, it could only be a good thing. She and Paul discussed it and, although finances were tight, they were convinced that it would be worth whatever it cost if it brought a bit of peace to Jason. Besides, they weren't going on some exotic foreign trip: it was just a week in a caravan at All Hallows, Kent, and in November it certainly would not be expensive. Paul would not be able to go, as he never can go away with the family – there are always animals on the farm which need his attention.

Secretly, when Jason was not around, Ann booked the trip for herself, Daniel, Jason and a schoolfriend of each of them. All the other boys were sworn to secrecy: the trip was to be a surprise for Jason. Ann even managed to pack a bag of his clothes without him realising. When his friends arrived on the doorstep early one morning, suitcases in their hands, a perplexed Jason did not know what to make of it – until he spotted his own case in the hallway. Within minutes Ann had four excited boys loaded into the car, and was taking her leave of Paul.

'I think I've got the soft option,' he said. 'The animals are going to be easier to handle than that lot.'

Ann was undaunted. This trip was for Jason's benefit, and if that meant she had to put up with four rowdy boys, she'd just make the best of it. She told her husband she'd be coming home for a rest in a week's time. Within a couple of hours they were picking up the key for their caravan, and Ann had to turn herself into a sergeant major to get them all to unpack and make up their beds, before they were free to explore the holiday camp.

The days went well, filled with roller skating, swimming and exploring. Jason was happy, if a little excitable, and this was a great relief to Ann, who for months had barely seen her son smile, but on the Wednesday night it all changed. Ann was woken by the sound of Jason screaming. The thin partitions between the rooms in the mobile home meant the sound was piercing, deafening. She rushed to the room he shared with his best friend, Mark. Jason was standing by the bed while Mark slept on, oblivious. Ann was thinking, 'Not again, not again,' as she stretched her arms out to her son, but Jason, realising she was there, stopped screaming and calmly held up his hand.

'Don't touch me. You mustn't touch me,' he said.

Puzzled, Ann asked why not?

Jason simply repeated it, 'You mustn't touch me.'

This was a new twist. At least, in the past, if she could do nothing else, Ann could always hug and comfort her son – but not now. She turned tearfully to leave the room.

Jason spoke softly: 'Mum, they're making me feel and see what they feel and see. I will be all right.'

Ann smiled lovingly at him through her tears, and went back to her own bed. She felt very much alone. Although she had taken the brunt of Jason's problems, keeping them from Paul whenever she felt she should, she always had the comfort of his reliable, solid shape in the bed next to her. When they did discuss their worries, Paul's pragmatism was a great bulwark against the worst of her fears. Now she was on her own, and in some way she had never encountered before, she was unable to reach Jason.

She lay awake in the dark, and after some time Jason came through from the bedroom he shared with Mark, and asked if he could stay with her. He climbed into the double bed, but before he lay down he told her again that she must not hug him or hold him. He said it in a remote voice, Jason's voice yet somehow, chillingly, different: a controlled, more adult voice. Weary, she drifted to sleep. When she woke, as the wintry dawn struggled through the thin curtains, Jason was still in the bed, but Ann vaguely remembered waking earlier, in the darkness, and finding him not there. She thought she had checked the other rooms, and he was not in any of the beds, but it was not a clear memory: she could not be sure whether or not she dreamt it.

When he woke Jason behaved as though nothing had happened. Usually, after a night like that, Ann would have expected him to be tired, depressed, difficult. Perhaps it was the presence of the other boys, and the excitement of being away, that lifted his spirits, because he ate a hearty breakfast, and was in just as much trouble as the other three for throwing bits of toast around the small kitchen. While Ann scolded them she was secretly happy: Jason's behaviour was so normal. She did not mention the events of the night, not even to Paul when she rang him later. Perhaps, she fervently hoped, it was a one-off, and Jason would be left in peace for the rest of the holiday.

That night she went to bed late, waiting for all four boys to be sound asleep before she switched off the television. It was long past midnight, so she fell asleep straight away. At 3am she was awakened by a noise. During the day, the roof of the mobile home was a roosting place for seagulls and crows, who would make such a noise up there that the boys decided they were having a football game.

This was the same sound, but it was pitch dark outside, and birds would not be moving about.

She lay motionless in fear and silence as the noise grew in intensity. Then her attention shifted: there were noises coming from the living room of the caravan: rustling noises, not as loud as the sounds on the roof, but as if things were being moved around.

Her fear disappeared: she was instantly convinced that the boys were up and playing about. She sat upright in bed and called out to them to stop messing about.

There was a sudden silence. All noise ceased the moment she spoke, and fear welled up inside her again. She listened to the silence for a few moments then, against her better judgment, got up to check on the boys. They were all sound asleep, even Jason.

She wandered nervously into the living room. Things had been moved. She sat down on the couch and stared out of the plain glass window through the darkness to the twinkling far-off lights of the estuary. She found them somehow comforting. Suddenly, she felt a physical chill sweep over her. There on the glass window pane was an image of what appeared to be a face. The gas fire, left on low to keep the cold at bay, produced lots of condensation, but the image was perfectly clear. The features were well-defined. It was a face – but not a human face.

As her fear wore off, Ann found a pencil and sheet of paper and copied the image as accurately as possible. She had been good at art at school, and her finished effort was a good likeness. She put the drawing away and switched on the television, watching programme after programme in an effort to stay awake so that 'they' would not come back. As dawn began to break, feeling safer in the cold light, Ann went back to bed and slept.

It was the noise of the boys helping themselves to breakfast that woke her. She went into the living room and Daniel, Mark and James lost no time in showing her the 'funny face' on the glass. Jason, knowing what it was, saw no fun in it, and said nothing. Ann laughed with the others, judging this the best way to treat it, but when breakfast was over and the boys charged outside to play, Jason lingered.

'I didn't think,' he said softly, 'that they would find me here, not here on holiday.'

Daniel's 'soldier man', the strange visitor who told him that his brother was 'an original soul'. Ann drew this sketch from Daniel's detailed description of his childhood companion.

Jason at the farm, aged 12 – just after his parents discovered he was an abductee.

Jason on Honey, the horse whose death he prophesied.

Paul leads Maverick, one of the Andrews's horses, along the half mile track from the farm to the road. It was from this track that he first spotted the mysterious men who watch the farm. They were standing in the middle of the field on the right of this picture.

Ann with two of the prize-winning Pyrenean mountain dogs, Chissum and Hannah. The farm where so many weird things happened is in the background, behind the trees.

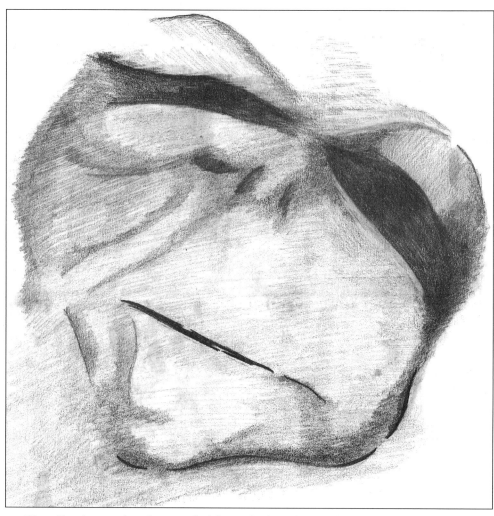

The alien image that Ann copied from the imprint on the window during the caravan holiday to All Hallows, when she was woken in the night by strange noises on the roof and in the living room.

He was very upset, but Ann tried to make light of it: 'It's coincidence. The shape on the window was just a pattern that resembles them, that's all. Besides, you weren't woken up, were you? Off you go and enjoy yourself.'

Jason hesitated, his fear and anger battling with the urge to join the others and have some fun. After a few seconds he smiled at Ann and ran out to join his friends.

The final two days of the holiday were uneventful, and the only other problem Ann faced was persuading all four of them that they really had to go home. The other boys were dropped off, and then back at their own house Daniel and Jason gabbled excitedly to Paul about their adventures. Ann listened: Jason did not mention his encounter with the aliens. When the boys had wandered off to see the dogs, Paul and Ann hugged each other. They had never spent a night apart before in all their married life except when she'd been in hospital, and it wasn't an experience they'd enjoyed.

While Ann was sorting through the washing, Paul went out to the shed and returned with an old walnut clock that had been in Ann's family for years. It was heavy and ugly, about the size of a portable television. Ann could vaguely remember it working when she was a child, but for over thirty years it had been broken. The boys had been allowed to play with it when they were little, and had removed many of its parts. As he carried it in it chimed the half hour, and Ann could hear it ticking.

She assumed Paul had spent the whole time they were away tinkering with it, but he assured her he had not fiddled with it at all. He said he heard it chiming in the boys' old toy cupboard. He took it out and it had kept good time ever since; he had not even wound it up, and had no idea where the key to it was.

Ann was as puzzled as he was. Neither of them questioned the sudden repair of the clock too deeply. Each had an idea about what had happened, but neither wanted to broach the subject right then. Paul took the clock back to the shed where it would, he said, be useful, while Ann carried on sorting the whites from the coloureds for the washing machine.

To this day, the old clock occasionally starts to tick and chime, although it does not keep going for very long.

CHAPTER 9

I SAW YOU THERE

Like his grandfather, Jason has a natural affinity with horses. They come to him as if to an old friend. Both he and Daniel were on horseback from the day the family bought the farm. Daniel is a competent rider, but Jason took to it instinctively. When Ann was little her father had to remind her never to blame the horse if she fell off: Jason knew this without being told, and he rarely fell. For a time he attended riding lessons at a nearby stables, and the owner told Ann that he had only a couple of times in his life seen such a naturally gifted rider.

As a young child his willingness to climb on the back of any horse worried Ann. At one time they were looking after an unbroken horse called Gipsy, a huge black and white sixteen-hand mare, which they had taken in because nobody else could handle her. Jason was only seven. While Ann and Paul were distracted doing their chores at the farm, Jason managed to steady the horse and climb on to his back: something nobody else had done. The horse charged around the field for some time, Ann watching with her heart in her mouth. She knew that if she tried to intervene Jason might end up being thrown and seriously injured. Eventually the horse tired, and with the small boy still clinging to its mane, slowed to a walking pace. Jason, unhurt and exhilarated, slid to the ground, patted Gipsy and wandered across to his mother as though nothing out of the ordinary had happened. Ann sighed with relief and gave him a lecture about never doing anything so foolhardy again. Jason looked puzzled.

'Why would a horse want to hurt me?' was all he asked.

Inevitably, over the years, he did have falls from horses, once fracturing his leg and another time dislocating a shoulder, but he accepts occasional injuries as part of dealing with horses. Ann can

121

never remember him complaining of the pain, or being afraid to get up on to a horse as soon as the plaster was off.

But one day Jason was afraid.

He was at the stables, riding his favourite horse, Patch. They were galloping, Jason enjoying the feeling of the strong horse beneath him and the warm air rushing past his face. Then he became aware of something else. *They* were there. The aliens, unseen, were with him, experiencing the ride, feeling what he was feeling. Ever since the moment on the holiday when he had screamed at his mother not to touch him, Jason has known that, from time to time, they share his feelings: 'It's as if they want to know what feelings are, what it's like being one of us. I know they won't hurt me. They just want to share everything.'

On the Sunday morning of the horse ride, he could sense they were with him, sharing the exhilaration of the wind in his hair and the sensation of speed and power that always thrilled him when he was on Patch. Jason did not resent their presence – in the previous weeks he had become accustomed to them being with him – but on this occasion the ride ended badly. Another horse came up behind Patch and spooked him, and both horse and Jason went down. Jason managed to roll clear of Patch's weight, and nearly crashed into a fence. He expected to feel immediate pain. Even if no limbs were broken, he was certain to be bruised and sore, but, to his amazement, he felt very little, then or later, even though his arm was bruised and there was a clear hoof print from the other horse on his shoulder for weeks afterwards. It was as though his uninvited guests had absorbed all the agony.

'They did not like it,' Jason chuckles, as he remembers the incident. Although he no longer hates his night visitors as vehemently as he did when he was younger, he enjoys the memory of them being hurt in the fall from the horse. He is baffled by the behaviour of the other horse, but believes it had a sixth sense which told it of his co-riders, and caused it to chase after and charge at Patch.

Although it was by no means the worst fall Jason ever had, something about the experience scared him, and he has not been riding since. The owner of the stables has tried to persuade Ann to take him back there again, offering to teach him without charge, but Jason refuses to go. He has climbed on to a horse a couple of times, but no longer gets any enjoyment from riding. He blames the aliens for depriving him of this pleasure.

'It's as if they won't let me enjoy it any more because they don't enjoy it and don't want to get hurt again,' he says.

Ann first heard of the fall when she collected Jason from the stables at the end of his lesson. She asked if he was hurt, and was dumbfounded when he replied that he wasn't but 'they' were. 'They didn't like the pain of hitting the floor, they don't like experiencing hurt,' he told her. Ann did not have to ask who 'they' were. She pulled the car over as soon as she found a parking place in the narrow lane and sat for ten minutes, quizzing Jason about the whole incident. It was one of the few times she had heard him openly discuss his visitors in daylight, but that was not what shocked her most. Her heart sank as she took in what he was saying: 'they' were with him during his everyday life, not just when they stole him from his bed at night.

She had been unable to shake the memory of him screaming at her to keep away from him during the caravan holiday, not allowing her to cuddle and comfort him. It had been perhaps the most desolate moment of the whole distressing experience of Jason's abductions: but now she was facing the same feeling, on a bigger scale. Jason was telling her about them being with him on a normal sunny Sunday morning, with other people around.

She asked, tentatively, almost dreading the answer, how often he was aware of them being with him.

He told her how he'd first felt they were there when he went on a long bike ride with Daniel and two of his older friends. They cycled a round trip of twenty-five miles, and what should have been a fun day was ruined for Jason because the aliens were with him. On that occasion he pedalled like mad in a vain bid to leave them behind, but now, he told his mother, he had learned it was easier to accept them. 'I have to allow them to experience my feelings – they can't do it unless I let them,' he said.

Ann could hardly take in what he was saying. Not only were they with him, but he was colluding in it, 'allowing' them to share his experiences. Looking across at her good-looking young son as he told her all about it, Ann had a terrible feeling of a chasm opening up between them. She was no longer able to reach out to him; 'they' were coming between her and Jason.

Back home, she did not tell Paul. Although he was sympathetic and supportive, she knew that Paul was always far happier when Jason's problems were in abeyance. He could lull himself into a false sense of security, enjoying the feeling that perhaps it had just been a temporary blip in their lives and it was behind them. He felt impotent in the face of what was happening to his son, and his own helplessness made him angry. Paul is a doer, a getter-on with things. He would joke with Ann about what he would do to any alien he found in Jason's room, and she'd laugh with him: but she knew his humour covered a deep unease. It was Paul's instinct to protect and provide for his family, and yet he could not protect Jason from being abducted.

The next day, with Paul at the farm and the boys at school, she rang Tony Dodd. It was difficult getting through: Mondays are always Tony's busiest day for UFO reports, as people ring in with the strange sights they have seen over the weekend. Ann persisted, and by lunchtime she was talking to the man she refers to as her 'lifeline'. She was so anxious about the new development that it was a few minutes before Tony could fully understand what she was telling him. In the end he cut through her confusion and alarm, telling her to calm down, take a deep breath, and start again from the beginning.

'Nothing is that bad,' he said, firmly, but to Ann, it was. In the hours between Jason telling her what had happened and finally getting through to Tony her imagination had been in overdrive, conjuring up scenes from an old black-and-white horror movie that had terrified her as a child: *Invasion of the Body Snatchers*. She envisaged her son turning into an alien-controlled robot.

'You've got to do something,' she pleaded with Tony. 'He's somehow letting them share his own body, his mind. They're experiencing things with him – and he's letting them.'

Tony calmly explained that this was not unusual: he had heard of it happening before. He shies away from the word 'alien', calling them instead EBEs, or extraterrestrial biological entities. The EBEs, he told Ann, were apparently incapable of feeling emotions of any kind but are interested in human experience of them. They need a human host to 'allow' them to share emotions. He reminded her

124

that Jason was in control, that he'd told her 'they' could only feel what he let them feel, and that therefore he was in no danger. Once again, he stressed that in all his years of dealing with abductees he had never heard of one disappearing for good, or 'going over' to the aliens in the way that Ann was imagining. In fact, he told her, it was a positive sign: perhaps Jason was coming to terms with his abductions, and was listening and learning from the experience, rather than fighting it.

Ann was reassured, but there was still a niggling doubt. Although she wanted to see Jason happy again, deep down she did not want him to become reconciled to what was happening. She feared he might even be starting to enjoy it.

She need not have worried about this. Jason was a long way from being comfortable with it. A few days later he again became very frightened of being alone at night, and his parents would often find him wrapped in his duvet sleeping at the bottom of their bed. He said he could feel 'they' were coming back. Paul shrugged it off, insisting to Jason that it was all in his imagination.

Then, one night they were both awoken by a very pale and frighteningly calm Jason, who told them: 'If you look out of that window you will see them.'

Ann and Paul were immediately afraid, expecting that they would finally see the entities that had terrified their youngest son for so long. They were both sitting up in bed but as they looked to the right, out of their bedroom window, they could at first see nothing. Paul was relieved. Then Ann spotted a bright light, at first no bigger than the pinprick of a star, visibly moving and becoming bigger and brighter and nearer. The very last thing they both remembered was their bedroom being flooded with a white light, and the 'star', by now as big as a football, framed in their window.

They woke simultaneously at about seven the next morning. The sun was shining, the birds were in full song. The dogs were clamouring for attention. It was such a normal start to the day that it took a few moments for the memory of the night to flood back into Ann's consciousness.

Then her first thought was of Jason.

She and Paul dashed along the landing to his bedroom, but there was no sign of him. Ann tore down the stairs screaming his name, only to find both of her sons looking up at her from the settee, puzzled.

'Did you have a bad dream, Mum?' Daniel asked. 'Only you look terrible.'

Ann caught a glimpse of herself in the mirror. He was right. She looked as if she had seen a ghost. She told Jason they wanted to talk to him, and he followed her upstairs, to the bedroom where Paul was waiting.

'You went to sleep,' Jason said in disgust, barely looking at Ann, 'but I had to go with them again. This time was different, though. They showed me how our government and other governments treat them. I saw people cutting into their eyes just to see what they are made of. I saw them being kept alive in glass tanks, and bits of them being put in sealed containers. I saw soldiers shooting at them.'

He poured out the story of his experience the previous night, telling how the aliens could not understand why they were being treated as laboratory specimens. He told his parents that he felt very angry when he saw what was happening to them, and how he wanted to make it stop, to punish those responsible.

He described being taken into an enormous room with hundreds of other people, all looking up at a gigantic screen. On it was a picture of the Earth.

Paul was listening attentively, but Ann was sitting rigid, a strange expression on her face. As Jason began to describe the huge picture of the planet she turned to him, clutching his arm urgently. She didn't have to listen to any more. She knew exactly what he was going to say: 'It suddenly blew up,' Ann whispered. 'It blew up, didn't it? And then there was a terrible low whistling sound, a desolate sound, like a strange wind blowing . . .'

She was staring at Jason as she spoke.

'That's what happened. Isn't it?'

Jason nodded, and he smiled with relief.

'I knew you were there,' he said softly. 'I saw you there.'

There was no smile on Ann's face as her concentration broke and she came back to herself. A look of horrified recognition spread across her features and her mouth dropped open. She, too, knew for the first time that she had been there, in the room with all the other people, watching the giant screen. The full meaning dawned on her: Jason was not the only member of the family going on night journeys to meet strange, non-human creatures. Deep and confused memories were stirring.

Paul was staring at her with a look of shock bordering on disgust. He'd resigned himself to his son having serious problems. He fought shy of the alien explanation, but he could see that Jason was genuinely disturbed and needed all the help and support they could give him.

But his wife, too?

He didn't speak to her as he dressed and left the house to go to the farm.

In the space of a few days, Ann had suffered two huge shocks. She was still reeling from the discovery that Jason was sharing his feelings with the aliens when she had to confront an even more profound realisation: she herself was an abductee. For a brief moment she wondered if she was simply telepathic with Jason, if she was thinking about him and worrying about him so much that she had somehow been able to tune into his thoughts and memories, but she soon knew this was not true. She, too, could remember being in the crowded room and seeing Jason there.

When Paul left, Jason gave her a hug: a reversal of their roles. He was mutely comforting her, in the way she had consoled and comforted him throughout his childhood. She shook her head as she pulled away from him after a few moments: she did not want to talk about it. Jason understood, and left her to get dressed and start the routines of the day, feeding the dogs and making breakfast for the boys. She went about her chores mechanically, her mind elsewhere. Slowly, bit by bit, events from her past began to slot into place. Her persistent childhood memory of the strange creatures in her room, which she had always known was not a dream, suddenly made sense, and she realised that she must have been abducted since then: it was simply that she had never remembered it before. Having read about other abductees, and having talked endlessly to Tony Dodd about his own experiences and those of others he knew, Ann was aware that Jason was unusual in remembering what happened to him so fully.

Most abductees do not remember, certainly not in any detail.

Some have confused fragments of memories, which, like Ann, they compartmentalise as 'dreams'. Many find memories are triggered by certain prosaic events, often years after the abduction. Professor John Mack details two typical cases in his book, *Abduction*. One man in his mid-forties was enjoying a pleasant walk when, for no particular reason, he recalled a summer holiday when he was a teenager. Over the next few weeks, in a series of flashbacks, he built up a picture of the abduction that had happened to him then, more than twenty-five years previously. Another man, in his late thirties, remembered a UFO sighting when he was nine only when he attended a family reunion and chatted to one of his sisters, who was with him at the time of that sighting and subsequent abduction.

Both of these men retrieved a fair amount of memories without hypnosis, but the full pattern of what happened to them was only revealed when hypnotherapy was used. In these cases, and in the many thousands of others where memories are masked, most experts believe the aliens have taken deliberate steps to confuse, delay and obscure the memories of what happened.

Just as they are obviously capable of inducing deep, almost paralysed, sleep in the families (and pets) of abductees, so they are able to obliterate memories. One of John Mack's abductees, under hypnosis, retrieved a memory of being told, telepathically, that he would remember 'when you need to know'.

It seems that many hidden memories of abduction are triggered at a point of crisis in the abductee's life. For Ann, the crisis was perhaps her heightened worry about Jason sharing his emotions with the aliens. Her fears that she would lose him for good (and even though Tony Dodd explained this was not going to happen, she still had a deepdown irrational terror of it happening) meant that she had, perhaps, reached the moment 'when you need to know'. She needed to be shown, from her own experiences, that it is possible to be a long-term abductee and survive, and live a relatively normal and well-balanced life.

It worked. It was when she pieced together her own experiences, and also realised that her own father had possibly been an abductee as well, that Ann was first able to come to terms with what was happening to Jason. Even though there are still huge areas of her memory that are submerged, there is a sense of relief and 'coming home' in being able to put an explanation on so many puzzling aspects of her life.

Professor Mack found that 'often abductees say that there are vast areas of their lives that they strongly feel are outside of conscious recall and yet powerfully affect them on a day-to-day basis.' Ann fits into this category: her affinity with animals, her heightened sensitivities (she uncannily understands other people's suffering), her worries about the damage the human race is doing to its own environment, are all present on a day-to-day basis in her life, yet she had, before knowing about the abductions, no knowledge of them being part of a pattern, one that derived from her abduction experiences. Yet when she realised she was an abductee, there was a deep sense of completeness and understanding – even though it was some time before she recovered from the shock enough to appreciate it.

Another explanation, given to another abductee, of why aliens block the memories of their abductees, suggests a more sinister but still plausible reason. US State Trooper Herb Schirmer, who saw a UFO while on night duty when he was investigating a disturbance among a field of cows in December 1967, had no idea he had been abducted until hypnosis was used to try to find out what happened in a missing chunk of time. He recalled being taken on board the craft, and told that his memory would be blocked because the aliens were aware that military powers on earth were hostile to them. They therefore chose their abductees randomly, and prevented them recalling the details of their encounters.

Abduction certainly appears to be random: there is no systematic attempt by the aliens to abduct, say, the earth's finest scientific brains – but as their intellectual processes obviously far outstrip those of humans, there would be little of particular interest to them in an appraisal of earth's technological or scientific pioneers.

It is more likely that the answer to what they are seeking lies in Jason's experience of 'sharing' feelings with them. One of Professor Mack's abductees explained under hypnosis that the aliens he met were humanoid, but that their development as a race had 'followed the path of almost rational intellectualising' and that they had 'lost much of their emotions and they want to get that back'. He said that the aliens were willing to share their intellectual powers with us if they could share the emotional development of the human race – which is very much in line with Jason's experiences. At times he appears to have a mathematical and numerical ability far in advance of anything you would expect from a young teenager with no particular aptitude for maths in the conventional classroom situation: at other times he is aware that the aliens are sharing his emotions and feelings, even physical feelings like pain.

Tony Dodd finds nothing surprising in Jason 'sharing' his feelings with the aliens. It is, in his experience, a relatively common part of the abduction experience: 'We don't know with any certainty why it happens, but it seems that they are devoid of emotions and fascinated by ours. They don't seem particularly concerned about our intellect – if they were, you would expect them to be abducting the human race's greatest brains. This is probably because their intellectual development is so far ahead of ours that even our cleverest people have insignificant mental powers to them. But in the area of emotions and feelings we appear to have something they don't possess, and either want or feel a need to understand.'

Why some abductees have more memories than others, without the use of hypnotherapy, is something that none of the experts have so far been able to explain. Jason is exceptional but not unique: there are others who have full recall of their night-time journeys; there are others who, like him, can anticipate when the aliens are going to come for them. It could simply be a trick of a particular memory: perhaps Jason and a few others are naturally resistant to whatever technique the aliens use to block memories (just as a few people are able to resist hypnosis). Perhaps, as Tony Dodd suspects, memories are blocked when it is of benefit to the abductee for them to forget. If they have to carry on with a 'normal' life, as he did when he was working as a policeman, or as Ann did as a wife and mother, it is much easier for them not to know about their abductions. However, that still does not encompass Jason's exclusion: he, too, would have benefited at school and in other relationships if his abduction memories had been blocked.

The abduction experience that Jason and Ann shared when they saw the planet Earth blowing up is such an important one, and yet at the same time such a typical one, that it is worth examining in detail. I have now read and heard many hundreds of abduction stories from reliable witnesses, and it is apparent there are three major themes running through the experiences. One is medical: abductees suffer medical examinations – samples are taken, implants are inserted into them – and the second is that they are used without being consulted for breeding purposes. These will be discussed in the next two chapters.

The third common thread is that the aliens are passing on an apocalyptic message to the human race. We are being warned that we are abusing our world, and that if we carry on this way the planet will not be able to sustain itself, or us. It is not always clear whether this is a prophesy, where the abductees are being told that this is a certain future towards which we are heading, or a caution, where they are being told that this is what may come to pass if we carry on behaving as we are. Certainly, this second interpretation is the one most abductees choose. They believe, perhaps because they have been told, that they are the bearers of an important message to mankind to mend its ways.

There are many examples. In 1980, Aino Ivanoff, in Finland, was abducted from her car and medically examined by aliens who told her that war would be the downfall of our planet. John Hodges, a Californian, was twice abducted from a flat in Los Angeles, and was warned about the dangers of nuclear war. British abductee Keith Daniel was told by the aliens, who took him in 1981 from the banks of the River Dee, that the Earth was approaching a holocaust.

One of the earliest detailed recordings of an abduction, from 1949, was that of Daniel Fry, a technician working on missile control at the US Government base of White Sands, New Mexico, where experimental military hardware is tested. He saw a huge UFO land, and was taken on board. The aliens were friendly, but told him he must spread the word about the dangers of nuclear war facing the planet. Fry was asked the obvious question: why, if the aliens want to change the course of human history, do they not intervene more publicly? His answer was that we have to control our own destiny; they cannot take over. Nick Pope, the MoD official who is now a UFO and alien investigator, draws an analogy with a child and a bird's egg: if the child 'helps' the chick by breaking the egg for it, the chick will not flourish. Similarly the aliens can only warn us, not 'help' us directly.

Professor Mack states: 'The transmission of information from the alien beings to the experiencers appears to be a fundamental aspect of the abduction phenomenon . . . The information that abductees receive is concerned primarily with the fate of the Earth in the wake of human destructiveness.' Several of the abductees whom he interviewed in depth, and whose hypnotherapy he supervised, had been shown scenes of the Earth after the devastation of a great manmade catastrophe, probably a nuclear war. Two of his subjects saw large black clouds suffocating the world's living systems, and others saw a scene very similar to the one both Jason and Ann were shown on the giant screen: the planet literally cracking open or blowing up.

The simple explanation, that we are being warned and should improve our relationships and behaviour accordingly, does not take into account what's in it for them: why do the aliens want us to change our ways? Theories abound: if Earth destroys itself the repercussions throughout the universe will affect other galaxies, other planets; they need us: this theory ties in with the breeding programme, explored later in this book; distinguished science writer Carl Sagan suggested that, to them, we are an adolescent world and we have to be taught, trained even, to take our place in a grander cosmic scheme of things.

This idea of benevolent alien cultures helping ours along is the most prevalent among the intellectual giants of UFOlogy. Dr James Deardoff, a physicist and meteorologist who is a research professor at Oregon State University, advances a complex argument that there are benevolent alien civilisations protecting us from more aggressive ones for their own reasons: perhaps because we are evolving in a similar way to them (which would explain why so many sightings of aliens involve some who look very like human beings).

He argues convincingly that if they landed here in full public view there would be mass hysteria, and, even if they avoided precipitating the sort of nuclear disaster they are trying to combat, they could trigger all sorts of other conflicts, not least against themselves. Even a gradual introduction of them over several months would cause shockwaves. Deardoff maintains that contact with us has to be very slow, over a period of hundreds or thousands of years (a long time to us as individuals but a mere tick of the clock for the universe).Contacting governments would cause panic, so information about aliens has to be leaked, very gradually, to the population at large by chosen individuals. Even the reluctance to believe, the mockery, the accusations of hoaxing, that greet such information are a part of the built-in checks and balances that ensure acceptance of aliens is a very long, slow, drawn-out process.

All this would seem to reduce the role of Jason and Ann Andrews to that of two tiny bricks in a massive bridge that has to be built before our human race can accept and communicate openly with our alien visitors, but that's a role they accept: neither of them sees themselves as standard bearers for alien cultures. If they have any grand motive, it is to further understanding about aliens. On a smaller, more earthbound scale, they simply want to help other families struggling with problems similar to those they have faced.

Another important aspect of Ann and Jason's both being abducted to the same place on the same night is that it highlights the generational nature of abduction. Most abductees have no knowledge or evidence of other members of their families also being abducted, but a sizable core are from families where at least one other member appears to have been an abductee. Ann will never be certain about her father, but the more she thinks about him, and the more she talks to Vi, her mother, about his life, the more convinced she becomes.

The cases studied in great depth by Professor Mack harvested many examples of brothers, sisters, parents and children also being abducted. He found it a common situation for a child to see a parent, or a parent a child, during an abduction (just as Jason saw his mother). Sometimes the child feels angry at the parent, or an older brother or sister, for not protecting them. More commonly the parent or older sibling feels angry and frustrated at not being able to protect the younger member of the family, especially when, in several reported cases, the young one was a baby or toddler.

One of the most celebrated cases of several members of the same family being abducted is that of an American woman called Debbie Tomey. She contacted Budd Hopkins, and in 1983 he published a book about her experiences, using the pseudonym Kathie Davis to protect her identity. She has since come forward and allowed her own name to be used. Her story has many interesting aspects, but one of the most striking is that she is aware of her own children also being abductees. Like so many others, she has been abducted repeatedly since childhood, and the pattern seems set for at least one more generation of her family. British abductee Keith Daniel is another who has a family history littered with possible UFO encounters.

Why particular families are singled out is not clear. It is perhaps totally random, but having found one abductee there is an interest on the part of the aliens in following the blood line, possibly for medical research purposes.

Ann Andrews knows of another child (apart from Jason) within her extended family who she believes is having abduction experiences. She has shared the details with me, but they are not for inclusion in this book. Although Ann believes that more and more people need to go public about their abductions, she does not believe anyone should be coerced into it. Besides, the abductee is a child, and it is a decision for her and her own parents as to how she will handle her experiences. Ann cannot interfere. All she can offer is a sympathetic ear, when the child wants to talk: 'The only thing I can do is to be there for her. I feel terrible when I remember all the years that Jason had to fight to get us to believe him, to accept what he was trying to tell us. I don't want anyone else close to me to have to go through all the loneliness and disillusionment he must have suffered. When she wants to talk, I will be here. Perhaps her own parents will accept by then, but if they don't, at least she will have someone she can turn to.'

CHAPTER 10

THE BABY THAT NEVER WAS

To appease Paul, Ann said nothing more about her own abduction memories. For a time, when he raised the subject, she pretended that she had simply had a premonition about Jason's description of the world blowing up, but she could tell from the look in his eye as he listened to her that he was unconvinced.

It was a bleak time for Paul. He had been struggling to accept Jason's problems, and he had started to come to terms with them. He had read the books he bought on the first day after the realisation of abduction, and more that Ann had found and recommended to him. He was not as easily convinced as she was, but the vast weight of evidence had won him over. He could also see how much happier Jason was, now that the problem had been diagnosed.

Now he had to face the fact that Ann, too, was being abducted. It was a strange feeling, almost like a betrayal. His wife, to whom he had been married for eighteen years, had a secret life from which he was excluded. It did not matter that she herself had not known about it: his resentment about it was not rational. He knew he should be helping and supporting her, but there was a large part of him that felt angry and rejected.

Worse, he blamed Ann for bringing abduction into his family, and hated himself for the feeling. Husbands and wives of partners who are found to be carrying genetic conditions which handicap their children often experience a similar reaction. They know their partner cannot help it, did not choose it, feels dreadful about it, but despite all their better instincts to comfort and console, there is a small angry part inside them that blames the other. All Jason's problems could be laid at Ann's door and, despite himself, he reproached her for it.

For a few days, there were long silences between them. Ann, who is naturally very sensitive to others and particularly attuned to Paul, kept quiet. Instinct told her that Paul needed space and time to adjust to another huge shift in his view of his family. On most other occasions when there had been friction between them it had dissolved rapidly, with a laugh and a joke. Neither of them sulked or bore grudges, and a shared sense of humour had seen them through a lot of difficult times. This, Ann knew, was something bigger, and not a time for jokes.

As always, for Paul, the solution lay in hard work. Up at the farm, shovelling manure and building fences in the fresh air, he found his sense of perspective reasserting itself. Of course it was not Ann's fault, he knew that, and he realised, with a guilty lurch, that however upset he was, she was going through something far more momentous. If he felt resentful about her double life, how must she feel? If he blamed her for Jason's problems, how much worse must it be for her, shouldering that blame? He was resting his arms on the gate, thinking about it all, when Craven, Ann's horse, trotted across the field and nuzzled him. Craven was usually indifferent to Paul, only making a fuss of Ann or Jason. It was as if, Paul thought, the horse was trying to tell him something.

'OK, old chap,' he said, 'you're right. She hasn't changed. She's still the Ann I married. She hasn't kept secrets from me – they've been kept from her.'

He drove home early, stopping to buy a bunch of flowers. Ann was with the dogs. She turned, saw his expression, and knew that everything was going to be all right. Paul hugged and kissed her, then led her through to the living room and made her sit down.

'I want you to tell me everything, all you can remember,' he said.

If it had been a bad few days for Paul, it had been worse for Ann. At first, she tried hard to convince herself that she had imagined being in the same room as Jason, watching the Earth destroy itself, but she could not deceive herself. She felt frightened, panicky, and she understood what Jason had been going through for so much of his life. She told herself all the reassuring things she told him, but somehow it was hard to take comfort from them. She went through, in her head, everything Tony Dodd had said, and she rang him as soon as she got a chance with neither Paul nor the boys around.

He repeated what she already knew: that most abduction is generational and that she wasn't losing her sanity; she was simply unlocking her own buried memories. Perhaps she was being 'allowed' to relive them, or perhaps she had simply reached a point where they were triggered: Tony did not know, but his inclination was to believe that the aliens, who had so successfully blocked the memories, were directly responsible for unleashing them. One likely reason, he felt, was that Jason needed her full support and under-standing – real empathy, not just sympathy – and she was being given back her own experiences to equip her to cope with his.

Gradually, over the following weeks and months, her memories became clearer. Small happenings which she had filed away at the back of her mind assumed new prominence, and filled out into complete incidents, now with a darker explanation than she had ever imagined.

Dominating all of these memories is the one that has always been clear to her: the time when, sleeping with her mother while her father was at work, a tall hooded being rose at the bottom of the bed, then moved round level with her, pushing back the hood to stare at her with large, almond-shaped black eyes. It is a memory that never went away, and always brought terror with it, even before any explanation was clear. Ann coped by pushing it to one side with a shiver, and busying herself with something, anything, else. She never believed it was a dream, but the other possibilities – that she was going mad and having delusions, or that she had genuinely met another life form unknown on Earth – were both too terrible to contemplate. She never wanted to explore it; she wanted to forget it, but her mind never completely allowed this. She might go for months, even years, without the memory recurring, but inevitably the image would eventually surface.

Now, more memories joined it, and this experience filled out. After the tall alien dropped the hood of his cloak, Ann now remembers lots of others, much smaller, fussing around her. Simply by touching her, they make her body weightless and she floats out through the closed window. She describes it as her whole body turning into liquid – a thick, heavy liquid like treacle – and being

squeezed through the window as if it was a strainer. There is no
pain or any feeling involved, but there is a sense of time being on
hold, as if everything is running in slow motion. By the time her
entire 'body' is on the other side of the glass she is whole again: the
liquid feeling has gone. She can feel the wind on her face, and she
can look around. Terrified of heights, she instinctively clutches at
one of the little aliens who are guiding her and he gently prises her
fingers off. More little ones are still guiding her, but Ann has not
been able to recall any more. She does not know where they take
her or what happens. She senses that there is a lot more to
remember: she can see it, as if at a great distance and very fuzzy.

She also remembers a childhood incident which Vi has since
confirmed. Ann was at a birthday party being given by one of her
small friends – she was eight years old at the time. A cartoon show
was the highlight of the afternoon, a big treat in those pre-video
days. The little girls watched a Popeye cartoon, in which the super-
hero sailorman was captured by a hooded old witch and imprisoned
in a dark cellar or cave. Suddenly, a bright light illuminated his
surroundings. At this point Ann started to scream uncontrollably,
and could not be placated. Vi was sent for, and it was not until Ann
was at home that she calmed down.

Another brief memory which Ann has now recalled in greater
detail also goes back to her childhood. She remembers being in the
local park with her father, on one of their regular weekend visits. It
was a bright day with sunlight dappling through the trees, and she
remembers feeling happy and secure, holding her father's hand,
the two of them swinging their arms. When they stopped walking
they came across three figures who seemed to be waiting for them.
They were tall, with fair hair and blue eyes, yet dark, tanned skin,
and even as a child of about eight Ann can remember thinking they
were lucky to have had a holiday somewhere hot. This was as far as
her original memory went, yet it filled her with panic and fear
whenever it flitted through her mind.

However, since unlocking her abduction experiences she has
dreamed of it many times, each time adding a bit more to a picture
which she now feels is complete.

The 'leader' of the group, who has thick wavy hair, is smiling.
Ann's father seems surprised to see them, but not shocked. He puts

his arms round Ann's shoulder and draws her closer to him. Nothing is said: in fact, the intense silence makes little Ann giggle, because it reminds her of a cowboy film, the silent showdown before the gunfight. Nobody, not even her father, takes any notice of her laugh, and she begins to feel frightened. She looks around: the park seems to be getting darker, and her vision is becoming restricted as deep shadows close in. Suddenly, she knows they are not in the park anymore, but she does not know where they are. She cannot feel the breeze on her face, or the warmth of the sun, or smell the newmown grass.

The three beings are still standing in front of her and her father. They are now wearing long white robes – they were normally dressed when she first saw them. The robes remind her of the pictures of Jesus which are handed out at Sunday School. The leader approaches them, with his hand outstretched to her father. Ann tries to hide behind her father's legs, but the leader sees her and looks down, smiling. He now stretches out his hand and Ann is compelled to look into his eyes. She wants to look, but at the same time she feels an urge to look away. However hard she tries, she cannot turn her head: it is as if his eyes have locked into hers, and she cannot break the link.

Without realising how it happened, she finds he is holding her hand and they walk slowly along together, still staring into each other's eyes. The being smiles: his face is human, and he has a normal mouth and lips, although his eyes are too large and dark for human eyes. Ann wonders where her father is, and why he isn't stopping this strange man from taking her away. The being never blinks, his hypnotic gaze never falters.

Ann cannot remember the journey, but finds herself being taken into a large room, like a church hall or function room, where lots of other children are noisily playing. The sounds are satisfyingly normal. The being lets go of Ann's hand and at the same time releases her gaze. She spots a boy of about her age – approximately eight or nine – and Ann feels happy because she knows him. She does not know how she knows him: he is not a relative or a schoolfriend, but there is something reassuringly familiar about him, and he reciprocates the feeling, smiling and walking over to her. Instinctively, Ann senses that the boy cannot speak. He takes her hand and she can feel his relief, as if he has been waiting for her to arrive. They squat down on the floor together to play with toys.

At this point Ann wakes, but she feels warm and happy: the fear and panic have gone completely. The memory of the boy somehow makes her feel contented and secure, as if he is someone very close to her, but she has no knowledge of him outside this recovered memory. Because of the happiness of this memory, Ann is sure that it is now complete. Despite the fact that parts of it are still unexplained, she knows that no more of it will be retrieved. On the days when she wakes having dreamed of playing with the mute boy, she is always happy and optimistic, no matter what is happening in her life.

Just as the boy seems inexplicably familiar, so, too, Ann feels she knows the tall being very well. She believes she has met him many times, and that he is the same alien who has guided Jason, and who was Daniel's 'soldier man'. She 'knows' too that he was familiar to her father, and that her father was not frightened of him. Although she has never completely come to terms with being an abductee, she feels that this being's interest in her and Jason is essentially benevolent, and in some ways he is their protector. However, she has ambivalent feelings about him: although she is confident he will not harm her, at the same time she knows that, to him, she and Jason are simply two objects of scientific interest. He may be kind towards them, but it is in the same way that a scientist is 'kind' to an animal being kept for experimentation.

Apart from these developed memories, Ann was also able to tell Paul about instant flashbacks, lasting no more than a moment, passing through her mind so rapidly that she cannot put a shape or form to them. Perhaps it is the image of a room, bare and clinical like an operating theatre; perhaps of being in the middle of a crowd, struggling to make herself inconspicuous; perhaps just a sense for a few seconds of looking into large, dark, mesmerising eyes. She knows that one day these may take shape and become fuller memories, but for the time being they are simply fleeting images triggered by everyday events, and gone as quickly as they come.

There was one, much more devastating, memory that came back to Ann. It was so vivid that she woke up sweating and crying, and it took some time for Paul to calm her down enough for her to tell him. It was the dream of her 'miscarriage', the night when she was so deeply unconscious that she was unaware that she was losing her baby. She finds it very distressing to recall.

When the dream opened, she did not realise it was about the loss of her baby, although she had a very strong sense of it being important. She saw 'them', the little ones, but they were in a haze. She could make out a taller one who seemed to be in charge, and she could hear a lot of shuffling noise, but the image was unclear, like watching a fuzzy television picture, and eventually it faded completely, and she slept soundly.

Suddenly she felt something: she was instantly wide awake and gripped by fear. There was a blinding light in the room, so powerful that she could see nothing, but she knew 'they' were around her. She was paralysed, unable to move, but her senses were on full alert. Something cold touched her legs, which she realised were spread apart. Then she felt a pain in her lower back and her stomach, and she knew what was happening. She was losing her baby. She did not want to be pregnant, but for it to end like this, without a choice and with such pain, made her eyes fill with tears. The tears rolled down her cheeks and she was unable to lift her hand to wipe them away. She cried, silently and constantly, until worry for her baby was overtaken by a conviction that she was going to die. She shut her eyes tightly, to close out the intense light, and tried to convince herself it was all a terrible nightmare, but the pain was real and undeniable, and she could hear the noise of movement around her.

Opening her eyes again she found the light was blocked by the shape of a head. For a moment she could not make out the face, as the bright light formed a halo around the head, but as her eyes adjusted she could see that it was a man, with a shock of pale blond hair, and piercing blue eyes. It was a handsome, gentle face, and she felt instantly reassured. He smiled at her, and placed his hand on her forehead. Instantly the pain, which had already subsided, disappeared completely, and with it all her fear. He stroked her hair, and although he did not speak, she 'heard' him tell her, 'It's for the best.' She felt herself agreeing with him, and she was overcome by a feeling of peace. Against her will, her eyes closed and she was deeply asleep.

When she woke from the dream, Ann felt angry and cheated, because the decision about the baby's future had been taken away from her. When she replayed the scene in her mind, she felt degraded and dehumanised, especially when she considered the implications. She told Paul. His eyes clouded with tears as he remembered the pain of losing the baby, and his fears for Ann's health, but his concern for his wife was tempered by a surge of anger at the aliens' interference, once again, in the life of his family.

Ann knew a little, because of her reading about the subject, about the 'breeding programme' that many of the extraterrestrial visitors to Earth seem to be engaged in, but this was the first time that she knew of herself or anyone close to her being involved. From time to time she had wondered whether Jason was being nurtured for this, pushing the thought away as soon as it occurred, but she had never imagined that she would be used, assuming that she was too old (even though she was only thirty-three at the time of the miscarriage) to be 'good breeding stock'. Now, logically, she realised that the aliens did not care about her age, the health risk to her, or the long-term effects of bringing up another baby. They had never intended letting her carry the baby to term, anyway, and however gentle the 'man' who removed it was, she knew that to him she was nothing more than a womb they had borrowed.

There were so many things to think about. Was the baby Paul's? She had heard of human-alien hybrids being created. She had also heard of human foetuses being taken and 'grown' in laboratory conditions, which was what she now imagined had happened to her baby. Deep down, she was sure it was Paul's: the possibility that she had been impregnated with alien reproductive material was too abhorrent to contemplate. Besides, she had no memories of this happening. The logical part of her mind knew that having no memories did not mean it had not happened – after all, her childhood memories were only just surfacing – but she clung to this as a liferaft, and she has only coped with the whole experience by pushing it away to the back of her mind.

Talking about it is difficult, even now. Paul knows it is a taboo subject: after their initial discussion, he has never directly mentioned it again. Ann had to brace herself reluctantly to talk to me about it, and even then she could scarcely go into details. In every other way she has been open and eager to help with research, wanting always to find out more about her family's problems, but this experience hurt her too much to allow her to dwell on it. Just once, she expressed her darkest fear: 'Where is my baby now?' she asked. 'What did they want him for, what have they done to him?' She does not know why she knows her baby was another boy, but she says she is completely sure of it, as if she has been told.

Ann's experience was intensely personal and therefore it is hard to reduce it to what, as part of the greater, worldwide picture, it is: another shard of evidence for the theory that humans are being abducted for breeding purposes. There are now masses of first-hand accounts of 'miscarriages' just like Ann's, and gynaecological 'operations' similar to the one Maria Ward's doctors believe was performed on her, which we will discuss later. Knowing that she is not the only woman this has happened to is some comfort for Ann, but not enough to make it acceptable. Like many others, she feels angry to have been involved in something without being consulted, and she describes it as feeling like a laboratory rat on whom experiments are conducted.

The 'breeding experiment' is probably the single most common element of all detailed abduction experiences. Both men and women abductees feel they have been involved in some way in a massive programme of reproduction that the aliens are carrying out. It is also the aspect of alien abduction that most causes the sceptics to scoff – yet in many ways it is the best documented and the most plausible. Ann's medical records confirm that she had a miscarriage: not, in itself, evidence that anything paranormal happened, but certainly proof that she is not imagining the whole experience.

One of the most significant factors in the reports of breeding experiments is how they first emerged. The stories of what was happening, mostly to female abductees but also to men, were being told from the earliest days that abduction stories were reported, but, because they carried such an extreme suggestion, these aspects were not widely reported until the late 1980s – eliminating any possibility of the earlier cases being influenced by each other.

As British researcher Jenny Randles has said: 'Prior to 1987 this phenomenon was unknown even to UFO researchers like myself.

We did have a fairly uncontaminated period for case collection. Any signs of such things within the records are very important, and it is quite astonishing to see to what extent this does emerge from study of the evidence. Often these cases had no publicity outside rare sources within UFOlogy or, indeed, no publication at all prior to 1987.'

The evidence she refers to includes that of Nebraskan state police trooper Herb Schirmer who, in 1967 reported being abducted, and being told by the aliens that they had a human breeding analysis programme to carry out on Earth; that of New York nurse Shane Kurz who, in 1973, was hypnotically regressed and remembered abductions over the previous five years during which gynaecological procedures had occurred, and she was told by the aliens that they were using her ova to provide them with a baby for genetic experimentation; that of a young couple from Essex who were abducted and told about genetic experiments; and that of an Italian woman living in Britain who remembered a complete abduction in which various samples were taken from her and she was 'raped' in an unemotional and mechanical way by a tall alien.

Men are not exempt from being involved in the reproductive experiments – although in the case of Carl Higdon, an oil driller from Wyoming, USA, he was excused, for a good reason. Higdon had an abduction experience in 1974 from which he emerged with a strong feeling that he had been rejected for the breeding programme that he had been told about: not surprising, since he had had a vasectomy. During the abduction he was aware not just of aliens, but of humans who were mixing with and working with his captors: he felt they were humans who had been bred by the aliens. This (the awareness of human beings co-existing with the aliens) is another aspect of abduction which has gained a lot of ground simply because of the frequency with which it is reported.

The examples cited here are just a small sample. There are many more, from across the world. As Tony Dodd says: 'They can't all be making it up, can they? They speak different languages, come from different parts of the world, are of completely different cultural mixes, including illiterate peasants who do not have access to television sets, and yet they all come up with such similar reports.'

Tony believes that Ann's miscarriage experience is crucially important: not just because of its obvious effect on her, but because she was sure that the person who carried out the removal of the foetus was of human origin, at most part-alien. Yet he was a human being with what we would call 'supernatural' powers: he could communicate with her telepathically, and he was able to soothe all pain simply by stroking her forehead.

The main reason that in the late eighties it became possible for UFO researchers and abductees to talk publicly about the breeding elements in their experiences was that American researcher Budd Hopkins published the well-documented story of 'Kathie Davis' (Debbie Tomey), in a book called *Intruders – The Incredible Visitations at Copley Wood.*

Hers is an incredible history of multiple abductions, starting at the age of six. At eighteen she was subjected to a (possible) artificial insemination, followed by the removal of the foetus after a few months. Some years later, during another abduction, she was shown a little girl, half-human half-alien, but very pretty in a doll-like way who, she was 'told', was hers. Later she was told this child was one of nine babies which had been bred from her tissue.

Before publishing this account, Hopkins spoke to several other women who reported very similar experiences. At the time (he was doing this research in the early eighties) the techniques that are now commonplace in our own hospitals for the creation of 'test-tube' babies were rare, and the general public knew little about them. Yet the procedures the women describe for the removal of ova, or of small early-stage foetuses, are medically credible.

Hopkins wrote: 'We are left with two possible lines of explanation. The first is a new and heretofore unknown psychological phenomenon in which women hallucinate near-identical scenes with near-identical semi-human babies . . . The other is simple . . . The women are actually remembering what they saw: their experiences are real. Both of these explanations, it is safe to say, violate conventional wisdom.'

The meticulous research done by Jenny Randles supports him. Before Hopkins's book was published, she had personally interviewed in depth six British women abductees, of whom three told of unexpected pregnancies immediately after abductions, followed by night-time 'miscarriages' three months later. Randles concludes that this is either a 'fantastic coincidence' or that 'these women were describing events that really happened to them.'

Many of the women who experience having foetuses removed see their own unborn babies, and often many others, stored in jars or containers. surrounded by fluid. They may also see larger 'babies' being reared in incubators. In almost all of the cases that Professor John Mack studied in great depth there is some evidence of reproductive procedures: sperm samples taken from men and intrusive gynaecological procedures used on women. One described seeing about forty small tanks, each with a foetus in it, submerged in liquid. Another saw rows and rows of incubators containing babies or foetuses, and she instinctively knew that one of them was hers.

Professor Mack wrote: 'Experiencers may also see older hybrid children, adolescents and adults, which they are told by the aliens or know intuitively are their own. Sometimes the aliens will try to have the human mothers hold and nurture these creatures . . . or will encourage human children to play with the hybrid ones.' (As Jason does.)

The most obvious question that arises from this consistent evidence of a breeding programme is: why? Why would an alien race, technologically so far superior to ours, want to inter-breed with us? What possible scientific purpose can it fulfil?

Several abductees believe they have been given the answer to this, by the aliens. They have been 'told' in the telepathic way that characterises such communications that the alien race are unable, or have lost, the ability to procreate.

One very neat theory that has gained some currency among researchers recently is the possibility of the visitors not being from outer space at all, but being time travellers from the Earth's future. They are, in other words, the human race after another millenium or two of evolution. We already have plenty of evidence that fertility in the human race is declining, particularly male fertility, possibly as a result of pollution. Although, with our overcrowded planet and mushrooming world population, we have a long way to go before this becomes a major global problem, there will come a time when our race will effectively die out. The assumption by many scientists is that we will overcome this by perfecting the already developed techniques of *in vitro* fertilisation using donor sperm and egg implantation. Perhaps that's what our descendants are doing, but because they have become completely sterile they are compelled to travel back to their own past to collect genetic material.

This theory also encompasses the constancy with which abductees report being given 'warnings' about pollution, nuclear holocausts, the dire future of the planet. 'They' are concerned about us, not because they are a remote species wanting to colonise our planet, but because they are our future, and their problems are the result of our despoliation of Earth.

There are other theories about why the aliens are carrying out a breeding programme. Nick Pope, the Ministry of Defence official who has written *The Uninvited*, which discusses the subject of abduction, states that any cross-breeding that is going on against the will of the abductees – or at least, without their consent – is 'not likely to be done for our benefit'. He focuses on the accumulating evidence that the aliens are fascinated by our emotions: that they are, themselves, unable to understand feelings and emotional responses, and that they, for some reason, want to study and perhaps experience these. Jason is clear about this: he knows that the aliens 'share' his emotions, such as the thrill and fear of riding fast bareback. They also seem interested in, but unable to empathise with, pain, and this too, may be something they want to investigate – but are they simply studying us disinterestedly, as a scientific project? Or do they want to take over the feelings we have for their own use, perhaps to help them get back to a strength they once had?

Nick Pope writes: 'Have they lost all the raw, primitive emotions that we have in abundance? For all our faults, we have a mixture of curiosity and determination that has taken us out of the Stone Age and into the Space Age in a matter of a few thousand years. Is this what they want from us?'

He also hypothesises that hybridisation may be necessary before we can be invaded by the aliens, as they perhaps do not have the facility to live in the atmosphere of this planet for long, and need to create a race that can survive here. A similar theory, but couched in much more spiritual terms, is put forward by Professor Mack. One of his case studies, an acupuncture therapist called Peter, appears to have been given sight of a future, following some enormous apocalypse, in which alien, human and hybrid races intermingle and a new 'tribe' is created, with biological and spiritual contributions from both aliens and humankind.

Professor Mack writes: 'What this suggests is that the alien-human relationship is something far more complex than a program of hybrid procreation. It appears to be a halting, difficult attempt on the part of an intelligence of which we know very little to create a merger of two species who seem to need and long for something each has to offer the other . . . To make the matter still more complex, there is evidence in Peter's reports and those of other abductees that we and the alien beings are derived or split away from the same primal source.'

What does all this theorising mean for Ann, who not only has to come to terms with losing a baby (and even though she did not want the child, the hormonal chaos caused by a new pregnancy and then a miscarriage should not be underestimated), but also now faces the dawning realisation that the foetus was removed from her, and exists somewhere? What's more, if her abduction experiences follow the pattern of so many others, she may yet have to meet her own child, in an alien setting, and form a bond with it.

She is not ready to face an experience like that. The testimony of other abductees suggests she will be given quite a bit of time – that any future meeting with her 'baby' is likely to be at least two or three years hence. Perhaps the abductors understand enough about human emotions to appreciate she needs time to get over not just the shock to her body, but the much deeper shock of realising she is part of the breeding programme of another race.

At the moment, she copes by not thinking about the 'miscarriage', or about the abduction that night. If she does think back, she can clearly remember the pain, but equally clearly remembers the anaesthetising effect of looking into the eyes of the 'man' who performed the operation on her. She remembers the kindness and gentleness she felt emanated from him, and allows this memory to console her. She does not think about the day-to-day existence of a child, but simply feels comforted that the atmosphere in which it was 'born' was one of peace.

As for Paul, he has a much greater capacity than Ann for pushing things out of his mind and simply getting on with the everyday routines. If he does ever think about the baby – was it his or a hybrid? what happened to it? – he never discusses it. To Paul, the shock of seeing Ann bleeding was enough to make him simply grateful that she is all right, strong and healthy again.

Neither Daniel nor Jason were told about their mother's pregnancy or the subsequent 'miscarriage'. They were both too young at the time to understand, but, as we have seen, Ann was shocked to discover later that Jason had talked to the first psychiatrist about 'the baby who never was'. It was six years after she lost the baby, and she cannot help but wonder if Jason knows about it because he has 'seen' his lost brother or sister.

As well as retrieving buried memories of abductions which happened to her years ago, Ann occasionally remembers an experience soon after it happens (although, unlike Jason, she never wakes up with a full picture of what went on during the night). One abduction memory which was quickly retrieved is regarded by Tony Dodd as significant, because once again it involves the participation of someone who appears to be human, and is 'helping' the aliens – reinforcing his belief that humans are being bred or cross-bred and are now adapted to living in the alien world (a belief shared by other experts).

For Ann, it started with a strong sense of foreboding, so great that she felt an urge, which she fought, to collect the boys from school to keep them 'safe'. Jason, who was thirteen at the time, shared her unease. He felt something approaching. The previous two days had been dominated by an escalation of paranormal activity: there had been sounds of movement upstairs when everybody was downstairs, light bulbs exploded, electrical equipment switched on and off, and the dogs were restless and growling at the slightest noise.

When Jason asked if he could sleep in his parents' bedroom that night, Paul and Ann both agreed. It was 3.45am when Ann woke up, a time when she often finds herself awake. Instinctively she glanced at the camp bed where Jason was sleeping, and was reassured to see the outline of his sleeping body. As she moved, she became aware of an acute pain in her lower left arm and wrist. It was so bad that she winced, and woke Paul. He switched on the light and inspected her arm: her fingers were swollen and would not move, her veins were standing out prominently, the skin of her hand and arm was red and an inch-long scar ran across the main vein in her wrist. There was a large red lump, about two inches in diameter, four inches up from her wrist. Paul slowly uncurled her fingers: there was no feeling in them. As her hand opened, they could see a patch of dried blood in her palm.

Paul's instinct was to call the doctor, but Ann refused. She took a couple of painkillers and told Paul to switch off the light. Throughout this, Jason remained asleep. Despite the paracetamol, Ann's arm was still hurting badly and she did not sleep for the rest of the night, partly because of the pain and partly because of her fear that whatever had happened might happen again.

She stayed in bed the next morning, and Paul got the boys up and ready for school. He told them their mother was unwell. Jason seemed angry and disturbed: he told Paul he had had an experience in the night, but that, unusually, he could not remember it, except to know it was different. He, too, complained of a pain, but in his lower right arm, but apart from a reddening of the skin Paul could see nothing.

Later, still in pain, Ann settled with a cup of tea in the living room, and idly flicked on the television. The first image on the screen was an advertisement for spectacles, and as she glanced at it she went cold. A clear picture of her experience started to unfold. She remembered waking slowly, and hearing noises, very loud, as if they were amplified. She became aware that she was sitting in a chair that was tilted backwards, like a dentist's chair. At first, she imagined she had been in an accident and was in hospital, because there was a hospital smell in the room: a mixture of disinfectant, antiseptic and anaesthetic. Lying back, as she was, she could see that the ceilings were high and there were fluorescent strip lights, which were not on. There were windows high up in the walls, and sunlight was streaming through. She could feel its warmth on her face.

Then all her attention was focused on the pain in her arm. Her right arm was resting on the arm of the chair, but her left was outstretched, palm upwards, across a table which was adjacent to the reclining chair. Turning her head to the left she could see a strap restraining her arm above the elbow. There were also five or six silver-coloured needles, about four inches long and spaced about an inch apart, protruding from the centre of her arm above the wrist. A clear tube had been inserted into her vein and blood was being drawn up it into a clear, sealed jar on the table.

Ann's only thought was to stop the pain. She reached across with her right hand and began to grab the needles one by one, throwing them down on to the floor. Suddenly there was a lot of noise, feet hurrying towards her. She knew, although she did not see them, that 'they' were there. She did not look round, because by now she was concentrating on getting the clear tube out of her arm. She felt sure the tube was the seat of her pain, but it was hard to release it. After a split second, which felt much longer, it moved, and she felt a searing pain deep within her wrist. The tube came free, and as it did so blood spurted upwards. She heard a voice say, 'Oh, no, she's awake.' There were more words that she could not make out, except that the tone was angry. Then she heard a voice say, 'Someone's got to answer for this.'

She felt the tube being wrenched from her hand, and then she saw a man's face. He wore a hood with a drawstring tightened around his face, and a mask over his nose and mouth, but he was still recognisably human, wearing black thick-rimmed glasses, normal glasses that you see every day, glasses just like those in the television advertisement.

The man began mopping up the bloody mess she had caused. She could sense he was angry that she had seen him, but he spoke to her with measured politeness. His voice was deep and authoritative, and he called her 'Honey', with a mid-Atlantic accent. She was struggling and crying, so she did not concentrate on his words, but she was aware of an intense feeling of cold, deep inside her arm. Something was wrong – the man started to panic. After that, her next memory was waking up in her bed at 3.45am, with the pain in her arm.

As she stared at the television screen, the innocuous advertisement for spectacles long replaced by some daytime show, she began to cry uncontrollably. When she calmed down, she dialled Tony Dodd's number, and was pleased to hear his down-to-earth Yorkshire voice answer. As ever, Tony persuaded her that her experience, however daunting, was similar to those of many other abductees.

Either humans were being bred to work with the aliens, or there was a measure of co-operation between certain government agencies and 'them'. Was the human she had met a servant to the aliens, an equal, a master? Tony Dodd told her he did not know, but he had long known of similar medical tests carried out on human guinea pigs in some unexplained joint venture between humans and aliens.

Ann was profoundly shaken by this memory, partly because she retrieved it so soon after it happened, and partly because of the obvious worry about human involvement. Ever since that day she has been nervous of anyone wearing spectacles with thick black rims.

CHAPTER 11

FOREIGN BODIES

As if to confirm everything Ann had been telling him, Paul had a strange experience that was all his own. It was late on a Friday night. As a taxi driver, self-employed but on the books of a local taxi firm, his busiest times of the week are Friday and Saturday evenings, when folk out for a good time want to be ferried to and from the pubs and restaurants of this affluent stretch of Kent. Many trips are pre-booked, but there are always lots of last minute requests, after the nightclubs and pubs close their doors. It is the most lucrative part of the week for Paul, and he regularly works until dawn comes up.

Being out at night means that he has, from time to time, witnessed strange lights in the sky. Several times he has used his mobile phone to call Ann, to check that everything is all right at home, after he has seen bright and unexplained lights. These are usually the nights that there are electrical disturbances around the house: power surges, the television jumping madly from channel to channel, every light bulb in the house blowing simultaneously. On one night, within seconds of Ann putting down the phone after speaking to Paul, the dogs became restless, one of them started to howl, another was growling at the door, as if there were intruders outside, and the four cockatiels began flapping uncontrollably around their cage, squawking wildly, feathers flying everywhere. On another occasion, Paul had two passengers in the car when a series of bright shapes passed across the sky. The light was so dazzling that he pulled to the side of the road and all three of them watched, the passengers as puzzled as he was.

However, on the Friday following his reconciliation with Ann, after the revelation that she too was an abductee, and his acceptance of it, there was nothing strange about the night sky. Paul had dropped off a fare, and could have driven back for more work, but instead felt an overpowering urge to go to the farm. He rarely visits the farm after dark, although occasionally, after spates of vandalism, he has popped in, but on this night, shortly after 1am, he felt impelled to go there. He did not know why: Paul is usually unaffected by the strange forces which surround his family. At first, as he drove up, everything appeared normal and he chided himself for worrying unnecessarily, until he saw that the horses were all huddled together, restless and not sleeping. Even Prudence, the pot-bellied pig, who likes her sleep more than anything except food, was awake and shuffling disconsolately about the yard. The hens and geese were awake, too, but silent. All the animals were unnaturally quiet, especially the geese which are usually such excellent 'watchdogs', cackling alarmingly when anyone approaches.

Feeling uneasy, Paul parked the car in the lane and leaned against the gate. Suddenly, he stiffened with shock, for without warning the sky lit up. A strange, circular, very bright object seemed to detach itself from the dense woods beyond the farm fields, and rise rapidly straight up into the sky. It hovered for a few minutes, then darted to the right and then back to the left, centring over the farm, and remaining stationary for what was probably only a few seconds, but seemed to Paul a threateningly long time. He raised his forearm across his brow and peered at it, but the light was so intense at the centre of the circle, radiating outwards to a diffuse glow, that it was impossible to make out the shape beneath the light or the source of the illumination.

The whole smallholding was clearly lit up by the object, immobile about sixty feet above it. The animals were no longer moving about restlessly, but standing stock still, like statues. There was no noise from them, but a low, steady humming sound. Like his horses, Paul was transfixed, held as if by a spell. Then the bright circle again darted upwards at incredible speed, dwindling in seconds to the size of a shooting star. Paul was plunged into complete darkness, until his eyes adjusted to the thin moonlight. He could make out the shape of the horses, now spreading themselves out in the lower field. The geese seemed to wake from a trance and became aware of him, waddling towards the gate with their usual harsh honks and gabbles.

Paul slowly turned and shakily walked back to the car, realising as he drove away that an hour had passed while he had been at the farm. Before he could tell Ann about his frightening experience he found her anxiously awaiting his return. She told him the whole house had blacked out, and even the street lights had gone out. Jason had woken and come downstairs to her, upset because he sensed an abduction was imminent. Eventually, although she had offered to let him sleep in her bedroom, he had gone back to his own room, telling her that it did not matter where he went, they could still find him.

The next morning, although he had no memories of an abduction, Jason had two large scoop marks on his leg, as if the flesh had been hollowed away from the bone without the skin being broken. He was tired and bad-tempered, and said he had dreamt he was at the farm. Paul noticed that his feet were caked with mud, and ordered him into the shower. It was when the boy took off his pyjama top that Paul noticed something else – there were deep scratch marks on Jason's chest, as if he had been fighting his way through undergrowth. As usual, all the marks on Jason's body were gone by the next day. Once again Ann noticed the strange, very sweet smell inside her car. Both cars, hers and Paul's, had flat batteries – even though Paul had been driving his only hours before.

She could not help but feel that Jason had been an unwitting presence at the whole weird episode that Paul had witnessed, but she said nothing to either of them.

After one particularly restless, disturbed night, Ann woke feeling more tired than she had been when she went to bed. She looked ill: she was pale, her hair was lank, she had no appetite and even less energy. Forcing herself to get up, she realised, as she swung her legs over the side of the bed, that her left knee was hurting. It looked swollen and red, and she had trouble bending it. Paul immediately noticed her limping, but she diverted his curiosity by telling him she had banged her knee on the bedpost. Something strange had happened in the night, but until she knew what it was she did not want to discuss it with Paul.

Ann knew there was something unusual about the pain. All night, as she tossed and turned, she had felt 'they' were nearby. As she

155

limped through the morning she consoled herself with the memory of how quickly Jason's unexplained ailments cleared up. The scoop marks on his leg, for instance, had vanished within four or five hours. Her knee, she was confident, would be the same.

However, the pain persisted all day. After dinner she was sitting in the kitchen, inspecting her swollen and discoloured joint, when Jason came in. 'You'll find a small scar at the back of your knee, Mum,' he told her, matter-of-factly. 'It's where they've inserted a tiny silicone chip. Don't know what it's for, but I remember when they put mine in. They said my knee would hurt for a couple of days.'

Ann got up, took a small mirror from the window ledge and with Jason's help manoeuvred it into a position where she could inspect the back of her knee. She could see a small V-shaped incision. She didn't question it; she knew Jason was right. True enough, two days later she woke to find the swelling had subsided, the redness had gone and there was no more pain.

The insertion of implants into abductees is one of the most controversial aspects of the abduction phenomenon. Like so many researchers before me, my reaction was initially to regard the implant as the ultimate proof, the 'hardware' needed to run the 'software' of the memories, the chunks of missing time, the strange electrical disturbances, the lights and other evidence that could not be transported into a laboratory. Implants, real bits of alien technology, would surely convince the sceptics, and also give the open-minded scientists something concrete to investigate. They would, I thought, give us a real handle on alien technology.

Many UFOlogists believe (with some substantial evidence to back them up) that we already live in a world of 'back-engineering': that alien craft (and perhaps even alien bodies) have been captured, and scientists have worked on them to discover the secrets of their advanced technology, using some of their discoveries in the development of military aircraft like Stealth and Aurora, as well as in other scientific breakthroughs. This is not the place to go into this vast subject in any depth (anyone who wants to know more should look at the list of titles appended to this book), but if it is possible to analyse the macro-technology of the aliens and their flying machines, then it must surely also be possible to investigate the micro-technology of implants.

Many abduction victims talk about the insertion of implants in various parts of their bodies, although the knee and the nose seem to be the most popular spots. Why the aliens need to insert these small devices into the humans they abduct can only be a guess. Some think it is to enable them to track their victims; this is consistent with the evidence that they do repeatedly abduct the same people, as if there has to be some continuity to their study of our race. Another reason could be that these tiny, sophisticated devices monitor the workings of the human body and provide them with constant feedback. If the aliens are, indeed, fascinated by our ability to experience emotions, perhaps these implants allow them to follow the physical effects of changing emotions. The most sinister explanation, and the least likely, is that they use the implants to control their victims. If they do, they operate them benignly. There may be some evidence of victims being 'called', attracted to go to certain places at certain times to facilitate an abduction, but even this seems unlikely as it appears to be possible for an abduction to take place at any time and from any place. So far, at least, there is no evidence of alien 'control' forcing abductees to behave in untypical and malign ways against their human will: if they do bend victims to their will, it appears to be by spiritual education, not force.

So we come back to the implants themselves. What are they? How do they work? What are they made of? I naïvely thought it was simply a matter of removing them from abduction victims and, even if we could not decipher their minute workings, at least we would have something to work on. So far, however, it has proved almost impossible to retrieve an insert. Why?

One of the best explanations comes in a paragraph in Professor Mack's book, in which he is dealing with the abduction experiences of a woman called Eva, who he interviewed at length and who had three hypnotherapy sessions. Eva 'knew' she had an implant in her head, and had had it since childhood. After her regression sessions she wrote to Professor Mack: 'Implants... are not likely to provide the definitive proof that abduction researchers are seeking. For to be sustained within our bodies they would have to be composed of substances that would not be rejected by our tissues, i.e., would need to contain elements with which we are familiar on Earth.'

Professor Mack went on to say that it is unlikely that a phenomenon of 'such intelligence, subtlety and sophistication' would leave a piece of technology lying around which we, of a much lower level of consciousness, would be able to investigate and understand.

Not all UFO researchers agree with him. Derrel Sims, chief of abduction investigations for the Houston UFO Network in Texas claims to have a collection of thirty small objects acquired from the bodies of abductees, most of which he says are being analysed scientifically in laboratories all over the States. He is cagey about revealing which laboratories and which scientists – sceptics use this as a reason to doubt him – but it is fair to say that the scientists have requested anonymity because of the mocking reaction of their peers should they admit to working on 'alien' material.

Sims teamed up with a Californian medical doctor, Dr Roger K. Leir, who enlisted the help of a retired surgeon to remove three implants from two abductees: two from a woman's foot and one from the hand of a man. The man claimed his headaches stopped as soon as the small disc, a quarter of an inch in diameter, was removed from his hand. Dr Leir claims there were many anomalies in the pathology report on the objects, which were removed in August 1995. These anomalies included the discovery of nerve cells in the tissue surrounding the implants: they were in parts of the body which should normally be made up only of fat and fibrous connective tissue. The presence of nerve cells suggests that the implants were communicating with the abductees' bodies for some reason, and this was borne out when the woman winced in pain if the implant was touched, even though it was no longer in her body.

Dr Leir had several independent witnesses present when the implants were removed: a lawyer, a psychologist, two writers, a photographer and a cameraman, all of whom have vouched for the honest removal of the objects – but this still leads to a verdict of not proven, because there is no hard evidence that the objects were implanted supernaturally.

Eva is not the only one of Professor Mack's abductees who believe they were tagged by the aliens. One man says he was shown the device, and 'told' that it was going to be inserted through his anus.

He also said that on subsequent abductions the implant had been removed and replaced. He described graphically the feeling of being an animal wearing a collar, a permanent means of identification and control. Another woman, under hypnosis, relived the agony of having an implant inserted through the side of her head and down into her neck, a similar position to the implant another man remembered being inserted to make it 'easier to follow me'.

British UFO researcher Jenny Randles investigated a case in Adelaide, Australia, which was one of the first cases to include detailed memories of an implant. A ten-year-old girl was abducted in 1971 and an object placed in her face, which caused it to be sore. She told her family and a local UFO researcher. Shortly afterwards a routine dental X-ray showed a mysterious object in her cheek. More detailed X-rays were taken, but nothing was visible – the girl believes the aliens removed the implant after it was discovered by the first X-ray. There is always a possibility that the object was a fault or shadow on the X-ray plate, but this was deemed to be unlikely. Jenny Randles has actually seen the plate, and points out that the victim did not recall the implantation after the X-ray, but reported it before.

Another abductee who claims the implant was removed just as it was about to be investigated is Ed Walters, an architect and builder from Gulf Breeze, a small town in Florida. He became a celebrity in the UFO world in 1988 when he and many other witnesses saw a dramatic series of lights in the night sky which lasted for six months, and brought hundreds of enthusiasts flocking to the town. Walters, who also claims to have had abduction experiences, believes he had an implant in his head for many years, and that the aliens removed this immediately prior to him being examined in hospital by UFO researchers.

Another possible explanation of why aliens use implants was given by John Hodges, a Californian who was twice (to his recall) abducted, once in 1971 and again in 1978. He claims the aliens communicated with him the reason for the implants: they are to increase the psychic abilities of the humans who have them. There is certainly evidence that abductees tend to have heightened psychic abilities: Jason Andrews has a history of predicting certain events. Both he and Ann have felt uneasy and been given glimpses, against their will, of impending disasters: they both foretold, separately, an aircrash in August 1997. Ann dreamed of the crash, and was even able partly to read a name that occurred in the dream: the location, she thought, of the crash. It began with GU. She told Paul that there would be crash in Guinea. The next day, a Korean Air Boeing 747 went down in a violent rainstorm in Guam, killing 226 people. It was the second time Jason had 'seen' a plane crash, having told his mother about the TWA Boeing disaster which killed 230 people on July 18th 1996. He was resigned to it happening, telling Ann there was nothing that could be done, and also telling her that there would be a US government cover-up: the plane exploded in mid-air, thirty-one minutes after takeoff from New York.

Ann has made other predictions, but always related to her own family. In October 1997 she warned Paul, as he was getting ready for work, to accept only local fares in his taxi. She had a feeling that he was in danger, but she did not know why. Later that evening she rang him, to say that she had 'seen' a large white lorry which she knew would be involved in a crash, and she had 'seen' Paul's car in front of it. The urgency in her voice impressed itself on Paul, who over the years has learned to take his wife's dreams and predictions seriously.

Ann found it hard to settle all evening, but when she went to bed she was able to sleep, feeling that the danger had passed. The next day, on the local news bulletin, there was film footage of a huge Safeways lorry which had spun out of control just outside Tonbridge, only a few miles away from the Andrews's home. It had ploughed into a house, causing substantial damage, but fortunately not injuring anyone. The lorry cab was white. Paul had turned down a taxi job which would have taken him along the road where the crash had occurred.

On another occasion, in November 1997, she dreamed that she could 'see' people inside the small caravan at the farm. She told Paul as soon as she woke the next morning, and they dashed up to Hawksnest. There had, indeed, been someone in the caravan: the windows had been smashed, the door was hanging open, and anything of value – horse bridles, rugs, Paul's tools – had been stolen.

Both Ann and Jason have a highly developed intuition about any of the Andrews's animals. Ann has always ascribed this to her father's

Romany legacy, and this may account for much of it, but there was one particularly unhappy event with one of their horses which Jason foresaw in advance, and which was not simply intuition.

It happened on May 1st 1996. As well as the horses they were keeping on the farm, Paul and Ann had two more which grazed a lush twenty-acre field about a quarter of a mile away. The field belongs to Billy and Sue Rutland, who live in a beautiful nineteenth-century oast house which Billy, a builder, converted. The Rutlands's teenage daughter Laura has a thoroughbred gelding, Tully, which lives in the field. To keep Tully company and to keep the grass down, Sue Rutland was thinking of buying another couple of horses, but when she heard that Ann and Paul needed extra grazing, she invited them to put two on to her land. It was a mutually satisfactory arrangement, and all three horses thrived on it.

In the spring of 1996 both the Andrews's horses, Honey and Lady in Black, were in foal, and on May 1st Honey gave birth. Paul was excited and relieved when Honey foaled, producing a gangly-legged colt they called The Rocket. Although other horses he owned had foaled, Paul was particularly fond of these two. He and Ann watched as The Rocket began feeding from his mother, and then left the pair alone to get to know each other.

They visited the new arrival every day. But four days after he was born, at the weekend, Ann was unable to accompany Paul. Paul's mother, Shirley, was staying with them to decorate the hall and staircase and Ann, despite hating decorating, had been roped in to give a hand. Paul was helping too, but slipped away for a couple of hours to see the foal and returned enthusing about how much his 'baby' had grown.

That night, Shirley settled to sleep on the settee in the living room, and the rest of the family went to bed upstairs. It was 3.30am when they were awoken by a scream from Jason's room, and then the sound of him calling out for Ann. When she reached his room, with Paul behind her, he flung his arms around her, sobbing. Over and over again he repeated, 'They didn't know she was ours.' Gradually Ann calmed him down, and he told her it was not another abduction, but that he 'knew' Honey was dead.

Shirley, disturbed by all the noise, called from the foot of the stairs and was reassured by Paul that it was only Jason having a nightmare. One by one the family all went back to bed, Jason reluctantly letting go of Ann. Back in her own room Ann asked Paul what he made of it. 'A bad dream. It's only a few hours since I fed Honey – I'd have noticed if anything was wrong,' Paul said, sleepily.

It was the phone ringing at 7am that woke them. Laura Rutland, sobbing, could only mumble four coherent words: 'Honey's dead, please come.'

When they reached the field they saw the piteous sight of the foal pawing at his mother's body. As they approached he backed away, whinnying in bewilderment. Blinded by tears, Ann did not inspect Honey. It was left to Paul to tell her later that the mare's stomach appeared to have exploded.

The following couple of days were taken over by the tragedy. The Rocket hungrily accepted formula milk from a lemonade bottle, while an appeal was made on the local radio for an adoptive mother for him. Eventually, the National Foal Bank came up with a mare who, like Honey, was a Welsh Cob, and whose foal had died. The Rocket was transported to Surrey, where a vet skinned the dead foal, leaving the ears intact, and draped the skin across The Rocket. Believing from the scent that it was her own foal, the mare allowed him to suckle, and within a couple of days the dead skin was removed: by this time the foal smelled so strongly of her and her milk that the mare accepted him. Six months later, a sturdy little chap by then, The Rocket was collected by Paul and brought back to the farm.

In the meantime Honey's body was taken away and the Andrews's vet performed an autopsy. Unfortunately, because of delays, by the time it was carried out it was impossible to say conclusively what caused Honey's death, but the vet said that he believed it was a double twisted gut – a relatively rare condition. He added that her stomach was 'such a mess' that it was impossible to be certain of the cause of death.

Ironically, just three days after a foster mother was found for The Rocket, Lady in Black gave birth to her first foal. He was weak and survived for only four days.

Jason refuses to talk about Honey, the new foal, or his night-time outburst. He will only say that 'they' did not know she belonged to him because she was not at the farm.

162

Ann, too, had a strange dream about one of the horses, a dream which subsequently seemed to be at least partially true. It was in November 1997, and she tells the story in her own words:

'Paul was working and I was very tired. I expected to fall asleep as soon as I got to bed, but for some reason I could not get comfortable, and I tossed and turned restlessly. Eventually I slipped into sleep. I was roused by the sound of a heavy vehicle outside, which sounded exactly like the dustbin lorry. I could even hear the whining noise of the crushing machinery on the back of the lorry.

'I sprang out of bed, convinced I had forgotten to put our dustbin out for them. It never occurred to me that it was the middle of the night, and that our rubbish is always collected on a Monday afternoon. As I passed the bathroom, in my slippers and dressing gown, I thought that I would empty the bathroom bin. I didn't put the light on, as the light from the landing, which is always left on for Jason, meant that I could see enough to find the waste bin. As I bent down to pick it up, the whole room was suddenly filled with light.

'In the next instant I was standing in a field at the farm, freezing in my nightclothes. A second later, without any sensation of moving, I found myself in a clearing in the woods. There were large spotlights all around the edge of the clearing, and I could plainly see about half a dozen men, dressed in navy blue or black coveralls. I accidentally brushed against one of them and he pushed me away rudely, saying to one of the others, "You wanted her here – you take care of her".

I walked slowly, as if in slow motion, while everyone around me bustled about at normal speed, across the clearing to a white box-shaped vehicle, like a Jeep or Land Rover. It had a bank of spotlights on the front, as well as the normal headlights. One of the men smiled at me, took my arm and led me to the centre of the clearing, where a makeshift animal pen had been built. It was surrounded by fencing about four feet high, and was about fifteen feet square, filled with straw.

'In the pen, lying down, was our stallion, Cardi (his full name is Chatshill Cadfarch, but he's always known as Cardi). I looked at him and thought that he was dead, yet I felt strangely emotionless. Then two of the men went inside the pen and knelt down, one by

Cardi's head and the other, with his back to me, alongside the horse's flank. I could not make out what they were doing, but within seconds Cardi woke up and staggered to his feet. He tried to shake himself but wobbled unsteadily, as if he was just coming round from an anaesthetic. I was aware that I ought to feel relief that he was alive, but again I felt detached and unemotional.

'One of the men opened the gate to the pen, and Cardi, after a moment or two, wandered slowly out and disappeared into the woods. Another of the men said "Let's wrap this up, people", making a gesture with his hand in a circular movement.

'I awoke the next morning with no memory of any of this. It was only when I went to empty the kitchen bin into the dustbin that I recollected the dream of the dustbin lorry, and then slowly, bit by bit, the rest came back to me. I told Paul about it, because I was afraid something had happened to Cardi.'

Paul instantly picked up on Ann's fear, and, trusting her instincts, the pair of them went up to the farm straightaway. As they drove up the lane, about half a mile from the farm, they met one of the girls who works at the local riding stable, leading Cardi. The groom explained she had taken a group out riding in the woods, and as they returned they had realised there was a riderless horse tagging along behind. Recognising the stallion, she was on her way to Hawksnest Farm with him.

After thanking her, Paul took the leading rein and Ann drove on, while he followed with the horse. When Ann arrived at the farm, all the other animals were clearly disturbed, even the placid cows. Paul was longer than she expected, and when he arrived he complained that he had to drag Cardi – normally a very active and energetic horse – all the way. He said the stallion seemed to be 'half-doped'. They inspected Cardi closely, but there was no sign of injury on him.

As well as the implant behind his knee, Jason also had one inserted up his nose. For some unexplained reason (perhaps simply because it is accessible, and is close to the brain) the nose is a favoured site for implants. Two of Professor Mack's case studies revealed under hypnosis that implants had been placed in their heads through their noses, one of them blaming his subsequent sinus and other nasal problems on to the implantation process. One of Budd Hopkins's most celebrated American cases, Linda Napolitano (often referred to as Linda Cortile, the pseudonym first used when Hopkins wrote about her case) was also believed to have an implant in her nose, which showed in an X-ray Hopkins arranged to have taken. The implant subsequently disappeared after she, her husband and both her children, all awoke one morning suffering from violent nosebleeds.

Nosebleeds are a perplexing symptom often found in abduction cases, happening both to the victims themselves and to close family members who have been present, but not aware, when an abduction has taken place. Dr Richard Neal, a medical doctor who is one of the founders of the Southern California UFO Research and Abductee Support Group, has been studying the whole subject since the 1960s, and has interviewed many abductees. He wrote: 'The nasal cavity, ears, eyes and genitalia appear to be the physical areas of most interest to the aliens. The umbilical region – the navel – is as well, but in females only. Many abductees have described a thin probe with a tiny ball on its end being inserted into the nostril, usually on the right side. They are able to hear a 'crushing' type sound as the bone in this area is apparently being penetrated. Many will have nosebleeds following these examinations . . . It is interesting to note that many of the individuals subjected to nasal probing now have a history of chronic sinusitis.'

Professor Mack was actually given an implant, a tiny object, that one of his abductees said she removed from her nose. On analysis it proved to be a twisted fibre made up of carbon, silicon, oxygen and traces of other elements. A university colleague of Professor Mack, a nuclear biologist, said it was not a natural biological specimen, but could have been manufactured. Professor Mack concluded that it neither proved nor disproved anything.

Others who have removed objects from their noses have not been able to get them to a laboratory for analysis, largely because many of them spontaneously disappear soon after being removed – as happened to Jason.

He had been unwell for several days, with a bad cold. He complained that his nose hurt, but Ann put it down to the normal problems anyone has when they are forced to wipe their nose

165

constantly. However, even after the cold symptoms had subsided, Jason was still grousing about a pain up inside his nose. Ann was surprised: Jason was always so stoical about physical ailments. She rubbed an antiseptic cream around the base of his nose, but he told her as she was doing it that it would not help because the pain was deeper inside.

The next morning, over breakfast he sneezed loudly, and then his nose started to bleed profusely. Ann rushed to grab tissues, which she thrust under Jason's nose. The tissues quickly turned deep red, and within a few second there was quite a pile of blood-soaked paper handkerchiefs in his lap. Daniel, unsympathetic as older brothers are, complained that Jason was putting him off his breakfast. He complained even louder – describing Jason as 'disgustingly gross' – when, after the bleeding abated, Jason began to pick through the bloody mess of tissue.

After a few moments Jason exclaimed excitedly, 'Here it is, I've found it.' Ann, Paul and Daniel gathered round as he picked something out of the sodden tissues. When Daniel asked what it was Jason answered by dropping into his brother's hand a tiny metallic object. They all stared at it: it was no bigger than the head of a pin. Jason gingerly touched the side of his nose and announced that it felt much better – and that he could breathe properly. Ann wrapped the minute object in a clean tissue, emptied a matchbox of its contents and placed it inside, but an hour later, when she checked, the box was empty apart from the paper. The tiny shiny implant had vanished, just as so many others have. Her excitement at having found some 'hard' evidence evaporated, and she rang Tony Dodd in dismay. He reacted without surprise, having encountered disappearing implants before.

Throughout Jason's story, there are numerous examples of him having scars or marks on his body which come and go mysteriously: the hospital doctors were puzzled, when he was taken in with suspected appendicitis; the general practitioners at the local surgery have seen the marks; so has the child psychiatrist. Ann and Paul have become so used to them that to outsiders they may appear indifferent. An angry red weal, which would have any other mother rushing to the local surgery with her child in tow, only makes Ann sigh and shake her head. The scars do not generally hurt Jason, and they disappear so quickly that Ann knows it is a waste of time seeking medical advice.

Although the marks do not usually hurt, Jason always seems to be aware of them the morning after they appear, and sometimes he complains of pain associated with them, as he did one night in June 1996. He climbed into bed with Ann and Paul in the middle of the night, in tears because of a pain in his right ankle, and in the morning there was a small deep-red mark, which looked more like a birthmark than a scar. Ann assumed it would go away, but it persisted for nearly a week. When Jason had to be taken to hospital anyway – he was bitten by a snake while playing in the long grass at the farm – Ann showed the mark to the doctor, who insisted it must always have been there. When Ann protested that she would have seen it, the doctor looked at her coldly, and Ann shrugged her shoulders, realising it was not worth arguing. The following day the mark had vanished, and Ann was tempted to take Jason back to show the doctor who had been so categoric that it was a permanent mark.

Despite such discouraging encounters, occasionally Jason suffers an unexplained injury that makes even his parents, hardened as they are by experience, react by calling for professional help. One night when Ann and Paul went to bed they found that Jason was missing from his room. They were used to this, and had even developed a capacity to sleep, knowing he was missing. He was always back in the morning, but, unusually, on this occasion Ann was wakened by the sound of him sobbing loudly.

She rushed to his bedroom, but Daniel was there before her. They both went across to Jason, who was lying face down, weeping.

'My legs. My legs hurt,' he sobbed.

Ann pulled back the duvet and saw that her son's legs were red raw from the ankles to just above the back of his knee. They looked as though they were burned, and the burns were blistering. She called Paul, told him to ring the doctor, and sent Daniel downstairs to get the medical chest. She rooted around in the box until she found the antiseptic cream and quickly and carefully covered Jason's legs with the ointment. He was still sobbing.

Paul announced that the doctor would come as soon as he had

finished his rounds, and that in the meantime Jason's legs were to be left uncovered. With difficulty Ann and Daniel got Jason up and helped him downstairs. They waited for the doctor.

It was nearly four hours before he arrived. By then, Jason's legs were almost completely healed. The doctor muttered something about a waste of time, and Ann and Paul felt guilty for bothering him. They realised again that whatever they were dealing with went beyond the normal medical experience of a local GP.

On another occasion Jason was at his school summer fête. Typically, he and a group of his mates were fooling around, and Jason managed to slip down the trunk of a tree, gashing his hand on the rough bark. He was taken to the St John's Ambulance first-aid post, where a concerned man placed five sterile 'butterfly' strips across the wound, warning Jason that he may have to go to hospital for the wound to be stitched if it did not seem to be healing. The first-aider put a dressing across the gash, and then bound the hand neatly with a white bandage.

Back home, Ann resignedly accepted that she was probably going to have to make a twenty-mile round trip to the hospital the next day. However, when Paul went into Jason's room to wake him, he found the bandage and the dressing folded neatly and lying on the bedside table. He called Ann, who assumed Jason had removed them in the night because they were too tight.

'No, it's more than that,' said Paul. He put his hand under the duvet and withdrew Jason's arm. As he still slept, his parents scrutinised his hand carefully. There was no sign of a cut, a scar or any evidence of the previous day's accident.

Just after Christmas 1996, Jason woke up one morning, when the weather outside was below freezing, with his bedclothes thrown back. He was hot, and his skin was red, just as if he had been sunbathing and had spent too long in the sun. There was no explanation for it, and again by the end of the day Jason had cooled down and his skin was back to its normal winter pallor.

The appearance of unexplained scars, lesions and marks is typical of a great many abduction cases, and blistering burns are not unique to Jason. When, in 1980, three women had a close encounter with a diamond-shaped object, hovering at tree height in front of them near the town of Huffman, Texas, they all suffered strange physical symptoms, including blistering and burn marks. The previous year, in Manchester, a woman out walking with her two children had a missing-time episode of about one-and-a-half hours, after seeing a brightly-lit crescent-shaped UFO. The following day the skin around her eyes was blistered, as if badly sunburned. Under hypnosis she recalled a whole abduction experience which included aliens shining a bright light in her face.

There are, in the annals of UFO research, hundreds of examples of unexplained scars appearing on abductees. They are usually straight scars, as if a cut has been made with a scalpel, or they are indentations in the flesh, as though tissue has been scooped out. Budd Hopkins, the pioneer of therapy work with abductees, soon realised that these scars, which the victim cannot recall as being caused by a conscious injury, are a common denominator in most cases of persistent abductions. When he referred cases to Professor Mack, who was initially sceptical about them, Mack noted: 'These experiences . . . frequently left physical traces on the individuals' bodies, such as cuts and small ulcers that would tend to heal rapidly and followed no apparent psychodynamically identifiable pattern as do, for example, religious stigmata.'

One of Professor Mack's cases is that of a young man who found small pimples, like insect bites, behind his ear where he remembered the aliens firing a laser beam into him. The pimples healed much more rapidly than insect bites, and were in a symmetrical formation. Mack also heard from another man who had a gash several inches deep on his leg after an abduction, yet it had virtually disappeared within twenty-four hours.

It may simply be a case of the aliens having technology so far superior to ours that they have perfected remarkable healing skills – but in that case it is surprising that the marks manifest themselves at all. Even if there is no physical benefit to the abductee in having rapidly appearing and disappearing scars, one woman who suffered a series of strange lesions and cuts was able to see a psychological advantage in something so tangible. The marks on her body mean she can reassure herself that what happened was real, that it was not a figment of her imagination and that she is not going insane. The scars are there the next morning, they are the testament of her own flesh – perhaps not sufficient proof for a disbelieving world, but enough to establish to her and her family that something very significant did take place.

For the Andrews family Jason's scars and marks have performed the same service, particularly in convincing Paul in the early days.

The scars and marks on Jason's body are not the only 'concrete' evidence that strange things happen to him in the night. On one occasion Ann went to wake him for school. With his curtains still closed and only faint light trickling in from the landing, she blinked her eyes in horror as she became aware that the whole of his pillow was seething with movement. Hurriedly switching on the main light and pulling back the duvet, she saw that his bed was full of hundreds of ladybirds. Some took off, flying around the room, blundering into Ann's face and hair, and making her scream for help. Jason woke up as Paul and Daniel charged to the rescue, and seemed unperturbed, even pleased, to see his legs and body covered by so many little red-shelled beetles. It took Paul and Ann half an hour of shaking the bedding out of the window and hoovering up the ones on the carpet and curtains, to be free of the ladybird invasion.

The only explanation put forward was that Jason had been returned from an abduction precipitately, and that he had perhaps been viewing an insect breeding programme when he was unceremoniously dumped back in his own bed with a whole consignment of 'samples' accidentally delivered with him. Infestations of ladybirds have been reported from time to time in various parts of Britain but on this occasion there were no other plagues of the insect in the area and the rest of the Andrews's house was unaffected.

Ann was grateful that it was ladybirds, not any other insect.

CHAPTER 12

MARIA AND JAMES

Sharing his experiences with others, by talking to people who believe him and take him seriously, has provided the greatest help for Jason. It is this more than any other single thing which has enabled him to come to terms with what is happening to him: the ongoing abductions that he probably faces for the rest of his life.

Tony Dodd was the first, and most important, contact that the Andrews family had, but after Tony came two other vital sources of help and support: Maria Ward and James Basil.

It was a colleague of Tony who put the Andrews family on to Maria, another abductee, who lives in Dartford, less than half an hour's drive away. Maria, an attractive woman in her thirties, married with one son, had already come to terms with her own experiences, which in many ways mirror those of Jason and Ann. She knows how difficult it can be facing up to abduction and talking about it openly. She has always, because of this, been willing to help others, and especially youngsters like Jason.

She has counselled thirty-five abductees, usually over many sessions, covering several years: 'Most of them come to me later in life, when they are on their second or third marriage, or they have failed to establish long-term relationships. They are coping in arrears with what has happened to them. They may have outwardly successful lives, but they have always been anxious and fearful, and they need help facing up to their experiences.

'I usually only see young people when they have very supportive parents, like Ann and Paul. They're unusual: it took a bit of time, but when they discovered what was happening to Jason they believed him, and they set about finding help for him. So many children find their problems are simply dismissed as "dreams".

Maria, like Ann, has Romany blood. Her father, a Hungarian gipsy, came to England as a young man and settled in Kent with her mother, who is of mixed English, Scots and Irish descent. Maria is the third of their four daughters and, like Ann, she grew up learning a great deal of natural folklore from her father. She saw small brown humanoids throughout her childhood years, dubbing them 'mud midgets' and later calling them 'fairies'. She also saw balls of intense light in the woods near the family home, and was often found, as a small child, outside in the garden in the middle of the night, even though all the house doors were locked. Sometimes she sensed someone in the room she shared with her younger sister, and assumed it was their mother, only to discover the next day that their mother had not been in. On one occasion her sister Lulu accompanied her when she was transported into the garden, and they both saw several large barn owls in the branches of the tree. They were not surprised, because they often saw owls in this tree. On other occasions Maria would know, because of a strange ringing sensation in her ears, that she was going to go somewhere in the night, and although she never remembered the details, she described it to her parents as 'going into the moon'.

Her experiences were accepted by her father and sisters, although less so by her mother, who thought the house was possessed by evil spirits. There was a great deal of poltergeist activity surrounding the family: objects thrown around rooms, doors slamming shut, strange smells pervading the air. Nobody was harmed, and Maria assumed it was normal – until she went to school. At her convent school she soon picked up on the fact that it was not done to talk about fairies and ghosts, and instinctively suppressed any mention of them.

During her teenage years she had heavy nosebleeds, so bad that eventually it was decided that she would be taken into hospital to have some of the veins cauterised. Once this decision was taken the nosebleeds stopped and the operation was unnecessary. In retrospect, it would seem likely that the implant which was causing the nosebleeds was removed before it was discovered – just as it was in many other, well-documented, abduction cases.

When she was nineteen her son, Andras, was born, after a difficult pregnancy. Maria had always had problems with menstruation, having irregular, heavy and very painful periods, but nonetheless she was shocked to be told that she would not be able to have any more babies. Her shock turned to bewilderment when she was told that a previous operation had left adhesions on her uterus, a common enough medical reason for failure to carry a baby or conceive. Adhesions are fibrous tissue that can form anywhere in the body, usually at the site of an old operation scar, and are only dangerous when they are sited close to a major organ like the womb, which can be completely closed off by this thickened tissue. Maria was astonished by the diagnosis, because she had never had any gynaecological operations. The doctors were able to show her a small scar near her navel which was, they said, the entry site for a laparoscopy, a keyhole operation by which internal organs can be explored. The medical staff looked at her in disbelief when she said she knew nothing of this operation.

Despite the problems with the birth, the years after Andras was born were peaceful and happy for Maria, although there were odd occasions when he, like Jason, was found out of his cot. Sometimes he would be playing with a ball, as though there were someone in the room throwing it to him. When he was a little older he told his mother about a lady who came into his room, and from time to time Maria found him disconcertingly floating in the air above his bed.

It was not until he was nine or ten years old that her own experiences restarted. Then she started having episodes of missing time, once waking to find herself lying on the floor, naked, with her clothes neatly folded next to her. Her last memory had been of saying goodbye to friends the previous evening.

Like so many other abductees, on another occasion she saw a ball of bright, white light come through a wall and into her room. She reluctantly followed it, and was sucked through the external walls of the house and upwards, above the trees, until she found herself standing on firm ground with three small brown creatures in front of her, looking exactly like the mud midgets of her childhood encounters. They led her through corridors and an anteroom to a domed room with a hard table in the middle. A taller creature, off-white in colour, joined the others and communicated with her

173

telepathically, angering her with its intrusion, uninvited, into her thoughts.

A variety of medical procedures were then carried out. She was prodded with a rod which had a bright green light at its tip, one of her fingernails was cut, an instrument was stuck into her finger, and a scanner-type machine was lowered over her, covering her body with a bluish light. At one point a thin filament with a light at one end was inserted into her neck, causing her excruciating pain. When she flinched, one of the beings touched her on the forehead, and the pain disappeared. They also seemed to remove something from her stomach, via her navel.

She was then left alone for a while. Finally, when one of the creatures came in, she found herself experiencing a whole range of emotions – with the distinct impression that these were being deliberately induced in her. Subsequently she was 'shown' a whole series of mental images, culminating with one of the Earth blowing up.

She was returned to her own home in the early hours of the morning. When she woke the next day she had bruises at the points where the green-tipped prod had been used, she had blood under her nose as if she had had a nosebleed, and her feet were dirty. A clump of hair from the back of her head was missing.

The detailed memories of this abduction, which happened in 1990, came back to Maria over the ensuing months. One trigger was a strange musty smell, like rotting leaves, which she realised she had been aware of all the time she was with the creatures.

Maria has had one session of hypnotherapy to help her recall the events that have been happening to her since childhood, but decided (as Ann did) that she was remembering enough without any outside help or prompting. She has had other important experiences since this one, but has so far only recalled snatches of them.

Maria's theories about abduction will be explored more fully later in this book, but one conclusion she has come to is that it is important to speak out, and to support others going through similar experiences: 'I knew as soon as I saw Jason that he was telling the truth. When Ann rang me she told me things about him that had all the hallmarks of close encounter experiences, but I told her not to give me details of incidents: I wanted to hear them from Jason. Often, unwittingly, we put our own perspective on to other people's experiences, and I wanted to be sure that I heard it from him, in his own words.'

The first time Jason met Maria, Ann and Paul were there, too. Paul was, as usual, suspicious. After all, he'd had reservations about the psychiatrist, and he believed his fears had been confirmed. He knew Maria was another abductee – and he recognised that Tony Dodd had given the greatest help the family had received – but he was unconvinced about letting her counsel Jason. Ann, always the optimistic one, had spoken to Maria on the phone and felt sure she would be able to help their son.

Maria had the kettle on, in readiness for their arrival, and when she ushered them into her cosy home all three of them instantly felt at ease. Jason had no inhibitions about telling her about his abductions. and at later meetings Ann would find that she, too, could open up freely. To his great surprise, Paul was won over by Maria's quiet and almost matter-of-fact acceptance of what she was hearing from Jason, and he, too, came to trust her completely. He felt so relaxed in her company that he would often fall asleep on her settee as she talked to Jason and Ann: Maria believes this was not just because he was tired, but because his role, as the stable non-abductee in the family, means it is better for all of them if he remains not as involved as Ann, whilst still being supportive.

'Paul is a big, bluff man, but underneath he has a gentle spirit, and that's a tremendous strength for Jason,' she says. 'Paul is at peace with himself, and that will rub off on to Jason. Ann has been Jason's greatest strength, because she is intuitive and sensitive, and because she now recognises that she has experienced many of the things that are happening to him. There is a very close bond between her and Jason, but we should not underestimate Paul's importance.'

The therapy sessions with Maria were of enormous help. They did not reduce the number of abductions Jason experienced, but they helped him recognise and accept them, and for Ann, it meant there was another vital lifeline, apart from Tony Dodd.

Maria found Jason shy at first, but she opened him up by telling him about some of her 'weird dreams'. Then she asked him to tell her of his. 'Some of the things he told me really were dreams,' she says. 'But others were abductions which he wrapped up as though they were dreams. Who could blame him? For years he'd been told that's what they were. When I asked if he was afraid he said he wasn't, but he could not tell me how he did feel. So I told him what I thought he felt.'

Maria believes that Jason, like most abductees, feels slightly embarrassed and ashamed because he is not as afraid as he once was, and has a 'sense of love and endearment for the experiences'. When she suggested this he started to cry, recognising the truth in her words. 'He felt he should hate it, should fight it, should be afraid, but despite having some of all those emotions, there was another one: a sense of liking it.'

Jason told Maria, as he told me later, that he resents the fact that the aliens 'don't ask my permission first'. Maria believes that it was this sense of being taken against his will, victimised, that caused his behavioural problems at school. He was once accused of bullying: she believes that was his natural response to being 'bullied' himself, by the aliens. Once she explained this to him, he understood it and there were fewer disturbances at school.

She also gave him strategies for coping with his experiences: 'He felt it was out of his control, so I suggested things which allowed him, in small ways, to regain control. I told him to have a voice-operated tape-recorder with him at bedtime, so that he could focus on recording the experience. I know all the problems associated with using electrical equipment, but I felt the actual recording was less important than Jason having something to do. For the same reason I told him that, if he was conscious during an experience, he should count. Thinking about the numbers would keep his mind focused.'

Another idea she passed on was to draw a pattern of dots on his thigh. This, she says, has confused abductors in other cases: 'They have come back with the dots joined up, or washed off. The night Jason's legs were burned was, he told me, one of the nights when he forgot to draw the dots on his leg.'

As well as practical strategies, Maria encouraged Jason to establish telepathic communication with his abductors: in other words, not simply to listen to them but to feed back to them his feelings about what they were doing. Although this two-way traffic is in its infancy, it has, again, given Jason something to focus on during an abduction.

'Jason does not need as much day-to-day counselling as he did at first, because he now understands what is happening, and because he has remarkably supportive parents,' said Maria. 'I am sad for him that he has been forced to jump through other hoops, like seeing a psychiatrist. So many young abductees are sent to see psychiatrists, behavioural psychologists, and other so-called experts. They are given tests for epilepsy, and many adolescents are diagnosed as psychotic – either schizophrenic or manic depressive. It is very distressing for them, because in the end, if nobody believes them, they really do question their own sanity.'

Jason enjoyed his visits to Maria, and his phone conversations with her. Ann, too, as she began to regain her own memories, found Maria a great source of support. It was on the way back from seeing her one night that Ann and Jason had a strange – but not frightening – experience. It was a dark, wintry night, and the narrow Kent lanes were almost deserted. Jason, in the front passenger seat, suddenly plucked at Ann's sleeve and wordlessly gestured at a large circle of light to the left of the car, moving parallel to them as if keeping pace. Ann wanted to stop the car, but Jason urged her to carry on driving. The 'star' followed them every corner and bend of the way. About a mile from home Jason called out to Ann to look at it again. She pulled over, and watched it split into two parts, with a beautiful multi-coloured shower of light breaking from it. The smaller piece, another perfect circle of light, darted towards the car and hovered just yards away from it, before shooting vertically up into the air.

As the light approached the car, the engine stalled. (There are many examples of mechanical and electrical failure when UFOs are visible.) When it disappeared, Ann turned the ignition and drove on, the main 'star' still keeping pace with them at a distance. The smaller star zoomed erratically about the dark sky, every so often returning to its base and merging for a few seconds with the bigger ball of light. When Ann and Jason arrived home they were surprised to see Paul and Daniel outside in the garden, watching the lights in the sky. They later discovered that they were not the only ones who had seen the strange aerial display, as the local television station and the local newspaper were inundated with calls from people who had seen it.

★　★　★

177

Apart from the counselling and support she gave to both Jason and his parents, Maria Ward performed another important task. She put Jason directly in touch with James Basil. James is another abductee and, importantly, he is much closer to Jason's age than Maria or Tony. He and Jason can relate to each other, talk more freely, guide each other through the similar experiences they have both had. James is four years older than Jason, and his abduction memories stretch back to when he was five years old, but, like Jason, he did not realise what they meant until many years later. For James, the breakthrough came in 1994, when he was fifteen.

I travelled to Bristol to see James at his family home, where he lives with his parents and two younger sisters. He is a student, working hard to make up for the blip in his education which occurred shortly after he discovered he was an abductee, when his energies and emotions were channelled into coping with the magnitude of the revelation.

He is a pleasant, shy young man who, like most abductees, would give a lot never to have been selected for the attention of the aliens. Like Jason, Ann, Maria and so many other abductees, he has struggled to come to terms with it, but has now adjusted his life to accommodate it. There have been rough times, when schoolmates have called him names, but these have given him a resilience that will stand him in good stead in life.

Like Jason, James has patchy memories of his childhood encounters. His first is of waking to find himself sitting up in bed, aware that there was a lump under the blankets that was moving. It seemed, at first, that perhaps a cat or small animal was trapped, but the family did not have a pet. Then the creature under the bedclothes emerged: it was a small humanoid, about three feet tall with a large round head and large, almond-shaped eyes, like a cat's. The nose was flat, and the overall colour of the creature was blue-grey. It stood at the end of the bed, looking at James and yet he somehow sensed it was looking through him, beyond him. He called for his mother, and as she emerged from her bedroom along the landing the creature floated into the air, soundlessly, and settled on the wardrobe.

When his mother came into the room she said there was nothing there, and comforted James until he went to sleep again. The following day she noticed two small scars on James, one on his right shin and the other on his stomach. When she asked him what caused them he said, 'The goblin.' Later James climbed up and took down a box that was on top of the wardrobe. In the dust, two footprints could clearly be seen, each small foot with three toes. He showed it to a friend, another little boy of about the same age, and then he showed it to his mother. She threw the box away and told the boys it was a hedgehog. She later said it may have been a mouse. Although he was only small, James clearly remembers the musty damp-leaves smell that he noticed during the night, when the alien visitor was in his room, and he can recall what he saw very clearly. The smell, interestingly, is very similar to the smell Maria Ward remembers.

Shortly after this incident the family moved house, to the home where they now live, and James remembers having an instinctive fear of the room which subsequently became his bedroom, and from which he believes he has been abducted many times.

One recurring memory is a typical abduction scenario: James wakes to find himself lying on his back on a flat, cold surface, which he believes is a large dark grey or brown metal table. He tries to get off, but his legs are too short to reach the ground and he ends up jumping down and trying to run away, but he is in a circular room, and unable to find a way out.

At other times he wakes on the table to find five creatures with large heads, four standing at the sides and one at the head of the table. They cover his face with a plastic sheet, and he has the terrible feeling of suffocating. He tries to speak, telling them to stop whatever they are doing or he will tell his mum. Years later, when he talked to his family, one of his aunts admitted that she, too, saw figures in her bedroom and sometimes woke on the hard table.

In another recurring memory he and a group of other children are taken down a white tunnel by some alien creatures. The one holding James's hand is of similar height to the one he saw in his bedroom, but has an orangey-yellow skin, black eyes, a tiny nose and a slit for a mouth. It appears to communicate with him telepathically.

With the other children he is taken to a room where human figures and aliens are floating in the air, in much the same way that the original alien floated across his room to the wardrobe. The human figures appear to be copying the hand and leg motions of the aliens, who were paler than the one holding James. He distinctly feels that the humans were enjoying the experience, and he was briefly allowed to join in before being taken back down the tunnel.

His mother thought these events were dreams. Like Jason, James knew this was not so, but he believed, as small children do, that his experiences were normal, that everyone had them, and therefore allowed himself to be comforted.

Later, at the age of thirteen, he remembers waking in bed, turning over and putting his hand on to another hand which was on the edge of his bed. It felt cold. His first thought was that it was a burglar who had broken in, but then a thought appeared in his head, as if planted there. 'If you don't disturb it, it won't wake up.' In some way he cannot understand, he knew the creature was asleep and within seconds James, too, was asleep again. The following morning he remembered more: this time there were two alien creatures with large white heads, and he instinctively knew that one was male and one was female. They floated him across the landing, and through the window he could see a UFO, with a ring of lights around the bottom. He was taken on board, but has no memory of what happened there. Then he was back in his bedroom and the two creatures were with him. One of them told him to go to sleep and he did, instantly.

In June 1993, when he was fourteen, James was lying in bed listening to the radio at midnight when he noticed a light on the ceiling and the window, a strip of light that moved across the room. It was coming into his room from the bathroom window, on the other side of the landing. He watched it for a few minutes until it disappeared, and then, fifteen minutes later, a round ball of light appeared, floating up the window. It had a white surround and orange inside it with a black-and-white centre. Within the orange segment were lots of small round shapes, which James described as 'like blood cells'.

It was further away than the strip of light had been, seeming to be hovering over the end of the back garden, about a hundred feet from the house. It winked out and then reappeared, then seemed to hop to the right, out of sight. James remembers no more until the next morning, when he discovered that the girl next door had seen something similar, hovering over the garden shed until it 'hopped' across the hedge into the field behind. Within a week or two all the local news bulletins were full of reports from the Bristol area of strange balls of light over the city, and there were sightings throughout that month.

The following winter James experienced what he refers to as 'the main memory'. He was in the bathroom, where the window looks out over the garden and the field beyond, when he noticed three objects landing in the field. They seemed to be small spacecraft with yellow windows and red lights on top. As he watched them his mind was suffused with the thought that he was not the only observer, that all around the world there were other humans watching similar things.

The three objects appeared to be about forty feet beyond the trees at the end of the garden, and James could see there was a creature in the middle craft, busily working on something with his head turned away from James. He turned round, and James frantically hoped he would not be seen, but within a split second three alien heads turned towards him, one from each craft. He believes they could 'hear me talking in my head'. He communicated telepathically with the middle one, and was told that he had seen too much. In less time than it takes to click fingers he was transported to the field, with one of the alien's faces just inches from his. He felt sick, dizzy and his vision blurred. As he stared into the creature's eyes he saw swirls of colour, and then blacked out.

When he came round the three creatures were standing in front of him. The one in the middle was about five feet tall, and the other two were about a foot shorter. The centre one had yellow/orange skin, a small nose with two tiny nostrils, black eyes with discernible pupils and a slit for a mouth, but with vaguely human lips – very similar to the one who led him down the tunnel in his recurring memory. The smaller ones had purple skin, shiny and hard-looking, flat heads and were much less humanoid. It was the larger one who communicated with James, while the others appeared to stare across him rather than at him.

As the taller one addressed James, a beam of blue light sprang from it and connected to James's chest. Another beam of the same light went from the alien up into the sky, where it formed a giant projection screen. On the screen appeared a series of diagrams and mathematical formulae – none of which James could understand – but these images gave way to a vision of a beautiful city in the middle of a desert, with golden sunlit buildings rising from the sand. As he watched the city, which he somehow knew represented the world, it blew up.

James asked the creature how he would remember all this, and the reply came: 'You will remember when you need to know.'

He could sense that the two smaller aliens were becoming edgy and impatient, and the middle one said, in the deep echoing voice that just appeared in James's brain, that he would not take much longer. The beam of light went off. James, profoundly moved by the pictures he had seen, begged the aliens not to leave him. The tall one told him: 'Don't worry, we will be back soon.' He told James they came from the sky.

With that, they each returned to their craft, which had been concealed in the darkness. The lights went on again, more muted than before but enough to illuminate the shapes inside. The three spaceships rose twenty feet in the air, their outlines gradually fading until they were completely transparent and James could see them no more.

The memory of this event came back to him several months later, although he is clear about when it happened to within a few weeks. After this memory surfaced, many more came back to James, replaying themselves as if on the screen in the sky. It was only when he saw a copy of *UFO* magazine, the one produced by Quest International, that he found someone to contact. Again, it was Tony Dodd, Jason's saviour, who was able to help James make sense of what was happening. Once again, Tony was able to reassure a frightened and confused teenager that he was not alone: as he had been told telepathically, there are indeed hundreds of people across the world having similar experiences.

'It was such a relief to know that I was not going mad, and that there was someone I could talk to who would believe me,' James says, echoing the sentiments of Jason and Ann Andrews.

James was put in touch with Maria, and ultimately she arranged for Jason to contact him. The two boys first spoke around about the middle of 1996, and they have been in fairly constant telephone

182

Sweetbriar Cottage, in Slade Green: Ann's dream home where the strange and frightening events started.

The dense woods beyond Hawksnest Farm, where watchful strangers have been seen and mysterious noises heard.

The four bizarrely mutilated mice, lined up inside the gate to the farm – just as the Andrews found them.

Cardi, the stallion Ann dreamed she saw being operated on by strange men in a clearing in the woods near the farm. The next day, Cardi was found wandering in the woods – but there was no sign of how he escaped.

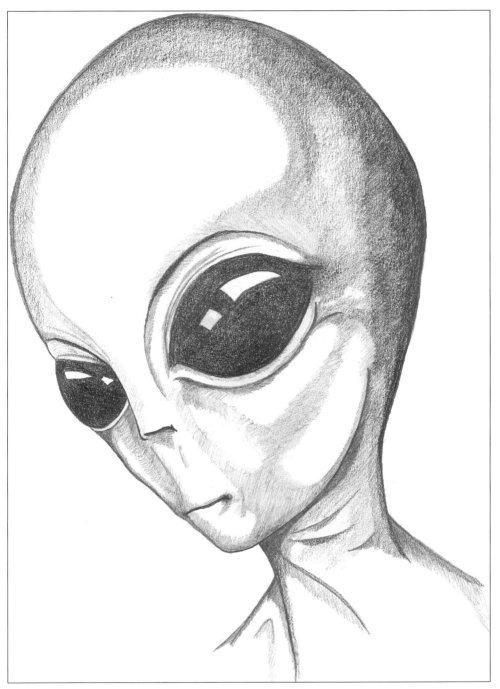

Ann's sketch of one of the 'little ones', the small aliens that regularly abduct Jason. They work in groups of six or seven with a taller figure controlling them. Ann has drawn this sketch from her son's description of the unearthly intruders who come for him in the night.

Daniel at 17: he knows his brother's experiences are real, and worries about him.

Jason at 14: his normal appearance hides his distress at being abducted.

contact since. James can offer Jason one major comfort: he has not been abducted since 1995, and since 1996 he has been able to sleep with the lights off in his bedroom. After his last abduction, he was given a telepathic message telling him: 'You have got to learn to live by yourself for a while.' He knows this could be interpreted as meaning he may one day be abducted again, but for a while he has a breathing space to concentrate on his college work, and deep inside himself, James is confident that his encounters with aliens are over for ever.

His later abductions took on a mystical dimension, with the aliens communicating with him about the future of mankind, in much the same way that they did with Professor Mack's clients, and with Tony Dodd himself. James also saw more strange lights, and experienced a classic 'missing time' episode.

James has found the contact with Jason mutually supportive, and he's pleased he's been able to help the younger boy. Occasionally they have seemed to be telepathic: James has been about to phone Jason when the phone has rung with Jason on the line.

'I believed Jason straightaway – he told me things that only an abductee could know. He rings me when he is upset, when something has just happened or when he senses something is about to happen. He seems to want to go on talking forever, as if that will keep them at bay,' says James.

Not only do the two boys have the actual abduction experience to share, but they also compare notes about other people's reactions to them: both have endured name-calling at school, both have been referred to psychiatrists because they have appeared, by conventional standards, to be disturbed, and both have had their education disrupted. James was away from school for months because of bullying. Jason, a more resilient youth, has not so far been so badly affected, but his schoolwork has undoubtedly suffered because he has been tired and unhappy on the days after abductions.

James believes that being abducted was, ultimately, a positive experience, which has given him a headstart in life, because he understands more than most people of his age. Like Jason, his home has been surrounded by other paranormal activity, with weird electrical effects. James is unable to wear a watch, as they simply stop working within hours of him putting one on his wrist. Like

Jason, too, the experiences appear to be generational: his grandmother had twelve children, of whom half have seen unexplained objects in the sky and have had other paranormal experiences, with one aunt probably also being an abductee.

There was another, unexpected, source of support for Jason. At Maria Ward's suggestion, Ann and Paul braced themselves to tell other members of their family what their son was suffering. Maria explained that the people close to Jason should be told, so that he would be free to talk to them about what he was going through, but she warned them that it would be unusual if all members of the family accepted Jason's story at face value. Ann and Paul should, Maria suggested, tell their relatives that, no matter what their own beliefs, it was vital that Jason be listened to and not mocked. One of the stresses of being an abductee, she explained, is constantly having to bottle up feelings and experiences for fear of being ridiculed. If, in his own close circle, Jason could avoid this, it would be of enormous benefit to him.

As predicted, the reaction from the family was mixed when Ann and Paul broached the subject. Paul's mother Shirley was confused, unwilling to believe in aliens, but happy to do anything for the benefit of her grandson. She could not promise to accept everything he said as true, but she could promise to be supportive and understanding, and willing to listen to him. Ann's two brothers reacted entirely differently, and not as Ann would have predicted. Stephen, whom she imagined would be sceptical, believes and accepts his nephew's story. David challenges and refuses to credit the alien theory.

Stephen and his wife Anita were at first unsure about Ann's story: it seemed farfetched and unlikely, even though they accepted the possibility of other civilisations existing in space. On a holiday to Greece they became friendly with another family, who came from Edgbaston, Birmingham, and after a few days the father confided that they were on holiday to rest and to try to bring some normality back into their lives. He, he told them, was an abductee. It took courage to confess it, and at first Stephen reacted predictably by scoffing and treating it as a joke. It was only when he heard the full story that he was struck by the amazing similarity to the stories that his sister was telling him about his nephew Jason, and when he returned home he rang Ann to apologise for not taking her seriously enough.

Ann's mother Vi has proved to be an enormous support from the first time Ann spoke to her, and registered no surprise at all. It was then that she shared with Ann her suspicions that Ann's father Stan was the genetic source of the strange goings-on in the family. Vi had seen at first hand the weird happenings that surrounded her much-loved grandson (she had been very keen to have the cottage at Slade Green exorcised), so although she had not anticipated Ann's explanation, she knew there must be something at the bottom of it.

It was not long before Vi witnessed more events which, if she had any residual doubts, fully convinced her that Jason is telling the truth. Vi is a devoted granny to all her four grandchildren – Daniel, Jason and their two young female cousins – and planned a caravan holiday in early July 1996 for all of them, with herself and one of her friends in charge. She was really looking forward to a whole week of spoiling her brood, and even Daniel, who considered himself too big for family holidays, was happy to go with Vi, knowing that she'd be more indulgent than his parents. When, at the last minute, Vi's friend had to pull out through illness, Ann was invited to fill the breach, to her sons' disappointment – they knew they wouldn't get away with as much with Mum in tow – but for Ann it was a much-needed break.

They drove to Minster, on the Isle of Sheppey, with the two little girls babbling excitedly the whole way. As soon as the adults had filled in the paperwork for the caravan, the four youngsters were off to the swimming pool, which was pleasantly empty so early in the summer season, setting the pattern for most of the days ahead.

It was Jason's thirteenth birthday on the Tuesday, so the previous night he went to bed early, in the twin room he was sharing with his mother. Ann, too, went to bed early, but in her case it was because of a severe headache. She fell asleep as soon as her head touched the pillow, and slept deep and dreamlessly until the early morning, when thin sunshine was filtering through a crack in the curtains. When she woke her headache was so bad that she could hardly see. She staggered out of bed, pausing to pick Jason's duvet off the floor and re-covering him, and made her way to the narrow galley kitchen to find some painkillers.

Turning on the tap for a glass of water, she was surprised to hear Vi call nervously, 'Who's out there?'

'It's only me, Mum. Sorry to wake you, I was just getting some aspirin,' Ann said.

The door to the room Vi was sharing with one of the little girls opened, and Vi emerged, holding a blood-stained tissue to her nose. Her long white nightdress had large blood stains down the front. She peered around as if making sure Ann was alone, and then made her way across the kitchen to the table, sitting down heavily on one of the chairs. Ann put on the kettle to make tea, and then sat down with her mother. Vi looked at her with fear in her eyes. Her nosebleed seemed to have stopped, and as she sipped her tea she told Ann what had happened in the night.

More than a year later, she told me the same story, and again her eyes filled with tears as she recalled the terror of that night. We were not in a strange caravan in the early hours of the morning, but in her neat living room, with all her familiar furniture and her much-loved collection of dolls around her: yet there was no escaping the fear she was reliving.

She had woken suddenly in the night. A hairslide she had used to clip her hair off her face was digging in, and she assumed this was what woke her. She pulled it free and leaned over to place it on the bedside table, but as she moved she noticed a very bright light coming from under the crack in the door. At the same moment she flopped back on the pillows, dropping the hairslide. She was unable to move, paralysed completely, apart from her eyes, which remained open.

'I felt so heavy and there was so much light, so much light. I really felt I'd had a stroke. I tried to call out for help but my face was paralysed. The light was bright, overwhelming. I lay there and heard all this noise, shuffling noise, coming from the living room. Then suddenly the light was gone, as if it had been switched off,' Vi said.

Immediately, she was able to move, but as she did her nose started to bleed, the worst nosebleed she has ever experienced (she has only had two or three in her entire life). There was blood not just on her nightdress, but on the sheets, pillow cases and Ann even had to scrub it out of the carpet. Vi stayed awake, terrified of closing her eyes, until she heard Ann moving about in the kitchen. She was scared the night-time visitors had returned, but there was no bright light and there was something comfortably normal with the noise Ann made opening the cupboard for the aspirin and running the water.

Ann persuaded her mother to return to bed, after taking off her nightdress and soaking it to remove the blood stains. As it was daylight, Vi agreed it was safe to go to sleep. Ann immediately checked on Jason, but he was sleeping soundly.

When the children were up and demanding breakfast, Ann cajoled them to be quiet, to allow their grandmother to sleep. She was surprised when one of her small nieces announced, indignantly, that: 'Nanny isn't the only one who needs some sleep.' The ten-year-old went on to say that she had been kept awake by 'all those noisy motorcycles going round and round the caravan'. She said she knew there were hundreds of them, because when she looked out of the caravan window she saw all their bright headlights zooming past. She'd been going to wake Ann, but had fallen asleep.

Ann tried to conceal her alarm when Jason appeared, sleepily rubbing his eyes. Daniel and the girls joined together in a muted chorus of 'Happy Birthday'. Jason opened his cards and presents, and his cousins excitedly ranged the cards on the narrow window ledge. Ann, sensing her son's distraction, sent Daniel outside with the girls, and as soon as they had gone Jason fell into her arms, sobbing bitterly.

'They came on my birthday, Mum. Why? Why can't I just have my birthday, a holiday?'

Ann hugged and comforted him, but they were interrupted by her six-year-old niece running in and demanding they go outside to see the 'big helicopter planes'. Jason went to the bathroom to hide his tears, and Ann followed her niece. There were eight Chinook helicopters flying low over the campsite. Following closely was a small black helicopter – neither Ann nor Daniel were able to identify it – which was flying extremely low. Ann estimated it was only about 100 feet above the roofs of the mobile homes, and it seemed to be circling the area. She left Daniel to look after the girls, who were fascinated by the air display, and went back inside. Jason emerged from the bathroom, saying he felt better, but he spoke in a curious flat monotone that worried Ann: she felt he was simply mouthing a platitude, that he did not feel better but was simply assuaging her worries. At that same moment Vi appeared, still pale but feeling much better in broad daylight. She wished her grandson a happy birthday, and gave him a hug. To her surprise, Jason pulled away from her arms, squealing in pain, and covering the left side of his body with his hands. Ann lifted his shirt, and both she and her mother were shocked to see a large, angry red swelling. Vi would have instantly called for a doctor, but Ann, by now so familiar with Jason's 'injuries', prevailed on her to wait and see. True enough, by the end of the day there was no sign of the swelling.

It was Vi who was unwell that day. Although she is not young, she is strong and fit and quite unaccustomed to being laid low by headaches, but a shopping trip had to be curtailed and for the rest of that day she was forced to lie in a darkened room. Every night for the remainder of the holiday she barricaded herself into her bedroom with suitcases.

Ann had another problem to deal with in the ensuing days. Jason, who had been known to have temper tantrums at school and at home, suddenly focused all his anger on his mother. He went out of his way to disobey her, to be insolent and rude at every possible opportunity. It was much more than the usual teenage resentment about the rules and regulations parents inflict on them. Jason was not railing against being sent to bed at a certain time, or being told to turn down the noise, or being forbidden to play dangerous games around the pool. His fury was personal and deep. Ann, who had always been his closest ally and friend, who above all was able to empathise with him, became the target for a bitter fury.

Embarrassed that her mother and her nieces were witnessing Jason's vitriol, she tried to make light of it. She responded to his outbursts by teasing him, trying to turn his temper into a joke. A highly-developed sense of humour is a common denominator in all the Andrews family, and each of them is verbally equipped to find a witty response to any situation. Whenever Daniel had been adolescently sulky Ann had always managed to laugh him out of it, but the technique fell flat with Jason, who scowled at her or subjected her to even more abuse. In the end, to minimise the discomfort of everybody, Ann kept out of his way and kept quiet.

Talking to Paul from the payphone on the campsite, she explained what was happening, and Paul agreed that it was best to get through the holiday and to tackle Jason when they were home again. Ann knew that her husband would not let Jason get away with calling her the names he was using, and she dreaded the confrontation. What puzzled her most, though, was why Jason had turned on her. His anger at the aliens was understandable, but why was it all concentrated on his mother?

They were having a meal in a pizza restaurant on the last evening when it all came out. Despite Ann's attempts to avoid antagonising him, he found an excuse for a row – and suddenly began to scream at his mother that if he had not been born to her 'they' would not come for him, he would be normal, he would be like all his friends. His face flushed and with angry tears starting down his cheeks, he fled from the restaurant, leaving the rest of the party shell-shocked and embarrassed as all the other diners watched the drama unfold. Daniel leapt up and followed his brother, muttering to Ann that it would be all right. Vi, shocked and angry, also went after Jason. However much allowance she made for the traumas she knew her grandson endured, Vi was not going to let him upset his mother like this. Ann, tears running down her cheeks, stayed with her little nieces, who had stopped eating and were looking worried. Ann told them that Jason was not feeling very well.

That night Ann did not sleep. She knew Jason was right. He had inherited from her the colour of his hair and the fairness of his complexion, and he had received a more deadly inheritance: he was an abductee. She felt wretched, both guilty and helpless to do anything about it. She also felt resentment, because she, too, was an abductee and it was not something she had chosen. She was as much a victim as her son. There was nothing either of them could do to change it, and however much she felt for Jason, she also resented being held accountable for it.

They were a subdued party travelling home. When they dropped Vi at her house she insisted she had enjoyed it, but there were tears in her eyes as she hugged her daughter. Later, she would tell me that it was then, after her night of terror and Jason's outburst, that she first fully appreciated what Ann and Paul live with on a day-to-day basis.

CHAPTER 13

THE PLANNING JUNGLE

Who – or what – wants to keep the Andrews family away from Hawksnest Farm? For years they have been fighting to move back on to the land they own – and for years they have suffered a mysterious series of setbacks.

When they were forced to leave the mobile home at the farm in 1990 they were sure it was a temporary move. They had bought Hawksnest Farm with the sole intention of living there, looking after their animals, bringing up their children and, in their dreams, still being there into their old age. It was the home where they intended to settle. They were never unrealistic: they knew that, by farming standards, it was only a small package of land, and they knew they would never become rich from it, but they had hopes of building it up, eventually expanding it. Besides, both Ann and Paul felt they had learned a valuable lesson when he lost his job. They had learned to live on a much-reduced income, and were happy to trade the credit cards and the material possessions for a different kind of happiness. It was quality of life they sought, not a huge bank balance. They don't drink or smoke or need to have a busy social life, so they are, as Ann says 'cheap to run'. They simply wanted to have an outdoor life, surrounded by animals, with just enough income to bring up the boys and keep food in the cupboards.

When the council rehoused them, the family saw it as a temporary measure. They reluctantly accepted it, as they realised they had been naïve not getting permission to live on the land in the first place, and also because the hard winter had made life in the mobile home difficult. Even before they moved, they confidently put in an application for planning permission to live on the farm in a mobile home, sure that this was little more than a formality. When they left, it was with a clear intention to be back within months, as soon as the planning details could be sorted out, but their application was turned down by Tonbridge and Malling Borough Council. It was a shock for both of them: they know of many similar small-holdings where the owners live in mobile homes until they get full permission to build a house on the site, and Paul and Ann had assumed they would be allowed to do the same. Unofficially, they had been told as much by one of the council staff when they drew up their application. So the notice telling them that permission had been refused was an unexpected blow, but they remained optimistic. They immediately lodged an appeal, supported by a letter from the local police confirming that vandalism and theft (and they had already been victims of both of these) would be inevitable if the property was uninhabited. Paul was particularly worried about the risks to his remaining animals.

The letter telling them the appeal had been turned down came when Ann was at home alone. She slumped on to the settee, for a moment unable to take in the meaning of the words. By the time Paul returned home, she was able to conceal the worst of her despair, but it was a grim evening for both of them.

Stunned, they were initially unsure what to do. Despite this major setback, there was little time to indulge their disappointment. There were financial problems, because as soon as they left the farm the bank trebled their loan repayments, and Paul was working all the hours he could to pay this off and keep the family financially buoyant. Ann's time was spent looking after the remaining animals, and bringing up her children. Added to the normal pressures and strains of family life with two growing sons, they had all the worries of Jason's problems.

Eventually, when the boys were old enough not simply to be less demanding, but also to be a positive asset in terms of helping on the farm, Ann and Paul decided once again to pour all their energies into rebuilding, re-stocking and eventually moving back to Hawksnest Farm.

This time, they were determined to do things right. The farm buildings had suffered in the intervening years, as they had never had the time or money to maintain them properly, and all their original plans for the farm had been put on hold after the mysterious death of their cattle, but there were horses, geese and Prudence the pig, still living very happily on the smallholding. On fine summer days, when the whole family went to the farm, usually with at least one of the dogs in tow, the old dreams were rekindled, and Paul and Ann would stand side by side, planning where they would house the cows, how many hens Ann would have, whether or not to breed pigs again.

The first step they took, before applying again to the council for permission to move back on to the land, was to commission a report from ADAS, the government's Agricultural Development Advisory Service. Since April 1997 ADAS has been privatised, so it is no longer an official arm of the Ministry of Agriculture Fisheries and Food, but at the time the Andrews consulted it, in 1995, it was government-funded and provided the greatest source of professional expertise on agricultural matters available in Britain. As Paul Andrews says, he was determined to make no mistakes: he wanted, for his own sake, to be sure that his plans for Hawksnest Farm were viable, and he also wanted to demonstrate to the planning authorities that he was proposing a sound and well-researched business.

ADAS sent Dr Elwyn Rees, a Senior Livestock Consultant, to carry out the report on the feasibility of Paul's plans. Dr Rees is a highly regarded figure in agricultural circles and was also, at the time, liaising between the government and cattle farmers over the BSE problem.

Paul's building plans for the new cattle unit had been professionally drawn up, and Dr Rees found no fault with them. His fifteen-page report made various recommendations, but very positively concluded that Hawksnest Farm could be turned into a viable cattle rearing unit, with 240 calves reared per year in batches of forty-eight. He estimated the Andrews would make more than £17,000 per year, and after the payment of fixed costs – repairs, insurance, water, electricity, telephone and contracting out muck removal – they would have an income of just under £13,000. They were not going to live like millionaires, but it was an adequate amount to keep the whole family, and it would be supplemented by the poultry, the sale of horses and possibly some pig rearing. Paul and Ann were sure they would survive – and thrive – if they were given permission to go ahead.

They also thoroughly researched the capital cost of the project. Paul had already bought quite a lot of second-hand building material, and he had also persuaded a friend, a professional building contractor, to help out by lending building equipment. This friend also worked out the costings, and concluded they could erect a satisfactory building for the calves for £25,000. Armed with the ADAS report and the costings, Paul visited a local bank manager who was impressed by his plans, and put in writing an offer to lend £46,000. With a rescheduling of their existing loan payments and the elimination of the rental payments on their house, they were only going to have to pay out an extra £40 per month.

They intended to do most of the building work themselves, with the help of friends and relatives (the Andrews are friendly with several professional tradesmen who were prepared to help out either free or at substantially reduced rates). Paul, a big man, relished the prospect of labouring on his own buildings, and both Daniel and Jason were rapidly reaching the ages where they would be useful on a building site. Paul and Ann knew that it would take them some time to complete the project by doing it this way, but it would save them a vast amount of money, and would allow Paul to carry on with his driving job to fund the work as it went along. If planning permission were granted, it would last for five years, an ample amount of time for their self-build scheme.

Confident once again that they would be given the go-ahead by the council, they contacted the farmer over whose land their access road runs, and he gave them permission to run in a water and electricity supply. They secured a quote from the local water authority for the cost.

The plans, with detailed back-up information, were submitted at the end of August 1995, with the fee of £1,440 required by the council. Once again, the Andrews felt that it was only a matter of months before they would be back at Hawksnest Farm full time. Once again, to the amazement of everyone concerned, they were wrong.

Over the ensuing months more details were requested by the council. Leafing through the huge file of correspondence Ann has meticulously kept, it is hard to understand why so many problems were raised. For a time, the council appeared to be obsessed with wanting to know how Paul and Ann intended to fund the development. Despite the evidence of the offer of a loan from the bank, plus the ADAS viability study, the main objection seemed to be that there were insufficient funds available. Both Vi and Shirley, each desperately keen to see the family back on its feet, had offered them substantial gifts, and Vi duly wrote to the council confirming this. The Andrews hoped to use these gifts to reduce the size of the bank loan they would need – but even without the money from Vi and Shirley, the bank loan would have been sufficient to cover their costs.

However, there were other objections. Aspects of the building design were changed several times to meet suggestions and requirements laid down by the council. A detailed breakdown of the capital costs had to be provided, practically down to the last nail Paul intended to use. To allay concern that the new buildings would be visible from the footpaths running next to the land (which are hardly busy with pedestrians at any time of the year) Paul took professional advice on how to revitalise the hedgerows, and which trees to plant to provide extra visual screening.

The objections kept on coming, and in the end, very reluctantly, Ann and Paul accepted that they would not be allowed to live at the farm. Being rehoused by the council so close to it had seemed like a godsend initially, but meant that it was harder for them to justify needing to live on the premises, although, as Paul stresses, where animals are concerned it is always better to live close to them. They removed the mobile home from their planning application again, confident that this huge concession would be enough to satisfy the planning officials.

'We felt that for some reason they really did not want us living there. Nobody would tell us why – we tried many times to get them to say what the problem was,' says Ann. 'In the end, we decided that the most important thing was to restart the business properly, and if that meant living away from the farm, we'd put up with that.

'It was a terrible decision to make. Living at Hawksnest had been our dream for so long, and it is hard to give up your dreams. But I would do anything to get Paul back into working with cows, because that is when he is at his happiest.'

In the end, with the help of professional planning advisers the

Andrews felt they had jumped through enough hoops, and that they would surely get the go-ahead for the calf unit. Their optimism and confidence had suffered many blows in the months that they had been battling to come up to the council's exacting standards, but even they were unprepared to be turned down, yet again.

The reasons given were that the smallholding would not make enough money to support the family, and that there was consequently a danger that the buildings would become a 'white elephant', and would either become a candidate for conversion to a house or become derelict. Ann and Paul had put forward a way around the conversion risk, by suggesting that the council grant permission with a restriction attached, that the buildings were only to be used for agricultural purposes.

They are aggrieved that their detailed financial breakdowns and the ADAS viability study appear not to have been given sufficient weight by the council, who relied in their decision on the advice of the Kent County Council official whose own calculations suggested they would earn less than £10,000 a year.

Ann remembers when they lived on the farm before, with far fewer cattle. She applied at the time for a government benefit for families on low income, Family Credit. Her application was rejected, on the grounds that the farm income was too high – an ironic twist that they should subsequently be turned down for permission to expand and improve the place because the potential earnings were deemed to be too low.

'How can they have it both ways? The farm earns too much for us to qualify for the benefits given to families on low income – yet it doesn't, according to the council, generate enough to support us. Why do they disregard the figures drawn up by the expert from ADAS, someone who knows all there is to know about farming?'

Another reason given for turning them down is that the small-holding is on Green Belt land, and that it has to be demonstrated, therefore, that its development is 'directly related to agriculture or other uses appropriate to a rural area'. It is hard to imagine anything more agricultural or 'appropriate' than rearing cattle, and Hawksnest Farm was listed as agricultural land before the Andrews bought it.

The County Council official whose professional opinion scuppered their dream also reported to the planning committee that he was concerned about their plans to go into rearing beef cattle while the BSE scare was on: an objection that the ADAS expert Dr Rees told them did not stand. His informed opinion (and he was extremely well-informed, appointed by the government to liaise between MAFF and the farmers) was that they would be in a highly advantageous position, rearing calves, as older cattle were being slaughtered and farmers were facing the need to re-stock.

It was in May 1996 that they were finally turned down. Ann wept that evening: the first time that she had given in to her feelings. During the months of struggle she had deliberately kept cheerful, building Paul's optimism at every opportunity. She knew how much the farm meant to him, even more than it did to her, and she knew how angry and impatient he was with all the red tape and bureaucracy they were forced to wade through. Several times she had to restrain him from exploding with anger when they were dealing with council officials who seemed determined not to listen to them. She felt the injustice no less than he did, but knew that it was better not to inflame the situation.

Paul's anger was exacerbated by seeing other planning applications sail through, with no question of the applicants having to provide the kind of detailed financial information that they had to produce. They were both bitter that the faith the bank and the ADAS expert had in them could be ridden over so roughshod. They were also puzzled: they felt they had been singled out for unusual and mysterious treatment. The subtext seemed to be that the council were afraid that they were only applying to build the unit so that, in future years, they could reapply to convert it into a luxury home.

There are, not far from Hawksnest Farm, examples of this being done: it has long been a speculator's way of getting around Green Belt legislation. Just down the road from the Andrews farm, a mobile home on a smallholding has been replaced, with council permission, by a grand five-bedroomed house. The great irony is that the Andrews never had any intention of doing it. They want nothing more than to live on their land and farm it. For Paul and Ann, happiness would be complete if they could step outside their home (albeit a mobile home) into a few fields full of calves, horses and poultry, with space for Paul's beloved dogs.

★ ★ ★

Was it the worry about Green Belt violations, or the lack of financial viability, that ruled out the Andrews being given permission to live at Hawksnest Farm – or was there another, more sinister, reason? The council will, predictably, say nothing more to me than that the reasons were given when the planning application was turned down, but Tony Dodd, Paul and Ann are suspicious. Paul says he has been told, unofficially, by a friend who has good contacts at the council, that the authorities are implacably opposed to the land ever being occupied. There was certainly a very rapid reaction when the family were discovered to be living there: they were rehoused, by the council, into a good house with a large garden, straightaway. Other families have to spend time in temporary accommodation, and there is, as with any council, a lengthy waiting list for three-bedroom houses. Even the problem of their dogs was instantly accommodated: the housing association which owns the house allowed them to move all three dogs (they now have more) in with them.

Ann remembers, ruefully, the time when they were desperate to be given a council house, before they bought the farm, when their cottage was threatened with repossession. They were offered a flat in an area where they did not want to bring up their young sons, and they would have had to get rid of their dogs. Although it was a different council, it is hard to believe that the pressure for housing is so different just a few miles deeper into Kent.

So what is so significant about the farm that there should be such determination to stop them living there?

Hawksnest Farm is close to the Ministry of Defence land, Mereworth Training Ground. The smallholding is separated from the MoD land by a stretch of woodland which is owned by an absentee Arab landowner, who contracts out the maintenance of it. As it is dense woodland, the maintenance involves occasional tree felling and pruning, but there is nobody permanently working on this land.

Mereworth Training Ground is used, as its name suggests, for training soldiers. It belongs to the Cinq Ports Training Authority, a regional Territorial Army area and, officially, it is the volunteers of the Territorial Army who use the site. Because of this, it is busier at weekends than during the week, with convoys of military personnel arriving late at night. It is fenced off from the woodland with barbed wire in places and there are notices warning the public to keep out. Inevitably, locals have wandered on to the land: children on bikes or horseriders who have failed to see the signs. When they have been spotted they have been shepherded off: escorted by army personnel to the edge of the MoD property. When Ann's brother David inadvertently rode on to the land, while out riding Craven, he was summarily escorted off, a soldier leading the horse and another, with a gun, walking behind. Children who have played on there have come back with empty bullet casings, and both children and adults talk of being told by soldiers that there are unexploded shells around. A fire that raged through the woodland adjoining Mereworth in April 1997 was no respecter of military boundaries, and the seventy firemen called out to fight it had to withdraw temporarily as the heat caused small explosions. When the firemen discovered from the soldiers who were at the training ground, that the bangs and crackles were only the residue of explosive left in spent cartridges, and that there was no live ammunition around, they carried on and extinguished the blaze.

Many local people have heard a strange high-pitched whining noise which emanates from the direction of the training ground. It is not constant, occurs infrequently, and is so high-pitched that some people are unable to hear it, but those who do are very aware of it. The Andrews, being the nearest people to the training ground when they are at the farm, hear it every few months, and it irritates them: as Ann says, you don't realise how much it is annoying you until it stops, when the sense of relief is enormous. She, Paul, Daniel and Jason have all heard it. It usually lasts for a couple of hours, and during that time the animals are restless and unhappy.

Sue and Billy Rutland and their children live a quarter of a mile away from Hawksnest Farm, in their converted oast house. They have heard the humming noise on several occasions, most notably in August 1996, when it persisted for about two hours in the late afternoon. Their teenage daughter Laura had a severe headache, which continued all evening, after the noise had stopped. In June 1997 Sue was again aware of the noise, and this time it lasted for only half an hour, in the morning. They are certain that it comes from the MoD land.

They have both also witnessed a strange light, which moved past their home, running parallel to the training ground. Billy saw it first, at half past eleven in the evening, as he walked home from The Chequers pub a few hundred yards away in the village of Crouch. He had only been to the pub for a couple of pints of beer at the end of a long working day and he was certainly not the worse for drink.

'I noticed what looked like a flock of birds or a shoal of fish in the sky. I couldn't make out what it was, so I stopped to watch it. It was a flat disc made up of wisps of light, between eighty and one hundred feet in diameter.

'It was turning – going one-and-a-half turns in one direction and then back. Then it would disappear and reappear. Each cycle took fourteen seconds – I timed it by counting, and it was absolutely regular.'

Billy watched it for twenty minutes, and then it began to move, still carrying out its turning manoeuvre, in the direction of his home. He followed it to the house – about a hundred yards – and woke Sue. She came outside with him and from their garden they both watched the light formation for another twenty minutes as it moved slowly across their land, standing still for a while over their stables, and eventually completely disappearing.

'It was the strangest thing I have ever seen,' says Billy Rutland. 'It was made up of feathery wisps of light, a bit like a chocolate whirl. They would build up in density, turn one-and-a-half complete revolutions, stop, then reverse the movement, and then disappear.'

Billy, who in earlier life worked on boats on the River Thames, is used to navigating by buoys, and used the standard technique of counting the time between the disappearance and reappearance. It never varied: it always vanished for exactly eight seconds, and the whole cycle always took fourteen seconds.

Neither he nor Sue have ever been able to explain what they saw.

'Billy woke me because he knew nobody would believe him the next day if he was the only witness,' says Sue. 'I'm sure, if we hadn't both seen it, we'd begin to doubt it ourselves.'

The Andrews have never seen anything similar, but they have on several occasions seen bright lights which hover over the MoD land.

Tony Dodd is cynical about the official version of the use of the land as an area for training Territorial Army volunteers.

'Where Hawksnest Farm is sited is typical of the kind of area which attracts UFO activity. There are more UFO sightings over and around woodland than anywhere else, and this holds true not just in Britain but across the world. There is also UFO activity around military establishments.

'Naturally, if aliens are studying our planet with a view to invading or colonising, they are more interested in our defence systems than anything else, so any place where there is military activity is a magnet to them.

'We do not know what goes on at Mereworth, because the MoD will not necessarily tell us the truth. Military areas which appear insignificant may not be so, but even if it is nothing more than a training area, that will be enough to make it of interest to aliens who, we know, are studying all aspects of human life.

'There appears to have been an orchestrated campaign to keep the Andrews off this land. Their cattle all died mysteriously, and every attempt by them to move back there has been blocked.

'If secret work is being carried out at the army base, it is possible that a leak of radiation killed the cows, and that's why their bodies were removed by men wearing cover-all suits. If that sort of experimentation is going on, it is obvious that the army would not want a family living close by: either because they would observe too much, or because they might themselves be in danger. They can cover up a few cows dying, but it would be more difficult if something happened to a family.'

Tony Dodd believes that the Andrews were a focus for alien interest long before they moved to the farm, but he is not convinced that their arrival at Hawksnest Farm was serendipitous: 'They both feel that they were drawn to buy that farm, even when there were others, some of them with better facilities, that they could have chosen. I believe it suited the purposes of the aliens that Jason and Ann should live close to MoD property: there are two things to study at the same time.'

CHAPTER 14

ANIMAL MUTILATIONS

Despite the deaths of their cattle, and the problems getting permission to build on their own land, Paul and Ann were still determined to make a go of the farm. In the spring of 1996 Paul decided to buy some more cows. He loves cows, enjoys handling them, and he'd successfully bred calves that made top prices at market before. Although he was being denied the chance to go into calf rearing on a proper scale, he had a barn in which he could overwinter a small number of cows and calves, and there was a pond and grassland for grazing.

He bought four pregnant cows, three Charolais heifers and an older Jersey cow. The family travelled to a farm on the Sussex/Hampshire borders to choose them, and then waited eagerly for them to be delivered to Hawksnest on June 30th. Ann and the boys were on holiday with Ann's mum when they arrived, but she phoned Paul every day to make sure they were settling in well.

The farmer who sold them, who was giving up his farm to retire, was confident they would calf at the end of September or, at the latest, early November. Jason enjoyed his holiday, but the journey home could not go fast enough for him: he wanted to see the cows. After a few minutes in the field with them he had established a relationship. They allowed him to stroke and cuddle them as if they were household pets. If Ann or Paul walked near them they would move away, but they seemed to accept Jason. He loved putting his hands on their ripening stomachs and telling his mother how he could feel the calves moving.

September came and went, and then October, without any sign of any of the four giving birth. In fact, all four looked thinner, less pregnant, their barrelled stomachs less obvious. Despite the fact

203

they were all in healthy condition, Paul was uneasy, and rang the vet when, by mid-November, there was still no sign of them calving.

The vet was due to visit them on Thursday the 21st. The previous Monday, when Ann and Paul arrived at the farm, all the six horses were missing. There was no great mystery: the horses had been let out before by young mischiefmakers who deliberately opened the gates. In the past, when Paul bred pigs, these too had been released on to the bridle path. One of Paul's enormous sows once lay down in the middle of a nearby lane, and refused to move even when two policemen told her she was causing a traffic problem.

The Andrews did not rush around looking for the horses: as on previous occasions, they all wandered back in their own time. Within a couple of hours only Squeakie, Daniel's mare, was still missing. This was odd, because Squeakie is timid and home-loving, and never leaves the farm even when the gate is wide open. When she had still not returned the following morning, Paul was afraid she had been stolen. While Ann worried about how to break the news to Daniel, Paul rang the police.

It rained heavily that night, and Ann slept badly, worrying that Squeakie, who needed the company of the other horses, was alone somewhere, wet and uncared for. The next morning, when they arrived at the main gate of the farm, Ann got out to unlock it. Outside the gate she was astonished to see, in the mud, deep cow hoof prints. There were a great many prints, as if the cows were moving around in a circle, yet there were no prints leading to the place or away from it – and there was deep mud on every side.

Puzzled by his wife's delay in opening the gate, Paul got out of the car and came to join her. He, too, was mystified. Then Ann pointed to another print, on the edge of the group. It was the shape of a boot print. There was only one, and the amazing thing about it was its size. Paul's own large feet were dwarfed beside it, and he estimated it was at least a size fifteen.

They were both worried, and hurried to the gate. The padlock was still in place, and the piece of string that Ann always tied around it (to tell them if anyone had tried to open it) was still in place. They went immediately to the barn, where the cows would be, sheltering from the night-time rain. The cattle were all there, but were clearly disturbed, snorting and backing off when their owners approached.

The horses, unperturbed, were grazing quietly. Ann and Paul were determined to find Squeakie, so they set off together through the thick woodland, calling for the horse, wandering along the outer edge, knowing that the mare would not voluntarily have gone deep into its dark tangle of undergrowth. They made their way through to a large, sloping field belonging to a neighbour, a fruit farmer. The slope ran away from them, so they could clearly see that the square field was empty. They didn't seriously think the horse would be there: the entrance to the field was next to the farmhouse, and could only be approached through the main farmyard, which was generally busy with people and dogs. Squeakie would have been noticed, especially as people knew this was the third day she had been missing.

Returning to their own farm, they could hear the other horses before they got to the gate. The horses were neighing and whinnying, as if they were calling out, and Ann and Paul could hear another horse answering the calls. They ran back along the track they had just walked, following the direction of the sound. There, in a corner of the square field they had inspected only minutes earlier, was Squeakie, white with sweat and shivering uncontrollably. They were both stunned: it would have been impossible to miss her. Not wanting to anger the farmer, Paul opened another, disused, gate, and led her out. He knows she did not get into the field that way, as the gate had obviously not been moved for a long time, and she couldn't have jumped it.

Back at their own land, they put a blanket over Squeakie to warm her, but she calmed down immediately she rejoined the other horses and she ate heartily. By the time Ann and Paul had finished feeding the other animals, they were exhausted. As they drove home, Ann told Paul that she had experienced a strong sensation of being watched and, to her surprise, he said he had felt it, too. It was, he said, the first time he had ever felt 'afraid' when he was on his own property.

The following day the vet arrived to see the cows, which were acquiescent and calm – different from the way they had been the previous day. After spending about an hour with them, the vet astounded Ann and Paul with his findings. Only two of the cows, he said, were pregnant. This was a shock. Both Paul and Ann knew that diagnosing a pregnancy is not always easy, and the old farmer could have made a mistake, but they had seen the swelling bellies of the animals, and had felt the calves kicking. But the vet's next announcement shocked them even more. One of the cows which was pregnant had about another ten weeks to go before delivery, and the other was only four or five months pregnant. As this was November 21st and the cows had been at Hawksnest since June 30th, this startling news meant that in both cases, it was just possible that the cows had been inseminated before they arrived at Hawksnest Farm, but only just: the farmer would not have been able to certify them as pregnant, as he had done. Nor would they have looked so obviously pregnant. The calves were duly born, one on a wet cold morning at the beginning of March and the second on April 17th.

The mysterious disappearance of Squeakie, the unexplained barrenness of two of the cows and the unnaturally long pregnancies of the other two were not the only baffling events involving animals at the smallholding.

In 1995, the farm cat went missing. The Andrews had acquired two cats from another farm, to help control mice around the animal feedstocks. When the cat, named Cosmic Creeper by Jason (after the witch's cat in one of his favourite films, *Bedknobs and Broomsticks*), disappeared for a couple of days, none of the family were alarmed: cats that hunt for a living often go walkabout. However, when Daniel and Jason were fooling around in the barn, Jason suddenly called out in alarm. Daniel rushed over to him to share the grisly discovery. The body of the cat was stretched out on a straw bale. She was not curled up, like a sleeping cat, and when they got close to her they could see a neat round hole in her head. She was stiff, having died at least a day earlier. Remarkably, there was no blood around the hole, which was obviously not a natural injury. The boys summoned Paul and Ann, and Ann held Jason tight, tears coursing down both their faces, as Paul took the body away for burial. Talking about it when they were alone, he and Ann decided that vandals had killed the cat, as a hideous prank. But

Ann felt deeply uneasy: to her, the cat had been stretched out as if on a medical slab, and the precision of the bore hole in her forehead did not have the hallmark of mindless vandalism.

A few months later a fox was found in the bottom field, with the same strange head injury. Again, there was no blood. Ann's unease increased. Something very strange was going on, but she kept her fears to herself, not wanting to alarm Jason or add to Paul's worries. However, there was nothing she could do to shield Jason from the next discovery, because it was he who made it. On Friday August 26th 1996, while on holiday from school, Jason went to the farm with his parents. He jumped out of the car to swing open the gate, then jumped back with a look of surprise on his face, which quickly turned to horror. There were four dead mice, laid out in an unnatural straight-line formation, near the gate. Each one had a small black hole, not much bigger than a pinprick in the forehead, the left eye missing, and the rectum neatly cut out. One of them was missing part of its stomach, another had its jawbone exposed as if the flesh had been cut away, and one had its left front paw cut off. It was hard to ascertain the mutilations to the fourth, as Jason had accidentally trodden on it. This time, alarmed by the ritual appearance of the injuries, Ann took a photograph of the mice and sent it to Tony Dodd, before disposing of the bodies which, after a couple of days, had started to rot.

At the time, Ann knew nothing about animal mutilations. When reading about UFOs and aliens she confined herself to material that seemed to relate to her and Jason's experiences. She was beginning to know quite a bit about abduction, but she knew nothing of other aspects of the subject. She was surprised by Tony's lack of surprise, but then discovered that he is familiar with strange marks and mutilations appearing on dead animals, particularly around the sites of alien activity.

The first modern animal mutilation report that was connected with the UFO phenomenon happened in Colorado, USA, in 1967. A healthy three-year-old mare was found dead, with the head and part of the neck stripped bare of flesh. It was so completely clean it looked as though it had been like that for days, and been bleached and dried by the sun, but the horse had been seen alive two days before, and the rest of the body was untouched. The head had been severed from the body with a clean cut that could not have been done by an animal. There were no tracks around the body, and no sign of any blood on the ground or oozing from the severed neck.

Because of the mystery surrounding the death of the horse, the body was sent to a pathologist, who discovered the heart, lungs and thyroid gland were missing. The wound appeared to have been cauterised. Years later the pathologist would recognise a similar cauterising technique when lasers began to be used for surgical procedures, but in 1967 these techniques were yet to be generally applied

What made the case of the dead mare more interesting – and drew international publicity – was that on the night she died several people in the area had reported UFO activity. There was a curious sweet smell – described by the rancher on whose land the horse had been grazing as 'like incense' – around the area the corpse was found.

Over the ensuing years there have been many reports of animal mutilation: in America, cattle are the most common victims; in Britain there are many stories of deer and sheep being subjected to strange injuries. Usually the report includes some strange lights or noises in the sky, or the animals are mutilated at a site previously known to have been at the centre of UFO activity.

The main characteristics that have been identified in mutilation cases are:

1. An absence of blood, often with small puncture holes in the jugular vein through which blood has been drained away. Some veterinary experts believe that in many cases the animals were alive but unconscious when this happened.
2. Cuts on the body showing advanced anatomical knowledge: the incisions to remove vital organs are made at the right places.
3. The use of surgical instruments. The cuts are clean, the wounds are often cauterised, and there is no sign of blood around them or, where bones are severed, of bone splinters and dust.
4. Internal organs removed, most usually the brain or the sex organs.
5. Sometimes, evidence that the animal has been sedated.
6. Occasionally, evidence of radiation around the site of the mutilation.

★   ★   ★

There was a great deal of interest in the media during the 1970s, when a whole spate of animal mutilations was reported across America, but when no explanation was found the subject dropped out of the headlines. However, the mutilations did not stop, and a few researchers continued to compile reports.

In America, television documentary maker Linda Moulton Howe, who has won awards for her work on environmental issues, collected together a mass of evidence of animal mutilations, initially assuming that she was investigating a government cover-up of contamination. She suspected that there had been a leak of radiation or some other contaminant, and that the dead cattle were random samples taken by the government to monitor the spread of the pollution. Her research, however, produced examples reported up to three centuries ago, and even then references were being made to strange objects in the sky at the time of mutilations.

The documentary she produced in 1980, *A Strange Harvest,* won her an Emmy television award, and set America talking, and she subsequently published a book: *An Alien Harvest: Further Evidence Linking Animal Mutilations and Human Abductions to Alien Life Forms.* She established that not only were UFOs routinely spotted at around the time of a mutilation, but there were also unmarked helicopters in the area soon afterwards. She presumed these were government helicopters. Her original theory, that the government was responsible for the mutilations, was, she believes, not right, but there is a government involvement in that they are monitoring, far more closely than they ever admit, the work of the aliens.

Her evidence is in line with most of the other serious UFO research which has been done, not specifically allied to animal mutilations. There is a consensus among respected and dedicated researchers that governments (not only in the USA but in all developed countries) know a great deal about the alien contacts with earth, despite blanket denials and cover-ups. This book is not the place to go into this whole subject in any depth: whole libraries of well-researched books have now been written exposing the links between governments and alien craft. Some UFOlogists believe there is an established line of communication between the two, but this is speculative. What there is, undoubtedly, is evidence that government and military agencies have more knowedge of alien activity than they ever admit to. There are so many reports of UFOs being bugged and followed by military aircraft, and so many well-documented reports of cover-ups, that it is impossible to ignore the evidence.

Among the many cases of animal mutilation that Howe investigated, there is one which supplies a possible explanation as to why aliens want to extract organs and tissue randomly from cattle and other animals – and which shows that her original hypothesis, about monitoring contamination, is not wide of the mark. The difference is that it is not government agencies that are monitoring it, but aliens.

A housewife who was driving home from bingo in Houston, Texas, in 1973, saw a large light 'hanging' in the sky. Her mother, sister, brother-in-law and teenage daughter were in the car with her, and also saw it. The woman, Judy Doraty, pulled over and got out of the car to look at the large stationary light. Everyone in the car remembers seeing it, and when they drove on it appeared to follow them, and was seen by neighbours and relatives. When Judy parked her car it moved on across a field, and then suddenly shot straight upwards and disappeared.

It was not until she underwent hypnosis seven years later, after constantly feeling disturbed by the events of the night, that Judy remembered what happened after she stepped out of the car to look at the light. She saw, although it was some distance from her, a calf being pulled up by the light, into a hovering spacecraft. She had a distinct feeling that she should not be watching, and the next moment she found herself inside the craft.

Two small aliens, with large heads and large piercing black eyes, were working on the calf, expertly removing organs and carrying out a systematic examination of its teeth, ears, eyes and reproductive organs. They talked to her as they worked, explaining telepathically that they were monitoring pollution. They said they were stationed here, and this was their job. They were concerned about manmade toxins entering the food chain, and they told her they carried out similar checks on all types of living creatures.

Judy Doraty felt they were humouring her, talking to her as if she was a small child. More than once they remarked that she would remember nothing afterwards. When they had finished with the calf she was horrified to see her daughter Cindy there, being placed on the bench by the two creatures and was relieved when they simply took some scrapings from the inside of Cindy's mouth. Then Judy and Cindy were both returned to the car, and continued their journey, remembering nothing except seeing the light.

That the aliens are monitoring pollution is a highly credible explanation, especially as we have already seen that they seem to be particularly interested in human fertility – the two humanoids had told Judy that it was the reproductive organs which would show the signs of the toxins – and we already believe that human male fertility is declining as a result of chemical pollution.

The aliens' assertion that they carry out similar tests on all living species has obvious implications for man. Tony Dodd believes that many unexplained disappearances could be the result of abductions that either go wrong, or where the human body is required for fuller investigations, and the victim is killed. There have been very few cases where a human corpse has been found with mutilation signs similar to those of the animals, but there have been one or two. He stresses that human beings disappearing completely after abductions is very, very rare: he believes that when aliens want human bodies to study they select victims who are dropouts and down-and-outs.

In Britain Tony Dodd keeps a comprehensive file on animal mutilations, to which the photograph of the mice found at Hawksnest Farm has been added. As well as sheep, cattle and horses, he has evidence of mutilations of deer, foxes, seals, hedgehogs, badgers, pigs and cats. Almost all have a neat hole in the forehead, through which the brain and a sample of the spinal cord have been removed, and have had the rectum cleanly removed, as if with an apple corer. Each time, there is no blood at the scene of the mutilation, and there are usually reports of strange lights and objects in the sky seen at the same time.

'It is so systematic it cannot be vandals,' says Tony Dodd. 'Something is going on, for so many animals to be mutilated in the same way, all over the world.'

The Ministry of Agriculture, the Royal Veterinary College and the National Farmers' Union all say they are unaware of any reports of mutilation. Tony Dodd is sceptical, having himself made reports. 'It could be that there is an explanation that is nothing to do with UFOs and aliens, but why don't they give it?' he asks.

Three magpies drowned in a water trough, ten dead rats floating on the top of a water tank – the bizarre happenings at Hawksnest Farm have become almost normal to Paul and Ann. They talk matter-of-factly about the sort of events which would terrify others. The strange sweet smell which plenty of others, and I, have smelled, comes and goes, especially around their animals. On April 30th 1997, Ann recorded in her diary that the smell was so strong around one of the cows, Cassie, that both she and Paul felt nauseous after tending to the animal. Two weeks later, the smell was very strong just inside the gate to the smallholding. It dissipated, but when Ann went down the field she discovered that Squeakie had foaled during the night, and that the smell was so strong on both the mother and baby that she could hardly bear to go close to check that the foal was all right. That evening both she and Paul had headaches, and neither of them could get the lingering smell out of their nostrils.

Four months after the birth of the healthy foal, Squeakie was looking thin. At first Ann and Paul assumed the flourishing foal was taking so much milk from her that she was not getting enough nourishment herself, but one day Ann noticed something hanging from the mare. She called out the vet, who discovered Squeakie had never expelled the afterbirth membrane. Normally, if the membrane is not naturally expelled after the birth, and the mare does not get treatment within twenty-four hours, the retained placenta decomposes, turns septic, and the mare dies within a few days. To the astonishment of the vet Squeakie had suffered no serious ill effects, and did not even need a course of antibiotics. She is, he told her owners, a miracle animal.

Every year, for one weekend in August, a motorbike club holds a rally at the far end of the smallholding and the bikers come from far afield. Despite initial misgivings by the Andrews's neighbours (and there is nobody living within several hundred yards of the farm) the Iron Horses Rally is peaceful and, to the amusement of those who feared the worst, the bikers tend to be in their thirties and forties and to retire to their sleeping bags relatively early. After the August rally in 1996 Ann was talking to a couple of bikers who had travelled from Belgium to be there and one of them asked if she knew they had paranormal activity at the farm. Ann, surprised, asked him what he meant and he and his friend told her that they had seen a bright light hovering over the fields, and then a 'fantastic light display' above the woods, from the direction of the MoD property.

(The bikers are not the only ones to notice the strange lights that appear over the Andrews's fields. When neighbour Sue Rutland was walking with her aunt to the nearest postbox one evening in September 1997, she saw a bright orange glow over the farm. Hurrying home, she called Ann, who summoned Paul from work. By the time the two of them arrived at the farm an hour later the orange light had gone, but there were two, dull white beams of light emerging from the woodland. The animals seemed unnaturally subdued.)

Jason and Daniel were allowed to attend the motorbike rally for the first time in 1996, with two of their friends. Paul has a small touring caravan on the site, which he uses as a base while working there, and the boys took sleeping bags and spent the night in there. Early in the morning, before any of the others had stirred, and while the bikers were all still crashed out, one of Jason's friends got up to relieve himself in the woods. Seeing a small 'child' dodge behind a tree as he approached, he followed it, assuming it came from the motorbike camp and had wandered away from its parents. When he got to the tree there was no trace of the 'child'. He searched for a few minutes, and then returned to the caravan to wake the others, saying he had seen a ghost. He now believes the farm is haunted, and refuses to sleep another night there.

A very similar incident happened ten months later, in June 1997, when Ann was holding a barbecue for other members of her family, including her mother, both her brothers, her two sisters-in-law and her nieces. It was a breezy day, but it still surprised Paul and Ann when an enormous tree crashed down from the woodland and on to their land, luckily not harming any of their guests or any of the animals. It was even more of a surprise when Ann's small nieces, aged seven and eleven, came back from the bottom field, where they had gone to see the horses, and asked who the 'little children' hiding in the woods were. Vi told them they must have seen shadows which looked like children, but Ann could tell from their faces that they found this hard to believe.

CHAPTER 15

AN ORIGINAL SOUL

By the beginning of 1996, both Jason and Ann had reached an uneasy acceptance of the alien activity which surrounds them. As Jason has become more accustomed to – and understands more about – the abductions, he has become more comfortable with the procedure. This does not mean he relishes or enjoys it. He says he wishes it would end, but he is no longer quite as fearful of it: 'It would be much better if it didn't happen, because I'm always so tired, but I now know that I always come back, and that although I don't like what they do to me they don't want to harm me.' Ann no longer fears that he will be permanently taken from her physically, and although she is still desperately worried when she discovers he is missing in the night, she is resigned to it. She has other, deeper, fears. Paul is less able to accept the abductions, and it is perhaps fortunate that he is, on the whole, less aware of it than Ann. She often wakes in the night, knowing that Jason is not there, but, unable to do anything about it, she goes to sleep again. If Paul is also wakened he veers between being understanding, and being angry that his life is taken over by something outside his control.

In early 1996, in the middle of an unhappy spell for Jason when the abductions seemed to be coming more frequently than ever, both Paul and Ann were awakened by sounds from Jason's room. When they got there they found Daniel sitting on Jason's bed, hugging a teddy bear that Jason has had since he was a baby. Although Daniel's cheeks were tear-stained, he was angry. 'The bastards have taken him again. I knew it was happening but I couldn't move, I couldn't stop it,' he said, punching his fist into the pillow. 'I hate them.'

Ann comforted him, reminding him that Jason always came back.

Paul, though, had absorbed Daniel's anger and feelings of frustration. He thumped the bedroom door and began to march downstairs. Ann followed him, asking him what he was doing. On many occasions Paul had been as philosophical as her about Jason's absences, but on this night his mood was entirely different. 'I'm getting the police,' he snapped at his wife. 'I've just about had enough. It's out of hand. This is not what normal families go through.'

As Ann tried to get between him and the phone he pushed her roughly away, and she slumped on to the settee. She was not hurt, but she was shocked: throughout all their married life, all the problems they had faced together, Paul had never been violent towards her or the boys. It had only been a push, but it was not something she had ever experienced from him before, and she began to cry.

Instantly, Paul had his arm round her, apologising. He, too, was shocked by his own behaviour: 'Oh, God, I'm so sorry. I just snapped. I sometimes feel I can't cope with this anymore. Why us? For God's sake, why this family?'

Feeling out of her depth, Ann rang Maria Ward, knowing that even though it was 3.30am Maria would be willing to listen and help. As she predicted, Maria was able to come up with comforting and calm advice. She spoke to Paul, telling him that however bad he felt, he had to cope, for Jason's sake. Going to the police, when they already knew what the explanation for the disappearances was, would only make matters much worse for the boy, she told him. The last thing Jason needed was a couple of uncomprehending and unsympathetic policemen turning up.

Maria then spoke to Ann again, and the choice of words she used gave Ann a jolt: 'Jason is special. I don't know how to explain this, but it seems to me that Jason has an original soul, and that's what they, those who take him away, are interested in.'

Ann remembered hearing Daniel use the same phrase 'an original soul', when he explained why his 'soldier man' had switched his attention to Jason. Maria was continuing, reassuring Ann that nothing terrible was going to happen to Jason, when the living room was suddenly filled with an intense white light. Ann had only switched on a small table lamp, because it was the middle of the

216

night, but the room was now bathed in brightness, and outside there was a loud crack of thunder. Instantaneously the light went out, and the thunder rolled away into the distance. Chissum, the largest of the dogs, whimpered at the thunder, and then went to the foot of the stairs, where his frightened whine turned into a joyous bark. Jason, rubbing his eyes, was walking down the stairs towards them.

Maria, who had been able to follow what was going on over the phone, laughed and said to Ann, 'What did I tell you? Can I get some sleep now, please?'

Jason sat down and told his parents and his brother what had happened to him.

'I met one of the tall people-like ones tonight,' he said. 'He showed me a really funny map and tried to explain exactly where they come from. He told me – in my head – that they have been watching us – you know, Earth – for hundreds and thousands of years. He was so interesting that I could have stayed for hours.'

'You did,' Paul interrupted.

Jason grinned and carried on.

'I saw loads of other people this time and, oh, yes, there was this little toddler there and the "little ones" were playing with him with a sparkly ball – like the one that came into our house, but smaller. This baby was laughing and chuckling so much at the ball that more and more of the "little ones" came over to see him. He was so funny.'

Jason smiled, enjoying the memory, and pausing for a few moments before carrying on.

'I felt really good at my experience this time. I felt nice inside being with the tall one. He said that he knew us all and I got the impression he was Daniel's soldier man, who used to visit him.'

About a week later Ann felt a strong premonition that something was about to happen. Jason had been restless again that evening, but had said nothing to suggest he knew an abduction was coming. He went to bed happily enough, and when Ann checked he was sound asleep. It was she who could not sleep. She lay next to Paul, who was snoring loudly, with a feeling of uneasiness that she could not explain.

She climbed out of bed to check on the boys again, but they were fine. The big dog, Chissum, was sleeping on the landing and did not stir, not even opening an eyelid, as Ann stepped over him. She gave him a gentle prod with her foot, and he let out a low grumble, but still, to her surprise, did not wake up. Back in her own bed, she was reassuring herself that all was well when she detected a dull, background humming noise. It was growing louder, as if it was approaching. Sitting up in bed, she nudged Paul awake with difficulty, as he was sleeping very soundly. He, too, could hear it, but he quickly put his head back on to the pillow and was snoring again.

Ann walked across to the window and looked out. There was nothing to see, but the noise now seemed to be all around her, inside the house. She remembers thinking, as she walked back to the bed, that it was astonishing that Paul could sleep through it – and then she remembers no more until the following morning.

When she got downstairs, Paul was gulping down a cup of tea before he rushed out to the farm, Daniel was reading a football magazine and Jason was eating a bowl of cereal. Daniel looked up and asked her if she had seen 'it' during the night.

'What?' she asked.

'The football,' said Daniel.

'It was a big, blue ball of light,' Jason continued. 'It just sort of hovered, as if it was inspecting everything. It moved around without bumping into anything.'

Daniel told Ann that the 'football' of light had explored all the upstairs bedrooms, including hers and Paul's. He was struck by the beauty of it, but when he stretched his hand out to touch it, it moved away. Jason said that he had not been frightened of it: he had known it was something other than an abduction experience, and that it would not harm him. Both boys said they had fallen soundly asleep before the ball of light had disappeared.

Another non-abduction experience that recurs for Jason is a dream. Because he describes it as a 'dream' his mother feels it is not a recovered memory, like her dreams. Jason has always been able to distinguish between the reality of an abduction and a dream: this is one of the ways in which he is not a typical abductee. In the dream he is sometimes at the farm, and sometimes out shopping in a supermarket. He picks up something with a shiny bottom, like a tin of food, and sees a mirror image of himself in it, but as he sees himself he also sees an alien behind him, and it is not the one he feels familiar with, not Daniel's 'soldier man'. He feels daunted and wary, and he struggles to block the mental communication that the alien is trying to establish with him. As he bends all his will to resisting the contact, he wakes up. Every time he has this dream – and it has recurred four or five times – he is frightened to sleep for a couple of nights, and he also stops eating properly, complaining of feeling nauseous.

Yet another recurring phenomenon was first noticed by Paul on a Friday night in April 1996, when he got up in the middle of the night to go to the bathroom and heard the sound of talking coming from Jason's room. Paul looked round the door, to see Jason sitting up in bed, talking fluently in a strange language, which involved lots of soft 'ummm' sounds. His eyes were wide-open, but he appeared to be in a trance-like state. Paul woke Ann, and they both listened for several minutes. Then Jason turned, fixed a steady gaze on Ann and said, in English, 'Oh yes, the mother.' Then he seemed to grow tired, and lay down after a while and went back to sleep, his eyes closed and his thumb in his mouth.

As Ann and Paul turned to leave the room, they were almost knocked over by Chissum pushing past them. He went across the room to his young charge and anxiously nuzzled at Jason's face. Without waking, Jason stretched out a hand and pushed him off, muttering at the dog to go away. The massive tail started to wag and, satisfied that Jason was now all right, Chissum turned and blundered out of the room to resume his position on guard at the top of the stairs. The tension broken, Ann and Paul laughed at the huge dog, and Ann gave him a hug before returning to bed, but the chill she felt when she heard him refer to her, coldly, as 'the mother', still returns whenever she remembers the incident.

The strange language has been heard several times, and at Tony Dodd's suggestion Paul attempted to record it. However, despite using reliable, modern equipment, the tapes always jammed. This is very common in investigations of the paranormal: members of the Society for Psychical Research devote a lot of time to trying to overcome the malfunction of electronic equipment during their research. Video cameras, tape-recorders, cameras programmed to work automatically, and even heat-recording equipment to monitor changes in temperature, have all been known to fail. UFOlogists are used to encountering films which turn out blank when processed, and it is always impossible to say with any certainty whether the fault is purely in the fallible human technology, or whether some outside interference has caused the problem.

Jason still, occasionally, has his late-night one-sided conversations. Despite listening closely, Paul and Ann cannot identify the language he is speaking: it does not sound to them like any of the familiar European languages. Whatever it is, Jason appears to talk it as easily as he does English, sometimes lapsing between the two as he murmurs to himself, so that his parents occasionally catch a clear, recognisable, everyday word such as 'pony' and 'farm'. Children brought up in bilingual households slip in and out of two languages without realising they are doing it, in exactly this way.

The first time she heard the new language, Ann was very concerned. The strange speech seemed to represent another way in which 'they' were taking over her son, and all her old fears about him 'going over' to them surfaced. This is by far her biggest anxiety, despite all the reassurance Tony Dodd gives her. The words 'the mother' haunt her.

Paul, too, had a disturbing exchange with Jason, in October 1996, which filled him with a persistent unease. After an argument, the normal sort of family row with a teenage son who was being bolshie, Paul shouted, 'You do what your father tells you, do you hear?'

Jason, instantly calm, fixed him with a cold stare.

'You don't understand, do you?' he said. 'I am more a part of them than I'll ever be of you.'

For a few days Paul mulled over these words, trying to make sense of them. He was unusually quiet and distracted. Ann, who had not been present when the row happened, sensed that something important had occurred, but had to prise the details out of Paul, who is normally so open and matter-of-fact about everything. She tried to reassure him that these were silly words, spoken in the heat of an argument by an adolescent trying to wound his parents, but she, too, felt a cold hand clutch at her heart when she heard them.

Eventually, after almost a week when he could not free his mind of Jason's pronouncement, Paul rang Tony Dodd. As ever, Tony was comforting, supportive and not at all surprised. Although, he told Paul, he had never directly encountered a child speaking like this before, he had read reports from America of abductee youngsters saying similar things to their parents.

For Paul, it remains the most upsetting and unsettling event in the whole catalogue of Jason's abduction experiences. It makes him feel, he says, like an irrelevance, as if all the energy he has put into bringing up and loving his youngest son has simply been a task performed for the benefit of others. The analogy he draws is with the dogs he breeds, which he loves and nurtures but never for one moment imagines he is genetically bound to: is he only fulfilling the same role for Jason?

However dark these thoughts, they only invade the foreground of Paul's mind occasionally. For the rest of the time he and Jason enjoy the same teasing, joshing, occasionally fractious relationship of any father and son – but there are times when Ann notices a cloud cross Paul's face, and a puzzled, almost frightened, look in his eyes as he watches Jason.

Tony Dodd has had to reassure Ann endlessly that in all his dealings with abductees, he has never encountered one who has switched allegiance from his human attachments. Many abductees go through a spiritual awakening and broadening, but this appears to be entirely beneficial, and not something which threatens their relationships (except where a preoccupation with the abduction experience leads to a rift with a partner who either does not believe or cannot fully comprehend the full importance of the events).

Ann now regards Jason's babblings in the unknown language (of which he has no knowledge in the morning) as a good sign. At least, she tells herself as she lies awake listening to the faint murmur coming from his room across the landing, if he is talking, he is there, in his bed, and not being abducted.

In February 1997 she had an important experience, which she feels she will, somehow, know more about as time goes on. Despite the bitter February weather, Paul and Ann always sleep with a window open in their bedroom. Paul was not working that night – which usually means that Ann falls asleep easily, reassured by his bulky presence in the bed – but on this occasion she tossed and

221

turned, drifting eventually into a sleep in which she saw herself as a child.

She was looking down at herself, asleep in the familiar bedroom of the house in Peckham where she spent her early years. She saw herself sit up, smiling, and then climb out of bed and pull on a dressing gown and slippers. The child version of herself looked so happy, and in her dream Ann was gripped with fear and frustration. She watched the small girl run lightly down the stairs, clapping her hands and giggling, following a ball of light which seemed to entrance her. The adult Ann tried desperately to tell the child not to go, not to be so happy about going, but she could make no sound.

Suddenly, Ann herself was awake, the fear of the dream still gripping her. As she surfaced into full wakefulness, Ann became aware of a figure at the far end of the bed, on her side. She momentarily buried her head in the pillow, convinced it was part of the dream, and then looked up again. The figure was still there, close to the window. She could hear the rain battering against the glass, and wind from the open pane at the top abruptly gusted the net curtain up, catching it over the head of the standing figure.

Panic-stricken, Ann struggled to wake Paul, but again he was sleeping too deeply to be roused. Clambering over him, she fled out of the room to check that Jason was all right. When she reached his bedroom she found her son sleeping peacefully, but as she turned to return to her own room she froze. She could hear the sound of shuffling footsteps following her along the landing, drawing nearer and nearer to the doorway of Jason's room. Ann, in terror, sat down on the chair next to Jason's bed. It is a small landing, always lit at night because of Jason's fear of the dark. Within seconds the footsteps reached the door of Jason's room, and the figure from the window appeared, illuminated by the landing light. It was a young man.

Ann's terror dissipated as she saw him. He was naked and soaked, as if he had been out in the rain. His expression was one of great fear and he held his hands out to Ann as if asking for help. Instinctively she stood up and stretched hers out to him. His hands were freezing cold. For an instant Ann was suffused with a great feeling of pity for the young man, and then she remembers nothing more until she awoke the next morning at 6am.

She believes – and so does Tony Dodd – that she met another

abductee who had been returned to the wrong house. When the aliens realised their mistake they corrected it.

There are many examples of abductees being returned wrongly, perhaps with their clothes the wrong way round or simply in the wrong room of the house – just as Jason, as a baby, was placed at the wrong end of the cot or on the floor beneath it. One abductee who has contacted Tony Dodd found herself in the early hours of the morning in the front garden of her home, with the doors locked against her. Nick Pope believes that the sloppy attention to detail shown by the abductors could, eventually, lead to concrete proof of an abduction, if a victim is returned to the wrong house or even the wrong country, and the aliens don't notice and rectify their mistake.

For two weeks after this encounter Ann refused to sleep in the bedroom, taking refuge on the settee downstairs with one of the dogs at her feet. Logically, she knows that the dogs have been unable to protect any of the family from the strange events which surround them, but for a time after this experience she found the snuffling bulk of a Pyrenean mountain dog gave her a sense of security. She has also tried many times to draw the face of the young man, but failed. She scans crowds looking for him, convinced that if he is an abductee he must live relatively near to their home, and that she will one day bump into him. She has a strong feeling that she will meet him again and she knows she will recognise him: but will he know her?

Jason's abductions go in waves, and after an unhappy start to 1997, March and April were relatively peaceful. It was halfway through May before he had another experience, and this time it was not an abduction but a variation which terrified him. Ann noticed that he was edgy, tired, bad-tempered: sure-fire signs that he was again having disturbed nights, but he had been better lately, more accepting of his abductions, and she was distressed to see him so obviously upset again. Eventually, she persuaded him to talk.

He was, he told her, trying to stay awake all night because he was scared 'in case it happens again'. Ann asked him what he meant, and he told her, crossly: 'In case I see me again.'

Baffled, Ann asked him to explain.

'It was last Thursday,' Jason said. 'I woke up suddenly, got out of bed to come downstairs and looked back for a second, and then I saw myself: still in bed, still asleep. I was terrified. I tried to scream for you or Dad, then I thought I must get downstairs to you. As soon as I thought it, I was downstairs, but I don't know how I got there.

'You were in the living room, and you were talking to Dad about us all going on holiday again, in a caravan in Hastings. You were asking Dad if he thought it was a good idea for my mate Alan to come with us, but Dad wasn't paying attention because he was listening to the news on telly. In the end, you hit him with a rolled-up newspaper.'

As he told her this, Ann went cold. She and Paul had discussed the holiday, but because no booking had been made – and they weren't sure whether they would be able to afford it – they had not mentioned it to the boys. She had been careful not to leave any brochures lying around. There was no way Jason could have known about it unless he had overheard them talking – and the fact that he had 'seen' her playfully tap Paul to attract his attention meant that he hadn't been outside the door, eavesdropping. He must have been inside the room.

Jason went on to say that soon after he 'entered' the living room, the dogs started whining and growling, and Chissum, the biggest and boldest, was snapping at him. Frightened, because the dogs are more comfortable with him than anyone, he wished he was back upstairs – and instantly he was. Again, Ann's mind went back to that evening.

'It was weird, because all the dogs were suddenly awake. The girls – the four female Pyreneans – backed away into a corner, whimpering. But Chissum was standing up, his hackles up, alert – as if there was some danger. We are used to him snapping in the air at flies, and at first that's what we thought he was doing. But there were no flies, and he seemed to be following something with his eyes, and lunging at it every so often.

'Paul told him to sit down and be quiet, and he normally obeys Paul, but on this occasion he wouldn't. Then, after a couple of minutes, he turned round, wagged his huge tail and settled back on the floor to sleep. The girls all came out of the corner and flopped down in their usual positions, and everything was back to normal.

'Paul said they must have been able to hear something outside.'

As Jason told her about his 'visit' to the living room, Ann was puzzled and afraid, but she kept her feelings to herself. She smiled and gave her son a cuddle, saying that she would speak to Tony Dodd, but she was sure it wasn't important. Jason was placated, but Ann, despite her brave front, was very concerned. She told Paul, and it was he who rang Tony who, as ever, was not fazed by their report.

He explained to Paul that Jason had had an OBE, or out-of-body-experience, a well-documented supernatural phenomenon which increasingly seems to overlap with abduction cases. There are known 'psychic stars' who are tested in laboratories and are able to go out of their bodies more or less at will, in one case being able to read a series of numbers placed on top of a high cupboard without ever physically leaving the bed.

Out-of-body-experiences are common at times of crisis – there are instances of patients being able to look down at themselves on the operating table, even being able to recall the conversation of the doctors and nurses afterwards – but they are not that uncommon at any time. As many as one in six people has had some sort of OBE, and it is quite 'normal' for the experiencer to be able to pass through walls, travel long distances instantaneously, and to pick up information they could not possibly have known any other way.

Only a very few people, though, have them regularly, and are able to have them at will. The prophet Elisha used his skill at going out of his body to spy for the Israelites during their war with the Syrians, and many primitive cultures accept that the shaman or medicine man can use OBE skills to find out about the movements and numbers of enemy tribes. We know that back in the 1970s the American military authorities started experiments with 'remote viewing', giving psychics map co-ordinates and asking them to describe the location, with some of them using out-of-body techniques to travel to the place. When Saddam Hussein announced during the Gulf War that the allies were spying on him by using psychic means it was generally regarded as another of the rantings of a madman: we now know he was speaking the truth, as remote viewing was being used.

It was, however, a completely new event for Jason, and although Ann comforted him she, too, had never previously heard of OBEs.

Tony Dodd was able to reassure the family that Jason's heightened psychic abilities make him a natural candidate for other paranormal experiences, as well as abduction. He also warned them that Jason's alien friends may have purposely given him the skill to have OBEs, for their own ends – although listening to his mum and dad discussing a holiday certainly was not very significant.

For once, Tony Dodd's words did not comfort Ann.

'I'm frightened that something may happen before Jason can get back into his own body. I don't like the idea of him being able to wander away from it. On top of all the worries of abduction, we've now got to cope with this.'

Within a couple of days of Paul speaking to Tony, Paul and Ann both woke early one morning to hear Jason calling them loudly, from his bed. When they got to his room he was in an agitated state. As soon as they had calmed him enough to be able to understand him, he insisted that Ann get a paper and pen and take down notes of what he was saying. He paused, and then explained: 'I'm trying to remember, I have to remember, I don't want to forget this. Write it all down, Mum.'

Then he told of a feeling of travelling, and finding himself in a light environment, despite it being night-time. He said he saw lots of corridors, long ones with shiny floors, like in a hospital. There were lights set into the ceiling, and these were on. There were no windows along the corridor, but plenty of doors, some of them double.

This is a transcript of the notes Ann took in the shorthand she remembered from her days working in an office:

All the corridors are empty, like in a dream. But this is not a dream, I know I'm there. I turn a corner, but I don't know how, and there's a low humming sound. I remember looking at something on the wall but I don't remember what it was. There is a very heavy dark-coloured door with a soldier or guard on either side. They are wearing dark blue or navy uniforms, with a white belt. Can't see their arms. They have white socks over their boots and white 'curtain tassles' on their shoulders – right, I think. Dark berets with no badges or signs on them. One man is white, the other is black.

I can enter the room without the guards knowing, but I don't know how. They don't see me. This is a large room – a hall. Very high ceilings but no windows. The floor is still shiny. There's a small switch panel by the door to the left and a bank of televisions and buttons immediately to the left of the switches. There are two more soldiers in front of the screens, both white. There's a small staircase leading from this balcony thing to the main room.

Now I'm in the big room and there are two people wearing white stuff next to these tanks. There's six, maybe eight of these tanks, and they look like dumpy little milk bottles. I can't remember clearly, but there are long shelves with smaller milk bottles with large numbers underneath. Each one has a number. There are lots and lots of little red lights on the ceiling, and some switch on and off as I look at them.

Some of the jars have things in them, floating in water or liquid.

At this point Jason became very upset and started to cry. His mother told him to relax and forget about it, but he snapped at her that he was determined to remember it all. He carried on:

I know what they are, I know what they are. They're bits. Bits of 'them', the aliens. I'm angry, very angry, and then all the red lights start to flash on and off and then there's a noise, like a ship's siren, and it goes on and on and it won't stop. People are rushing around and more people come in but nobody seems to know what is happening.

The very last thing I remember is a fantastic flash of light, then I'm in the light and I have this incredible sensation of speed and I can't hear the siren anymore. Then I wake up, and I yell for you and Dad because I didn't want to forget anything.

Having told them, and being satisfied that Ann had taken it all down he allowed her to tuck him in and he went to sleep. Back in their own room Ann, who tries hard to hide many of her fears from Paul, broke down in tears. Paul cuddled her until she calmed down enough to tell him her fear that, in some way she could not explain or understand, she felt more threatened by Jason's OBEs than by the abductions. Sobbing, she told Paul of her fear that one day Jason would fail to find his way back to his sleeping body.

Paul reassured her as best he could, and when her sobs subsided they discussed the events that Jason had insisted his mother write down. They had both noticed that Jason had seemed happier, less agitated, than he did after an abduction. The only conclusion that they could draw is that Jason's OBE took him to a laboratory where military personnel were carrying out experiments on samples of captured aliens. Jason had already told them of being shown, by the aliens, the experimentation the human race inflicts on them, and how it made him angry: now he seemed to have the facility to see it without being abducted first. Tony Dodd, as ever, was right.

When she looks back on that night, Ann's emotions are mixed. She is relieved that Jason seems comfortable with what happened to him. She also understands his feelings of anger over the way his 'friends' are being treated. But she feels overwhelmed with sadness that he should be identifying with 'them', and she has a deep-seated fear that one day he may switch allegiance completely.

'Tony tells me it can never happen, Paul tells me to put it out of my mind, but I can't. It is my biggest fear of all. I know it is better for Jason to be comfortable with his experiences: but I am terrified that if he becomes too relaxed, we may lose him forever – if not in body, at least in spirit.'

So far, Jason's OBE has not been repeated, and he is no longer frightened of it occurring. In some strange way he seems happier in the knowledge that it was probably engineered by the aliens, than he was when he thought it was a whole other dimension to his own life. He is reconciled to being an abductee; he did not relish the prospect of 'being spooky in other ways', as he puts it.

The next event to disrupt the family centred not on Jason, but on Daniel – or, more accurately, on his cat. Daniel's cat was one of the two farm cats acquired to keep the mice down at Hawksnest Farm, but during a cold winter a couple of years ago he was taken to the house, and he decided that is where he is staying. In the way of cats, he has called the shots about who he belongs to and where he lives: it was the cat who chose Daniel as his master, and it is in Daniel's bedroom that he has made himself at home. He is not a friendly cat, keeping a safe distance from the dogs and flicking his tail in contempt if anyone tries to make a fuss of him. Daniel is the only person he holds in affection, and it was Daniel who chose his name: Fadius Dudus Maximus, an imperial name for an imperious and lordly cat. He's known as Dude because he is, as Daniel says, 'a real dude'.

It was just after midnight on the night of Tuesday May 27th, that Dude had his own encounter with something inexplicable. Daniel had just arrived home from a friend's house, and because it was a half-term holiday from school Jason was up late, watching a video with his parents. A high-pitched screech made them all jump and Paul turned down the sound on the television. There was another scream: they could tell it was an animal, not a human being. Daniel rushed to the back door, practically falling over one of the dogs. All five dogs were alert, watching, and the big one, Chissum, rose to his feet, growling.

'Dude,' was all that Daniel said as he rushed out.

Paul shrugged, turned the television back up, and commented that the cat was no doubt in a fight with a neighbour's moggy. 'You know how unsociable that cat is,' he said. Ann was ready to agree and carry on watching the film, but she became aware that Jason was staring into space, and was clutching the arm of his chair until his knuckles showed white. Then he walked across to sit next to her, taking hold of her arm and pulling it round him. She remembered, for the first time, that when he woke up that morning he had said he had a 'bad feeling' that 'they' were about.

At that moment Daniel yelled from the garden for Ann. She dashed out. He was holding the cat in his arms, but it was hissing and spitting and staring intently at something on the other side of the wooden garden fence. Ann put her hand out to stroke Dude, hoping to calm him, but he lashed out at her, sinking his claws into her arm. She told Daniel to take the cat in, and she stared into the darkness, trying to make out what was upsetting the animal.

Back in the house, Dude would not settle. He perched on the window ledge, his tail swinging, his hackles up, growling at the blackness outside. Paul did not take it seriously, announcing that the cat had finally met its match, probably a fox. Daniel, in the meantime, had been upstairs and reappeared with a baseball bat and a torch, and marched back outside, closing the door behind him.

After ten minutes or so, Ann got up from the settee again. 'I'd better get the great white hunter in. It's late. He'll be disturbing the neighbours soon,' she said.

The garden was quiet, but she saw the beam of the torch by the fence. When she called him Daniel turned, switched off the light and followed her back inside without saying anything. In the warmth of the living room lights, Ann could see that he was shaken.

'I heard a noise,' he said, 'so I shone the torch at the fence where Dude had been looking. There was something crouching there.'

Seeing Paul about to speak he carried on:

'No, Dad, it wasn't a fox, or another cat. It was alive – I know it was alive – but it looked like . . . like . . . like a leaf. It sounds daft, but it was eighteen inches across, leathery and with lots of veins, just like a big leaf on a wet day. But it was alive. I kept the torch on it and raised the bat, because I was angry at it for upsetting Dude. Then I hit it, I know I hit it . . . but I didn't, because when the bat came down it just sort of faded away, disappeared.'

He looked at his parents, expecting Paul, at least, to make some glib comment, but after everything the family has seen over the years, none of them dismissed it. Daniel continued to puzzle over it until Paul ordered both him and Jason to bed. Dude leapt gratefully into Daniel's arms to be carried upstairs. The dogs refused to go out into the garden for their final late-night patrol. Paul locked up extra carefully, and Daniel slept that night with his light on and the baseball bat by his bedside, the cat prowling restlessly along the window ledge.

The next day, Daniel tried to put a logical explanation on to the night's events. It was a hallucination because he was tired, it was nothing more than a catfight, it was an animal, like a hedgehog, but he knows that none of these are true. Telling me about it months later he says: 'I know I swung at something. I know it was there and then it wasn't. It's, like, you notice something more when it has gone. I was aware of it being there and not being there and I can't explain it, but compared to what Jason has to try to explain, this is nothing.'

Daniel is a sensible boy, doing well in his first serious job, studying in the evenings for extra qualifications. He is well-balanced, with a cynical sense of humour, not taking anything too seriously, but he never underestimates Jason's problems.

'Like most people, there's a little bit inside me that tries to come up with other explanations, which says it cannot possibly be aliens, things like that don't happen, but that's only two per cent of me. The other ninety-eight per cent has seen it all happening. I've talked to him, I know he's telling the truth. I believe Jason, and I believe that the only real possibility is that it is aliens. I didn't need to see Dude's reaction that night – I already knew.'

Whatever it was that spooked Dude, the cat does not always react so angrily to uninvited guests. A month or so after the incident in the garden Jason half woke up to find Dude walking up and down on his bed, miaowing. He sleepily pushed the cat away, surprised that it was with him: it never settles anywhere other than Daniel's room. The cat persisted, purring and making a fuss around Jason's face, until he roused himself and sat up. As he did so, he saw one of the tall aliens, the ones he describes as 'monks' because they are enveloped in long cloaks or robes, and four of the little ones. The cat not only accepted their presence, it seemed to be making a fuss of them, and Jason had the feeling that it deliberately woke him up. The large alien stared at him, while the other four busied around, picking things up, putting them back. Then Jason remembers no more until the next morning.

He now dislikes Dude, believing that somehow the cat has turned traitor. He has told his mother that he much preferred the old Dude, the Dude who was terrified of something in the back garden.

There is no conclusion to the story of Jason Andrews and his family. If you talk to Ann Andrews, as I have done for many months now, several times a week, there is always something unusual for her to report. It may not, by the standards of this remarkable family, be very significant, but it is always enough to make anyone who lives in quieter times feel deeply uncomfortable.

Take, for example, a set of keys Ann uses every day, when she visits a house in a nearby village. She has a standing arrangement to walk the dogs while the owners are at work. The keys went missing – not in itself an unusual event, but inconvenient because it involved having another set cut. Determined that this second set would not stray, Ann insisted Paul witness her putting them in her purse, which she left in the kitchen. The next morning, the keys were lying on her bedside table upstairs.

As another example, there is the caravan holiday in Hastings which Ann took with Jason in June 1997. This time Ann's mother Vi, her sister-in-law Ruth and her two nieces accompanied them, and everything seemed to be going remarkably smoothly. Small incidents, such as the teapot disappearing and turning up inside the fridge, were blamed on the children. When they protested their innocence, Ann laughed it off: she did not want to spoil Jason's break by inquiring too deeply.

As his birthday came closer, Ann could see Jason was worried: the previous year he had been distraught that 'they' had followed him on holiday. He begged his mother to let him go to an all-night disco organised as part of the holiday park entertainment. She agreed, partly as an extra-special birthday treat, and partly because she felt his need to be with other people during the difficult hours of the early morning. It was arranged that Ann would pick him up at 4am, much the latest he had ever been allowed to stay up.

For the rest of the family, back in the caravan, it was a strange night. Ruth was wakened by a loud hammering noise, and as it increased the others – Ann, her mother and her nieces – all woke up, too. The noise seemed to be coming from all over the van, even underneath, but there was no sign of anybody out there. So early in the season, all but one of the surrounding caravans were unoccupied.

Eventually, the noise died down and they all went back to sleep. Ann had, for a moment, been tempted to go and fetch Jason from the disco, but she checked her fears and told herself he was in the right place, away from the caravan. When she collected him, dead tired but full of the excitement of the party, she knew she had made the right decision. He knew nothing of the strange noises, and she did not tell him. He got up late the next day, to celebrate a perfect, and uninterrupted, birthday.

As Jason gets older, he is inevitably growing away from his parents, in the natural way that all adolescents do. He talks to them less, has whole areas of his life that they are not closely involved in. It is normal and healthy: but unlike most mothers of adolescent sons, Ann has deeper worries.

She believes that Jason is learning to cope with his abduction experiences without her help, or the help of anybody else. There are mornings when she is sure, from his tiredness and his general demeanour, that he has had an experience, but he no longer feels the need to share it with her, or have counselling from Tony Dodd or Maria Ward. He phones James Basil, and she hears him telling James of things she does not know about. It is, she says, as if an 'invisible barrier' has come down between Jason and the rest of the family.

In many ways, Ann is glad that her son is handling his experiences without the terror and misery he used to feel, but she has a residual worry, one that has been mentioned several times in the course of this narrative. She is afraid that Jason is 'going over' to the aliens. She knows that he will always physically return, but she wonders if his loyalties are becoming split, if he is being used as their ambassador – a notion that an incident in September 1997 seemed to confirm.

Throughout the summer of that year the future of Hawksnest Farm was in doubt. Paul and Ann were wrestling with a feeling that they must cut their losses and sell up. After investing their souls in the place for nearly ten years, it had become clear that they would never be allowed to develop and run it the way they wanted.

Logically, when they were finally turned down by the council for permission to build and stock a calf-rearing unit, they felt it made sense to go. They knew then that the farm could never be their sole source of income: they would always have to do other work to subsidise it. They knew, too, that they were never going to live there again, and this was the bitterest blow of all. The Housing Association house they live in is comfortable and convenient, but it has never felt to them like a home: they have always regarded it as a temporary staging post before moving back to the farm. Ann admits her heart is not in the place: she did not choose it, she feels no inclination to spend time and money doing it up.

However, even though they accepted that it would be sensible to cut their losses and sell the farm, it took another frightening experience to bring them close to selling their dream. It was on Sunday August 17th 1997 that it happened. Paul and Ann were at the farm, tending the animals but also taking advantage of being away from the boys to discuss the family's future. They had just been told unofficially, by a friend of Paul's, that no matter how many times they applied and however they chose to vary the application, the council would never relent over planning permission. There was, the friend had discovered, an unusual determination over this by the authorities. The words he used were: 'You are banging your heads against a brick wall.'

Deep down, after eight years of wrangling with the council, Paul and Ann already knew this, but they love their small parcel of land so much that they had chosen to ignore it. Now they had to face up to the future. Besides, they both felt that the farm was in some way a magnet for the alien activity, even though it did not necessarily happen there. Perhaps it was best to accept defeat, sell up and start again, somewhere else.

It was a hot afternoon, and they took Hannah, one of the Pyrenean mountain dog bitches, with them. She was in season, and they did not trust the boys to keep her away from the male dog, Chissum. She settled down in the shade of the small caravan, one eye open, keeping watch as Ann and Paul saw to the other animals. When they finished, they sat near the steps of the caravan, drinking coffee and mulling over their plans. The beauty of the place, on a sunny summer afternoon, made it harder for them to be ruled by their heads, not their hearts, and their talk was going round in circles.

Suddenly Hannah started to growl, rising to her feet, the growl graduating into a deep, furious barking. Paul and Ann stood up and stared in the direction the big dog was looking, but they could see nothing out of the ordinary. The geese were resting in that area of the field, and Paul commented that there could not be anything wrong or the geese would be making their usual racket. Hannah was undeterred: she did not move across the field, but she barked angrily, panting with the exertion in the heat, until Paul was worried about her. Eventually the barking subsided, but she continued to look into the distance and whimper. It was only then that Paul realised the geese were too quiet: just the noise of the dog would normally have been enough to raise them into uproar. As he and Ann watched, they could see the whole flock was motionless. One large gander had a wing outstretched, as if he had been cleaning under it, but the movement was frozen.

Then their attention was caught by a rustling noise from the woodland near the geese: they were only able to hear it because

Hannah was quiet now. They both caught a glimpse of something grey moving through the bushes, near to the flock of immobile birds. Then the shape moved quickly away, deeper into the woods, and as it disappeared the geese came back to life, cackling and fussing about in their normal way.

Hannah, still unsettled, eventually lay down again, but her head was raised and her eyes were open, watching. Paul and Ann were shaken, Paul asking Ann to confirm what they had seen several times before he would accept that it was not an hallucination. They brought the horses up from the bottom field early that day, and instead of splitting up to halve the length of time the chores took, they did everything together. Although it was such a lovely afternoon, they did not linger at Hawksnest, as they usually do. For the very first time, the farm did not give them a feeling of peace and relaxation and pleasure at owning it. They both felt afraid. Back at home, they made up their minds. They put the farm on the market the following week.

There was plenty of interest from potential buyers, but as soon as they began discussing the sale in real terms, they both realised that they were not yet ready to part with it. When Paul tentatively mentioned his doubts about leaving it, Ann felt enormous relief: she, too, was secretly hoping nobody would want to buy it so that they could stay there. Much to Jason's delight, because he loves the farm and is happier there than anywhere, they have decided, for the moment, to give it another go.

Five weeks later Ann was to experience a reprise of that strange afternoon when the geese were paralysed, but this time, it was even more distressing for her, because it involved Jason making one of his disquieting pronouncements. She and Jason were at the farm on Saturday September 20th, seeing to the animals. Dusk was closing in, and Ann was getting ready to go home, when the geese began cackling from the far end of the field. Jason, grinning, caught hold of his mother's arm and began to walk towards the noise.

'They only want to show us something. We should go,' he said.

Ann realised that the geese, and all the other animals, had gone suddenly and completely quiet. They were all facing the woods beyond the far field. She peered at the gloom of the bushes, but could see nothing. Afraid, she shepherded Jason to the car. He was unwilling, and kept repeating that they should go because there was something 'they' wanted them to see. Ann had to push him into the passenger seat of the car. As she turned the key in the ignition she realised, with a sense of rising panic, that the car engine was completely dead.

Jason, very calm, tried to climb out. Hastily, Ann locked all the doors. Turning the ignition several times she was eventually rewarded by the engine revving into life, and with a sense of relief she drove down the track. Jason turned round to watch the farm, and said, 'Look, there's another of them.' Then he turned reproachfully to Ann: 'We should have gone to see them.'

Back home, Jason was his usual self: in trouble for gobbling his meal too fast, wanting to go out to see a friend, rowing with Daniel about what to watch on television. Ann, as ever, was able to put the troubling incident to the back of her mind, but in the middle of the night she woke. Paul was not yet home from his weekend taxi driving. Some instinct told Ann to go to Jason: as she entered his room he was sitting bolt upright in bed, smiling.

'Are you all right?' his mother asked.

'Yes, we are whole,' Jason said, in a flat monotone, the smile never leaving his face. He seemed to be looking through Ann, beyond her, yet his eyes were fixed on her. Soothing, she told him he looked tired, and that he should lie down and try to get some sleep.

Jason raised one hand, as if to tell her to be quiet, and then spoke:

'Understand: I am them and they are me. The few are the many and the many are one.'

With that, he lay down, curled up in his usual sleeping position, and closed his eyes. The following morning, he had no recollection of anything happening in the night.

Ann has puzzled over the meaning of his words. Tony Dodd believes 'the few' are the abductees and 'the many' are the aliens, and 'the many are one' means that the whole body of aliens and abductees is acting in concert.

For Ann, the words themselves are less relevant than the way in which Jason delivered what appeared to be a portentous message. Is he, she worries, becoming a mouthpiece for his alien friends?

CHAPTER 16

EPILOGUE

When Jason confided in one of his friends at school about his abductions, within days he was being laughed at in the playground, and dubbed 'Spaceboy' and 'ET'. It was unsettling, but Jason is a resilient boy, and has survived with his 'school cred' intact. At times, when a burst of paranormal activity around him is at its height, he appears to be electrically charged: touch him, and you get a mild electric shock. I have experienced this at first hand. His mother Ann was actually burned by him, badly enough to leave a red scar on her arm. Unfazed, Jason charges his schoolfriends 10p a time to give them an electric shock.

It is this kind of Just William reaction to his problems that gives those who meet him, like me and Maria Ward, the greatest hope. He may be going through the strangest experiences and he may one day, as Tony Dodd predicts, be able to add a great deal to what we know about his abductors, but nonetheless, he's still the boy described in the opening paragraph of this book: a normal teenager who just happens to lead an abnormal – in some ways – life.

It is impossible to assess what the future holds for him, but it seems clear from the experiences of all multiple-abductees (those who are abducted regularly) that there is an important spiritual dimension to the phenomenon. The scenes Jason has been shown, of damage inflicted on the Earth itself, and of work being carried out by humans on aliens, may well be part of some orchestrated propaganda campaign by the visitors to our planet. They are trying to tell us something, by choosing a few individuals who are fed information to pass on to the rest of us. We are in no position to speculate on the quality of this information, but it does appear that they have a consistent message.

Professor Mack expresses it very eloquently: 'The alien beings . . . seem to many to come from another domain that is felt to be closer to the source of being or primary creation. They have been described, however homely their appearance, as intermediaries or emissaries from God . . . The acknowledgement of their existence, after the initial ontological shock, is sometimes the first step in the opening of consciousness to a universe that is no longer simply material. Abductees come to appreciate that the universe is filled with intelligences and is itself intelligent. They develop a sense of awe before a mysterious cosmos that becomes sacred and ensouled. The sense of separation from all the rest of creation breaks down and the experience of oneness becomes an essential aspect of the evolution of the abductees' consciousness.'

Tony Dodd agrees that being abducted should be regarded not just as being a victim, a part of some strange medical monitoring being carried out by aliens, but as the start of a spiritual journey. He has recorded the messages that he 'receives' in his brain from alien intelligences, and the recordings have been used to bring a great deal of spiritual comfort to many people, particularly to patients in hospices who are facing up to the end of their time on Earth.

Nick Pope, the Ministry of Defence official who came into UFO research because of his job, and was initially sceptical, also believes that the interest of alien races in Earth is a bid to 'civilise us as a species'. He discounts the explanation that the aliens are simply carrying out scientific experiments in order to breed from our tissue as unlikely to be the primary cause of abductions. As one of the most established UFOlogists, Jacques Vallee (whose book, *Passport to Magonia*, kickstarted much serious academic interest in the phenomenon) points out, if the aliens simply wanted genetic material they could get it in one hit, without the prolonged and awkward business of abducting individuals. Nick Pope, like Professor Mack, found that the abduction 'victims' he interviewd almost all recorded a growth in spiritual awareness and a greater interest in environmental issues.

Maria Ward and James Basil, the two abductees who have been so generous with their time to Jason, also both feel that whatever they have been caught up in, it has been a journey of enlightenment, and that their lives are enhanced because of it. Maria's view of the universe is holistic, like Professor Mack's: she believes that we have interacted with other intelligences since the beginning of creation, that their hardware (spaceships, strange grey bodies with big eyes, etc) may be 'alien' to us but that their existence around us is natural and familiar. Maria does not like words like 'UFO', 'extraterrestrial' and 'alien' because she thinks they erect a barrier around the very real experiences she and the other abductees have. Labelling them determines the way others will react to them, and because there is so much scepticism about, it makes it hard, she believes, for those in need of help in understanding their experiences to come forward.

Over the years she has spent counselling other abductees she has seen a pattern emerge, which falls roughly into three stages: there are childhood abductions, which tend to be childish in their content; there are adolescent abductions, which are much more physical (and the stuff that science fiction concentrates on); and then there is the final, spiritual dimension. Her analogy is with school: the abductee progresses from one class to another. All abductions involve a physical element, but eventually the experiencer is able to accept this and can, if they choose, derive enormous spiritual benefit from the other aspects.

Her prediction for Jason (and she made it to Ann at their first meeting) is that Jason will probably be abducted until he is between sixteen and eighteen years old. He will then be left alone for some years, either until he is married with children of his own, or until he is in his early thirties: 'It is as if "they" know that these are critical years for human beings to grow up and develop their own personalities, so they leave us alone, but their interest starts again as soon as we have our own families.'

She says that in the adolescent, physical stage – when the abductions usually involve a sexual or breeding aspect – Jason may find it hard to talk to his parents, which is why he finds James so valuable: 'Not only has he got to come to terms with his own feelings and reactions, but he also, perhaps, has a sense of betraying his parents, especially Ann, if he admits that he does not find the experience totally unpleasant. And besides, teenage boys are not inclined to tell their mothers the intimate details of their lives, even if the situation is "abnormal".'

She believes 'the others', as she calls them, have been involved with the development of the human race since creation. 'There is for me and others, a deep sense of recognition, of familiarity with them. I know that Jason feels this, and he should go with this feeling rather than with his fear. Fear narrows the goalposts, reduces everything. If he is in a state of panic during an abduction, it is the panic he will remember afterwards. If he can accept it, he can move forward. I'm confident that Jason will progress. He's a boy with great strength and energy, which will see him through, and if he can learn to benefit from his abductions, he will have a happy, rich, spiritual life.'

Maria believes that Ann, too, will eventually come to terms with her own abduction experiences: 'Ann is naturally intuitive, very sensitive, and open. She picked up Jason's distress signals very early on, much more than most mothers do. I think, once she has got through the business of bringing Jason up and helping him accept the way of life that lies ahead, Ann will start counselling others. She has a capacity to feel for others and to understand them. At the moment her energies are focused on Jason, and on her own recovered memories. She has a lot to take on board, but eventually she will have time to help others, and then she will find her true role.'

James Basil had his last experience in 1995, and he was told, 'You will have to learn to live by yourself for a while.' He does not believe he will be abducted again, although he accepts and respects Maria Ward's theory that he is simply in a dormant stage, being allowed to grow into his human personality without any outside interference. 'I believe they stopped coming when they could see that I had learned from the whole process, and was ready to move on. I stopped being frightened and stopped fighting the experience. That's when I had my last contact, with one of the small ones, and I knew that he was as frightened as I was. He was young, and he let me reach out and touch his face. In the past, I'd have wanted to kill him, but this time I felt so sorry for him – and I believe he was sent to me as a test, an ambassador, to see if I had moved on enough to feel equal with them.'

James has formulated two theories about the nature of his visitors. One is that they are time travellers, human beings from our own future. The second is that they exist in concrete, objective terms, but that they are running from a subjective source: in other words, every abductee has some input into the existence of the aliens, who move between reality and unreality in ways that redefine human experience (and to which, he believes, we should all be more open).

His thoughts are abstruse and philosophical, and he, too, accepts the holistic nature of the experience. It was and is a part of his life, essential to it and not imposed from outside, but a core element of all human existence.

He feels that he has been given a head start because of this understanding of life, the universe and human spirituality. He is confident that Jason will one day feel the same: that although the original feelings were of fear, out of them comes something far greater, a deeply mystical appreciation of life. 'The next couple of years are very important for Jason. If he can learn not to be afraid, he can learn to grow and gain from it all. I can sleep with the light off now – but I was seventeen before I could do that. He can choose: this can either be a time of great fear or of great enlightenment.'

For me, the whole process of researching and writing this book *has* been a time of great enlightenment. I started, as so many outsiders do, desperately looking for material proof: like Paul Andrews I wanted to touch an alien, take a photograph, have an insert analysed. Such proof is very elusive, as every other researcher has found, but perhaps looking for this kind of 'evidence' is, in itself, to contradict the nature of the experience of abduction. If we are dealing with higher levels of intelligence than our own, why would they need to leave fingerprints, clumsily attesting to an event which they choose to shroud in secrecy (abductions almost always happen at night, under cover of darkness, with all potential witnesses rendered unconscious)?

What the Andrews family, collectively, provide is a different kind of proof, a proof that cannot be dissected under laboratory conditions, but is no less valid. They *know* that what has happened to them is real – and not only that – they, and I, have now met many other people who have had compellingly similar experiences. If so many people have been there, and if similar stories can be traced back to the beginning of human civilisation, and if they cross all cultural, social and racial backgrounds, there is a sheer volume of evidence that cannot be ignored or dismissed.

The people involved in the alien abduction phenomenon are not cranks or weirdos. Sitting in the audience at the first (of several) UFO conferences that I have attended, I was struck by the ordinariness of the people around me. They were not the brown rice, open-toed sandal brigade, nor were they anoraked loners. They were men and women of all ages, whose conversation ranged around grandchildren, cars, football and pop music, yet who were there because of a common denominator: they all believe that if the sun is just one of millions of stars in the Milky Way galaxy, and that this galaxy is just one of billions in the universe, and that, as the Astronomer Royal says, we only 'know' ten per cent of our own universe, and that there may be more universes beyond ours, then it is highly unlikely that there is not, somewhere out there, a developed life form, ahead and beyond us in technology and the development of intelligence.

I was also struck, during my research, by the quality of the people working in the alien abduction field: people like Professor John Mack, one of the most highly regarded psychologists in the world; Professor David Jacobs, a history professor at Temple University, Philadelphia; Tony Dodd, a level-headed police sergeant. Men like these are academically disciplined and rigorous in their approach.

Most convincing of all are the abductees themselves, most notably Jason and Ann Andrews. Jason has struggled all his life to find a voice to express his fears and his knowledge of what happens to him: it is not a path he chose. Nor did Ann: they would both (and Paul and Daniel) gladly change places with those of us who sleep easy in our beds all night every night. Their simple courage and conviction cannot be bottled and analysed, but you only have to be around it for a short time to be completely convinced by it.

This book is the story of Jason and Ann Andrews, and the last words should go to them. Looking at everything that has happened to him in his short life, Jason says: 'Perhaps I have been chosen, perhaps I am special, and maybe one day I will understand, but right now I'd just like it to stop. I want them to leave me alone. I want them to let me be ordinary.'

Ann says: 'We have travelled a long way in the past few years, and it has not been an easy journey. I don't think the future is going to be easy for Jason, but I hope, by telling the world about it, we have made it just one little bit easier for other children to be believed, and to get the help they need.

'We can't turn the clock back and make it all unhappen: it was destined from the moment Jason was born, from the moment I was born, and my father before me. All we can do is look for a way for Jason to come to terms with it. His needs come first.

'For me, too, there is still a lot to achieve. I have to make sense of my own experiences before I can truly help him. The journey is not over: we have a long way further to go.'

BIBLIOGRAPHY:

Further reading about the subject of UFOs and abduction:

Good, Timothy, *Above Top Secret: The Worldwide UFO Security Threat,* Sidgwick and Jackson.
Good, Timothy, *Alien Update,* Arrow.
Good, Timothy (editor), *The UFO Report,* Sidgwick and Jackson.
Hopkins, B., *Intruders: The Incredible Visitations at Copley Woods,* Random House (New York).
Howe, L., *An Alien Harvest: Further Evidence Linking Animal Mutilations and Human Abductions to Alien Life Forms,* Linda Moulton Howe Productions.
Jacobs, D., *Secret Life: Firsthand Accounts of UFO Abductions,* Simon and Schuster (New York).
Mack, Prof. John, *Abduction: Human Encounters with Aliens,* Simon and Schuster.
Marrs, Jim, *Alien Agenda,* HarperCollins.
Pope, Nick, *Open Skies, Closed Minds,* Simon and Schuster.
Pope, Nick, *The Uninvited,* Simon and Schuster.
Randles, Jenny, *Alien Contact: The First Fifty Years,* Collins and Brown.
Spencer, John, *Perspectives: A Radical Examination of Alien Abduction Phenomenon,* Macdonald and Co.
Spencer, John, *The UFO Encyclopedia,* Headline.
Vallee, Jacques, *Dimensions: A Casebook of Alien Contact,* Ballantine Books (New York).
Vallee, Jacques, *Passport to Magonia,* Contemporary Books (Chicago).